D0369874

Praise for the Original Edition of
The No-Cry Sleep Solution

"Humane, sensitive, and baby-centered. It is refreshing to see and to be able to endorse an approach toward tender infant and child caregiving that does not claim to know who and what every baby should be or what every parent should do to achieve parenting success. *The No-Cry Sleep Solution* speaks to the uniqueness of each parent and child in a loving and knowledgeable way."

> —*James J. McKenna, Ph.D., Director, Mother-Baby Behavioral Sleep Center, University of Notre Dame*

"A wise and wonderful answer to every tired parent's prayers. Finally, a sleep solution that is loving, gentle, intuitive, safe, and successful. Elizabeth Pantley teaches parents how to build, step by step, a pleasurable nighttime experience without the restrictions that have turned parents away from sleep advice. *The No-Cry Sleep Solution* should be a part of every prenatal and baby class!"

> —*Nancy Eggleston, Community Producer, StorkNet.com*

"Offers a marvelous balance between acknowledging the meaningfulness of infant crying and recognizing the reality of parents' exhaustion. Parents will find confirmation of their suspicion that the crying of babies should not be ignored and affirmation of their own power to help their baby learn how to sleep."

> —*Michael Trout, Director, The Infant-Parent Institute, Inc.*

"At long last, a book that deals sensitively with a sensitive issue: how to get babies to sleep without resorting to letting them 'cry it out.' If you are one of those parents who stumbles through your days groggy and cranky after seemingly endless nights with a sleepless baby or toddler, or if you are simply a parent who would like to prevent that scenario, this is the book to read. It offers real-life, workable answers to one of the most challenging and confusing situations that parents face."

— *Tricia Jalbert and Macall Gordon, Executive Editors, Attachment Parenting International*

"It has always bothered me that every 'sleep through' method touted by so-called experts was *cruel* to babies and young children. Elizabeth Pantley has answered the sleepy prayers of parents all over the world and provided a sensitive and caring method that actually works! To all the tired parents out there: This is the book of your dreams!"

— *Gaye E. Ward, Founder, Gayesy's Attachment Parenting*

"Finally! A book to help all parents gently and lovingly guide their babies to better sleep. Elizabeth's techniques and approaches are an excellent way to encourage a child into a healthy sleeping schedule. This fantastic book is for everyone, regardless of parenting style, feeding situation, or sleeping arrangement."

— *Tammy Frissell-Deppe, Author,* Every Parent's Guide to Attachment Parenting

"Clearly stated, without guilt trips or shortcuts, this book is as pleasurable as it is helpful. The bond that you will develop with your baby as together you overcome the sleepless nights, and the insight that you will acquire by adhering to Pantley's program, will no doubt prove an asset for years to come, enhancing your ability to positively influence your child's development. This book goes way beyond its stated goal. In short, it's a must."
—*Richard Rubin, Editor, Baby-Place.com*

"Finally, a gentle, loving answer to baby sleep woes. Elizabeth Pantley's suggestions make sense—and they work! In this positive and practical guide, she demonstrates how understanding your baby's innate needs and learned responses will help you work together to get the soothing rest you all need."
—*Nancy Price, Cofounder, Myria Network: Myria.com*

"Whether Baby sleeps in a crib or the family bed, *The No-Cry Sleep Solution* is full of supportive, encouraging, and sensible ideas that respect the needs of both baby and parents. The book reflects the fact that each family is unique and requires more than a one-size-fits-all solution to sleep issues. Parents will welcome Elizabeth Pantley's empathetic insight and parenting experience."
—*Judy Arnall, Founder,*
Whole Family Attachment Parenting Association

the no-cry sleep solution

*Gentle Ways to Help Your Baby
Sleep Through the Night*

Second Edition

Elizabeth Pantley

New York   Chicago   San Francisco   Athens
London   Madrid   Mexico City   Milan
New Delhi   Singapore   Sydney   Toronto

1 2 3 4 5 6 7 8 9   LCR   25 24 23 22 21 20

ISBN   978-1-260-46212-8
MHID   1-260-46212-9

e-ISBN   978-1-260-46213-5
e-MHID   1-260-46213-7

Interior design by Nick Panos

McGraw-Hill Education books are available at special quantity discounts to use as
premiums and sales promotions or for use in corporate training programs. To contact a
representative, please visit the Contact Us page at www.mhprofessional.com.

This book is dedicated to my husband, Robert, for all the things you do as father to our children—things that may sometimes seem insignificant but are the pieces of life I cherish most in the special place in my heart that only you know. This book is for you, my husband, for:

Wrapping our first child, Angela, in her very first diaper. Your delicate and vigilant movements that day make this a memory I cherish from my first moments as a mother. For all your years coaching her in softball and in life, and for bringing her under your wing in the family business and becoming her true mentor.

Carrying newborn Vanessa in a sling as we shopped the mall. For placing your hand under her diminutive body as you walked, for peeking at her face between sentences, and for that look of love and pride that glowed in your eyes. For now supporting her endeavors in film with passion and an honest, wholehearted belief in her possibilities. And because that first glow of pride gets brighter every year.

Singing to David all those silly songs that made him laugh. And singing them with as much gusto and emotion the tenth time around as you had the first. For the pride you express in his growth as a remarkable, capable man. For listening and learning equally as much as teaching. Perhaps most for all the connection and joy I hear when you two are talking together as the best of friends for hours and hours . . . and hours.

Rocking baby Coleton to sleep, even when your arms fell asleep before he did. And for never, ever ignoring a call of "Daddy" from a toddling little boy, no matter how busy you were. For forever guiding and listening as if he were your only child and not your fourth. For giving him respect for the things he knows and being willing to ask his advice and honoring his opinions.

Coaching our children and others in sports, with a heart as big as all the world. For the day when the opposing pitcher struggled on the mound and broke down in tears: How can I forget the scene as you emerged from the dugout with a box of tissue and draped your arm around her shoulder, encouraging her to finish the game?

Guiding our children in their studies with the perfect balance of seriousness (those goal-setting meetings filled with spreadsheets) and fun (helping with homework while eating popcorn and watching the Mariners play baseball). For helping each one choose the college that provides the unique experience that they may not even know that they are searching for.

Inviting child after child into our home. And then, when your invitation includes the entire softball team to sleep over, staying up late so I could go to bed early. For opening wide the doors so our grandson can be enveloped in our loving home and arms, and begin forming the next generation of kind, gentle parents.

Teaching the importance of thoughtfulness, caring, respect, and family by hugging Grama when she most needs a hug, surprising her when she most needs a surprise, and saying "thank you" for every deed great or small.

Revealing to our children the secrets of a long and lasting marriage—trust, honesty, respect, and affection—so that they may emulate ours and grow up to cherish marriages of their own.

Understanding that a baby's bedtime ritual takes precedence over dinner parties; that a perfect French braid is as important as getting to the field on time; that breakfast out with Dad on Sunday morning is an essential ingredient to a happy childhood; and that a closed door to a teenager's room sometimes represents a more earnest invitation than an open one. That even as adults our children can call on you anytime for advice or just a listening ear.

Demonstrating that there really is a secret about a father's love for his children. As George Strait so beautifully sings, "Daddies don't just love their children every now and then. It's a love without end, Amen."

Contents

Preface to Second Edition

You are holding in your hands the fully revised and updated second edition of my classic sleep book. *The No-Cry Sleep Solution* has helped almost two million parents and has been joined by seven other books in the No-Cry series—including three others on the topic of sleep. The No-Cry books have been translated into twenty-eight languages—since babies are the same the world over.

Through my work with parents, my studies and research, and my personal experience as a mother of four and proud Nana of one, I have learned so much about babies and sleep. I've logged in the many questions that arrive in my inbox daily, and asked almost 1,000 parents to complete surveys in regards to the No-Cry sleep methods. I've used this opportunity to provide you with answers and solutions addressing the topics most frequently asked about.

It is my sincere hope that this book provides you with absolutely everything you need to gently, kindly, and lovingly help your baby to sleep well, so that you can sleep well, too.

Foreword to
the Second Edition

I've been there—a weary mama, desperate for sleep, worried that I'm doing it all wrong, feeling like I'll never get my life back again. I've watched the sun rise through bleary, sleep-deprived eyes countless times as I breastfed my six children through those long, lonely nights. The tears and the struggles and the endless stretches of night and day, and day and night, all seemed to meld into one another in a cacophony of crying and feeding and walking and rocking and bouncing and kissing tiny faces while silently begging them to sleep. I've wondered if there was a better way than just waiting-it-out, while also knowing beyond a shadow of a doubt that I'd never let my tiny humans cry-it-out. Because building the trust that would be the basis of our lifelong relationship outweighed all other concerns for me.

Looking back, I can only imagine how genuinely helpful and comforting it would have been to have a gentle companion offering me support and guidance as I stumbled, exhausted, trying to figure things out all on my own. *The No-Cry Sleep Solution* by Elizabeth Pantley can be that gentle companion for you.

This is *the* book for those preparing to welcome a new little life, those already in the deep trenches of sleep deprivation, and those who need assistance gently shifting to a new stage of sleep development. From your first sleep log to your first successful night's sleep, Elizabeth's nonjudgmental, time-tested guidance will be there for you.

The No-Cry Sleep Solution was the first and original no-tears, anti-cry-it-out, no-cry solution book. At the time of its release, the only other books addressing infant sleep promoted one of two methods: wait-it-out or cry-it-out. But Elizabeth developed a gentle sleep approach in the space between, based on years of research, trial and error, and extensive input from parents in the trenches themselves who applied her methods and reported back on their results. And now she has expanded and updated her original into this remarkable second edition.

In the space between wait-it-out and cry-it-out there is a sleep solution that will work for you and your little one, and *The No-Cry Sleep Solution* will help you find it. Written with kindness and compassion by an experienced mother of four and grandmother of one, you'll feel the hand of a best friend guiding you on your sleep journey.

With each one of my very, very different children, I did eventually find a better way. It took a lot of trial and error, testing and tweaking, adjusting and readjusting, but with each new baby's arrival, I kept at it until the two of us settled into a rhythm that worked for us. Schedules weren't for me. And routines felt forced. But a synchrony of two, heartbeat to heartbeat, moving into a rhythm of life that worked for both of us, felt so natural that the work needed to discover our rhythm quickly faded into memory.

Instead of trying to figure things out on your own with your weary, I'm-so-desperate-for-sleep-I-could-cry brain fighting you every step of the way, Elizabeth has clear, well-researched, proven steps to guide you to a sleep solution that will fit the unique needs of you and your child. It's not a one-size-fits-all schedule or a rigid routine. It's a slow dance into a rhythm that works for you and your little one.

Three of my babies are young adults now, and three are still at home. My youngest is nine. All grew into independent sleepers in their own time. Now it's your turn. Congratulations on finding this guide to gentle sleep, parents. Enjoy the dance!

—*L. R. Knost*

L.R. Knost, writer, researcher, award-winning author, human rights activist, children's rights advocate, founder and director of Little Hearts/Gentle Parenting Resources, editor-in-chief of *Holistic Parenting* magazine, mother of six, and cancer warrior, is the author of four parenting books, *Two Thousand Kisses a Day*, *Whispers Through Time*, *The Gentle Parent*, and faith-based *Jesus, The Gentle Parent*; the children's book *Petey's Listening Ears*; and her soon-to-be-released memoir *InHumanity: Letters from the Trenches* detailing her traumatic childhood and the long road to healing.

Professional-Speak

"Instead of raising children who turn out okay despite their childhood, let's raise children who turn out extraordinary because of their childhood."

L.R. Knost

Foreword to the First Edition

Sleep—or more accurately, the *lack* of sleep—is one of the most challenging aspects of parenting during the first year or two of a baby's life. The biggest hurdle is getting the baby to sleep through the night. Parents who are sensitive to their baby's needs are reluctant to try any technique that requires that they let their baby cry, so they often struggle through a fog of sleeplessness. This "nighttime-martyr parenting" often leads to frustration and resentment, resulting in unnecessary feelings of guilt and obscuring a family's joy over the new arrival. At a time when new parents should be enjoying the process of getting to know their baby, this lack of sleep leaves parents doubting themselves.

I've always thought that it would be wonderful to have a menu of ideas that parents could try until they hit upon a magic antidote to help their baby sleep all night. Elizabeth Pantley has created just such a menu in *The No-Cry Sleep Solution*.

The beauty of this book is that parents can create their very own sleep plan based on their baby's makeup as well as their own. Parents can choose from a variety of sensible, sensitive solutions that respect both baby and parent, striking a balance between a baby's nighttime requirements and the parents' very real need for a full night's sleep. The ideas are firmly rooted in the concept that the early years are the time to help your child develop a healthy sleep attitude—one that regards sleep as a pleasant, peaceful, necessary state that's not to be feared.

You've most likely picked up this book because your baby is keeping you up all night. Your lack of sleep has probably affected your ability to function fully throughout the day. Elizabeth Pantley, an experienced mother of four, clearly understands where you sit today, having sat there herself on occasion. She's created a book that is clear, easy to read, and uncomplicated. The steps are set up so that even the most sleep-deprived can understand and apply the solutions.

At long last, I've found a book that I can hand to weary parents with the confidence that they can learn to help their baby sleep through the night—without the baby crying it out.

—*William Sears, M.D.*

A Note from Author Elizabeth Pantley

Dr. Sears is one of my parenting heroes. His books came to my aid when I was a nervous and inexperienced new mother many years ago. His wisdom helped me learn what it really means to be a parent, and his gentle insight showed me how to do the job in the most loving and successful way. I am deeply honored that he finds my books helpful to parents and that he was willing to write this foreword. My perception is that most parents know Dr. Sears—and those who don't, should.

Dr. Sears is one of America's most acclaimed and respected pediatricians. He and his wife, Martha Sears, R.N., are the parents of eight children and are grandparents as well. They are the authors or collaborators of over thirty parenting books, all of which I enthusiastically recommend. A partial list of Dr. Sears's work includes *The Attachment Parenting Book*, *The Baby Book*, *The Successful Child*, and *The Discipline Book*. You can visit his website AskDrSears.com.

Acknowledgments

I am very grateful for the support of the many people who have made this book possible, and I would like to express my sincere appreciation to:

Christopher Brown and the entire team at McGraw-Hill—thank you for your unwavering support and guidance.

Judith McCarthy for believing in my work from the very beginning.

Meredith Bernstein of Meredith Bernstein Literary Agency, New York—thank you for your high-energy enthusiasm, your vision, and your persistence.

Vanessa Sands, Pia Davis, Christine Galloway, and Kim Crowder—thank you for lending your experience and comments to the original edition—the roots of this book.

The nearly one thousand parents who provided input, ideas, questions and suggestions for this updated edition, and to the original group of test parents: Alice, Alison, Amber, Andrea, Ann, Annette, Becca, Becky, Bilquis, Carol, Caryn, Christine C., Christine Ga., Christine Gr., Cindy, Dana, Dayna, Deirdre, Diane, Elaine, Elvina, Emily, Gloria, Jenn, Jenny, Jessie, Jill, Julie, Kari, Kelly, Kim, Kristene, Lauren, Lesa B., Leesa H., Lisa Ab., Lisa As., Lisa G., Lorelie, Marsha, Melanie, Neela, Pam, Penny, Pia, Rene, Robin, Sandy, Shannon R., Shannon J., Sharon, Shay, Staci, Susan, Suzanne, Tammy, Tanya, Tina, Victoria, and Yelena—I'll always remember you and your babies.

Judy Arnall, Maribeth Doerr, Nancy Eggleston, Tammy Frissel-Deppe, Macall Gordon, Tricia Jalbert, Dr. James J. McKenna, Nancy Price, Richard Rubin, Michael Trout, and Gaye E. Ward—thank you for your encouragement.

Dolores Feldman, my mom—thank you for being a blessing in my life, every day. I love you.

Photo Acknowledgments

I would like to express my sincere appreciation to the parents and photographers who provided the glorious baby photos that grace these pages.

Thank you to the parents:

Aaron, Alessia, Alyson, Andtre, Annie-Jo, Anthony, Avie, Avril, Brian, Britt, Brody, Casey, Charles, Charlotte, Chinda, Chris, Christina, Clarence, Dania, Deaan, Deborah, DeShawn, Eagle, Eliza, Emilee, Erin, Ernest, Flavia, Frank, Gagan, Glen, Hannah, India, Jacob, Jae, Jahir, Jamelia, Janelle, Jason, Jenifer, Jervis, Jesse, Jessica, Jose, Joy, Juana, Kathleen, Koza, Kristina, Krystin, Laura, Liesl, Lisa, Luvern, Magdalena, Major, Marc, Marvin, Meera, Megan, Michelle, Nelson, Nibha, Paris, Peter, Phillip, Porshe, Prashant, Rhonda, Roberto, Robyn, Ryan, Sa'Keenha, Sam, Sanacha, Sandi, Sarah, Shawn, Sheria, Spencer, Stefanie, Stormy, Sylvia, Tanner, Tom, Tony, Trang, Trevor, Ty, Varsha, Will, Winny

Thank you to the photographers:

Anika, by Kimberlea Millar, Kimberlea Isabella Photography, kimberleaisabellaphotographyonline.com

Elara and Olivia, Everly, Sumair, and Tommaso, by Amber Noble, Amber Theresa Photography, ambertheresaphotography.com

Amelia, Antonella and Izadora, Aurora, Drew, Kayden, Penelope, Saajan and Yasmin and Maya by Carrie Ferris Photography, carrieferrisphotography.com

Chantelle by Christiana Casuscelli, Red Poppy Studios, redpoppystudios.com.au

Ahsha, Alexander, Mila and Lily, Samarth, Sophia by Trudi Lynn, {Photography} by Trudi Lynn, photographybytrudilynn.com

Nico by Michelle Gonzalez, Michelle Gonzalez Photography, michellegonzalezphotography.com

Winter by Casey Bell, Casey Bell Photography, caseybellphotography.com

Emma Rose and Keagan by Amy Jandrisevits, A Doll Like Me, adolllikeme.com

Saunders by Anna Fly, Anna Fly Photography, annaflyphoto.com

Maddison and Paige by Bec Gordon, Bec Gordon Photography, becgordonphotography.com.au

Frankie by Paula Riddel, Riddel Photographers, riddelphotographers.com.au

Camden by Laetitia Lues, Laetitia Lues Photography, facebook.com/laetitialuesphotography

Zoey and Willow by Sarah Long, Joyful Photography by Sarah Long, joyfulphoto.com

Callen by Natalie O'Donnell, Natalie O'Donnell Photography, natalieodonnellphotography.com

Raylan and Conor by Tiffany Bridges, Tiffanyleigh Photography, tiffanyleighphoto.com

Fernanda by Dania Maciel, Dania Maciel Fotografia, facebook.com/daniamacielfotografia

Steele and Alyson by Michal Chesal, Baby K'tan, babyktan.com

This book is designed to provide parents and caregivers with a variety of ideas and suggestions. It is sold with the understanding that the publisher and the author are not rendering psychological, medical, or professional services. The author is not a doctor or psychologist, and the information in this book is the author's opinion unless otherwise stated. Comments attributed to parents may represent a compilation and adaptation of reader letters and survey answers. Names are changed to protect the privacy of the parents and children.

This material is presented without any warranty or guarantee of any kind, express or implied, including but not limited to the implied warranties of merchantability or fitness for a particular purpose. It is not possible to cover every eventuality in any book, and the reader should always consult a professional for individual needs.

Information and suggestions regarding bed-sharing, swaddling, white noise, pacifiers, bedding, and all other topics covered are included for your review, consideration and personal decision on whether to use each idea or not. You must determine which ideas are safe and practical for your baby and your family. Please do your own research when making these choices for your family.

Readers should bring their baby to a doctor for regular well-baby checkups, talk to a medical professional about Sudden Infant Death Syndrome, and learn how to reduce their particular baby's risk. The safety list and references to bed-sharing in this book are not intended to be construed as permission to use this parenting practice, but are provided as information for those parents who have researched this issue and have made a choice to sleep with their baby. This book is not a substitute for competent professional health care or professional counseling.

Introduction

Do any of these describe your baby?

- It takes *forever* to get my baby to fall asleep.
- My baby will only fall asleep if I do one or more of the following: breastfeed, bottle-feed, give a pacifier, rock, carry, swing, bounce, jiggle, or take a ride in the car.
- My baby wakes up frequently throughout the night.
- My baby won't nap easily, or takes very short naps.

Does this describe you?

- I desperately want my baby to sleep better.
- I won't—I can't—let my baby cry it out.

If so, this book is written for you. It will explain the steps you can take to gently help your baby sleep through the night. So, prop your eyelids open, grab a cup of coffee, and let me explain how you can help your baby sleep—so that *you* can get some sleep, too.

How do I know so much about children and sleep? I am the proud and lucky mother of four children who shine the light on my life, whether they're asleep or awake. There's firstborn Angela, who was twelve when her youngest sibling was born and is now a mother herself. Not far behind her are Vanessa and David, young adults whom I also count as my close friends. And then there's Coleton. Ahh, Coleton. Our little surprise treasure who reminded me of all the wonderful things I love about babies. And who also reminded me that with babies . . . come sleepless nights. I began my journey to become a sleep expert as a very tired mother of four, looking desperately for answers to better baby sleep.

1

With two of my children, I would not have needed this book. David followed such a textbook pattern of sleep that I barely remember that time in our lives. Vanessa was one of those *very* unusual babies who, miraculously, was sleeping ten straight hours by the time she was six-weeks-old. (I wouldn't believe it myself if it were not written in her baby book!) My oldest and my youngest, though, were frequent night wakers. While I was in the process of convincing Coleton, my youngest, to go to sleep at bedtime—and *stay* asleep, *all* night—I discovered many wonderful, practical, loving solutions and created the original *No-Cry Sleep Solution*. As my children grew I helped other parents on their own journeys to better sleep through my books, articles, chats, emails, and interviews. When my firstborn daughter had a baby—my first grandchild!—I was given another opportunity to learn firsthand how to use gentle, no-cry methods to gain better sleep. As an author and parent educator, I take pleasure in sharing these solutions with you in hopes that you'll also help your little one sleep better, so that you can sleep better, too—without any stress or tears for either of you.

Professional-Speak

"A little-known reality is that exhaustion is a key trigger of more than 500,000 cases of postpartum depression a year. Deep fatigue also pushes women into breastfeeding failure, mastitis, marital conflict, divorce, child neglect, weight struggles, missed work, car crashes, and other accidents."

Dr. Harvey Karp, Author of *The Happiest Baby on the Block*

How This Book Will Help You

Through years of research, personal experience, and work with many thousands of families, I have assembled and organized a wide variety of gentle ideas into what I call the No-Cry Sleep Solution. It's a ten-step plan to help your baby sleep through the night. It's not a rigid, unpleasant process. It does not involve letting your baby cry—not even for a minute. Rather, it consists of a customized plan that you create for your own family based on the ideas and research I present here, all within a simple and easy-to-follow framework. It's a method that is as gentle and loving as it is effective. Let me first tell you why I became passionate about writing this book.

When my first child, Angela, was a baby, I faced your dilemma. She did not sleep through the night, and her napping was abysmal. She woke up every two hours throughout the night for my attention and required a vast repertoire of actions to coax her to take a short cat nap. As a new and inexperienced parent, I searched for solutions in books, articles, and conversations with other parents.

Coleton, eighteen-months-old, and David, nine-years-old

I soon discovered two basic schools of thought when it comes to babies and sleep. One side advocates letting babies cry until they learn to fall asleep on their own. The other side says that it is normal for babies to wake up at night; it's typical for them to resist naps, and that it is a parent's job to nurture the baby—all day and all night.

In a nutshell, the two methods can be summed up as "cry it out" or "live with it." I wanted neither. I knew there had to be a kinder way, a road somewhere between nighttime neglect and daytime exhaustion that would be nurturing for my baby *and* for me.

Those many years ago, after all of my research about babies and their fragile needs, I felt guilty and selfish when I began to wish for an uninterrupted night's sleep and peaceful daytime naps. It was nearly impossible to reconcile my own instincts regarding Angela's nighttime needs with the fatigue that hampered my daytime parenting. Time passed, and eventually my

Chantelle, twelve-days-old

daughter did sleep through the night—but not until after her second birthday. We never did figure out how to help her nap well.

Cry It Out

During my struggles with my first baby I heard over and over again how I could solve all my problems if I sleep-trained her. Cry-it-out advocates make it sound so easy. "A few nights of crying, and your baby will be sleeping all night, every night," they say. If only it *were* so simple! My research has shown that very few parents experience this effortless success. Many deal with months of crying for hours each night (for baby *and* parent, in many instances). Some babies cry so violently that they vomit. Some parents find that the nighttime crying affects their baby's daytime personality—making them clingy and fussy. Many find that any setback (teething, sickness, missing a nap, going on vacation) sends them back to the previous night-waking problems, and they must let the child cry it out over and over again. Most (if not all) parents abhor the process. Many (if not all) parents who resort to letting their baby cry it out do so because they believe that it is the only way they will get their baby to sleep through the night.

My One Personal Experience with Cry It Out

At one point during Angela's period of sleeplessness I *did* cave in to all the pressure from friends, family, and even my pediatrician, who recommended that a few nights of crying would solve our problem. (If you're reading this book, you know this pressure, too.) So one dreadful night, I let her cry it out.

Oh, I checked on her often enough, each time increasing the length of time before I returned to her side. But each return visit struck me with my precious baby holding out her arms, desperately and helplessly crying, "Mama!" with a look of terror and confusion on her tiny face. And *sobbing*. After two hours of this torment, I was crying, too.

I picked up my cherished baby and held her tightly in my arms. She was too distraught to nurse, too distressed to sleep. I held her and kissed her downy head as her body shook and hiccuped in the aftermath of her sobbing. I thought, "This approach is responding to a child's needs? This is teaching her that her world is worthy of her faith and trust? *This is nurturing?*"

I decided then and there: they are all wrong. Horribly, intolerably, painfully wrong. I was convinced that this was a simplistic and harsh way to treat another human being, let alone the precious little love of my life. To allow a baby to suffer through pain and fear until she resigns herself to sleep is heartless and, for me, unthinkable.

I promised my baby that I would never again follow the path that *others* prescribed for us. I would never again allow her to cry it out. Even more, I vowed not to let any of her brothers or sisters-to-be suffer the horrible experience we'd just endured.

And I never have.

Thirteen Years Later: The More Things Change . . .

At twelve-months-old, my fourth baby, Coleton, was not sleeping through the night. Following in his older sister's footsteps, and *beating* her record, he was waking up nearly every hour for my attention. Now an experienced parent and professional parent educator, I found that my beliefs about letting a baby cry it out had not changed at all. But knowing that so many other parents feel the same way, I was certain that the intervening years would have produced new solutions. I thought I would find useful, concrete ideas in a book, and I began my search.

Nearly a month later, eyes glazed over with fatigue, I evaluated my finds. Before me sat a stack of articles and books—old and new—with the same two choices to address my dilemma: either let the baby cry it out or learn to live with it.

What Experts Say About the Cry-It-Out Method

I did find much new data that reinforced my abhorrence of letting a baby cry it out. And every year, more and more experts come forward to explain the risks of using a cry-it-out sleep method with your baby. Dr. Paul M. Fleiss and Frederick Hodges in *Sweet Dreams: A Pediatrician's Secrets for Baby's Good Night's Sleep* (McGraw-Hill) have this to say about such training programs for babies:

> Babies and young children are emotional rather than rational creatures. A child cannot comprehend why you are ignoring his cries for help. Ignoring your baby's cries, even with the best of intentions, may lead him to feel that he has been abandoned. Babies are responding to biological needs that sleep "experts" either ignore or deny. It is true that a baby whose crying is ignored may eventually fall back asleep, but the problem that caused the night waking in the first place remains unsolved. Even if parents have checked to make sure that the baby is not sick or in physical discomfort, unless they pick up the baby, interact with him in a compassionate way, soothe him, or nurse him until he falls back asleep, the underlying or accompanying emotional stress will remain.
>
> The most sensible and compassionate approach is to respond immediately to your child's cries. Remind yourself that you are the parent, and that giving your baby reassurance is one of the joyous responsibilities of being a parent. It is a beautiful feeling knowing

that you alone have the power to brighten your child's life and ban-ish fear and sorrow.

Dr. William Sears, in *Nighttime Parenting* (Plume), says that letting a baby cry it out creates "detachment parenting" and goes so far as to warn parents against this approach. "Parents, let me caution you. Difficult problems in child rearing do not have easy answers. Children are too valuable and their needs too impor-tant to be made victims of cheap, shallow advice."

The Biology of Cry-it-Out Sleep Training

Will a sleep-trained baby eventually stop crying and go to sleep? Of course. Does that mean the process was successful? Not necessarily.

Researchers have begun to examine the effects of sleep training on babies, and what they have learned demonstrates that when a baby cries he is just as distressed as he appears.

There are physiological ways to gauge the effects of these pro-longed, unanswered periods of crying. One method is to measure the level of the stress hormone cortisol that is released during the crying spells. Studies have identified a distinct rise in cortisol levels when a baby is left alone to cry to sleep. Even more impor-tantly, these levels remained high even after the crying ceased. This is particularly important to note because excessive levels of cortisol can negatively affect a baby's developing brain.

What Parents Have to Say About the Cry-It-Out Approach

As I spoke with parents about this book, many came forward to share their personal experiences with letting their babies cry it out.

Professional-Speak

"A baby is not capable of settling himself to a state of inner peace and well-being. What he can do, however, is eventually give up in the absence of response and go to sleep after endless exhausted, unanswered cries for help.

A baby who is trained out of his instinct to cry when being separated from a parent should never be mistaken for being in a state of calm. His stress levels have gone up, not down. Studies show that after being left to cry, babies move into a primitive defense mode. This results in an irregularity in breathing and heart rate, both of which can fluctuate wildly, and high levels of cortisol."

Dr. Margot Sunderland, Director of Education and Training at the Centre for Child Mental Health London, Senior Associate Member of the Royal College of Medicine, Child Psychotherapist, and the author of over twenty books in the field of child mental health, including *The Science of Parenting* (Penguin Random House, 2016)

"When we tried letting Christoph cry it out, he cried for two or three hours every night for eleven nights in a row. He became fearful and fussy all day long. Since we gave up that awful idea, we've all been sleeping better."

—Amy, *mother of ten-month-old Christoph*

"We tried letting Emily cry herself to sleep when she was nine-months-old. It worked for a few days, and I got really excited. But then she went right back to her old pattern. It's never worked since."

—Christine, *mother of eighteen-month-old Emily*

"With my first child, I worried about doing things the 'right' way and so I tried to do cry-it-out sleep training. I discovered that there are so many relapses even after doing it—traveling, sicknesses, bad dreams, new situations, etc., etc., etc.—that it wasn't worth it to do it in the first place. Doing it once was bad enough; I couldn't stomach multiple cry-it-out sessions."

—*Heather, mother of fifteen-month-old Anna*
and three-year-old Brandon

"We tried the cry-it-out method; our pediatrician told me to just let him cry all night if necessary. Well, he cried off and on for four hours, slept until 2:30 A.M., and then cried off and on until I got him up at 6:00 A.M. It was absolute torture! I found the 'crying' part of the idea works, but there was no 'sleeping' for either of us. We found a new pediatrician who supports more gentle sleep methods, and now we are all happier."

—*Silvana, mother of nine-month-old Salvador*

"With our firstborn, we dutifully worked at getting her to sleep in her crib and finally did let her cry, believing we were doing the right thing. It was not the right answer for her at all. At one point, she cried for more than an hour and was literally foaming at the mouth. I was so sick over this and (obviously) still feel bad about it. From that point on, she slept with us. She is almost three now and sleeps well in her own bed. If she has a nightmare, she is welcomed into our bed. I am currently breastfeeding and co-sleeping with our son. He is not the best sleeper, but I feel strongly that my parenting does not end at night, and if crying is the only solution I'm not interested."

—*Rachel, mother of ten-month-old Jean-Paul*
and three-year-old Angelique

How Does a Baby Feel About Crying It Out?

No one can really tell us how a baby feels about crying to sleep, but many people guess—taking advantage of a baby's lack of voice to present their own case. In my research for this book, I viewed a video by a sleep "expert" who stated, "Letting your baby cry herself to sleep is not physically or physiologically harmful, even if she cries for hours." This apparently is his attempt to make parents feel better about letting their baby cry. I was so appalled that I immediately conveyed this information to my husband, who is a caring, supportive, and involved father to our children. The statement haunted him so much that he responded the next morning via email with his answer to any parent who hears this advice:

> If you believe what this "expert" says then you are going down the wrong road with your child. Don't think for a minute that your tiny baby is not affected by this attitude. This insensitivity to your child's feelings can be born here and bred into other areas as he grows. If he wants you to hold him during the day, and you're too busy with other things, you can convince yourself that he won't be permanently harmed by your inattention. As he gets older, when he wants to play ball with you but you're otherwise occupied, you can rationalize that he's better off playing with his friends. If he wants you to attend a school function and you are too tired, you can argue that your presence really isn't necessary. You are setting up a pattern in babyhood that will follow for the rest of your life in your relationship with your child. There are times to encourage independence in your children, but parents should choose those times with wisdom.

On that same video, the author offers this terrifying statement to sleep-deprived parents. "She will *never* learn to fall asleep unless you let her cry." Really? Tell this to my four children who now sleep through the night. Tell this to the millions of babies who *do* eventually sleep through the night without ever having to cry it out.

No one truly knows how crying it out affects a baby in the long run. After all, one cannot raise a baby twice and note the difference. So, if we are even slightly unsure, why not err on the side of gentle, respectful choices?

Renewed Resolve, but Tired Nonetheless

Reading books and research papers had strengthened my resolve *not* to let my baby cry himself to sleep. Nevertheless, with the perspective of experience—as a mother of four—I refused to feel guilty for wanting a good night's sleep. I wanted sleep. I wanted answers.

There *had* to be answers.

My research began in earnest. Predictably, I found abundant information about babies and sleep. Observations and laments were easy to come by. But solutions? Variations of the same two schools of thought appeared over and over: cry it out or live with it.

Parents, though, seemed to fall into only one main category: sleep-deprived and desperate. Here's how Leesa, mother of nine-month-old Kyra, described her condition:

> I am truly distressed, as the lack of sleep is starting to affect all aspects of my life. I feel as though I can't carry on an intelligent conversation. I am extremely disorganized and don't have the energy to even attempt reorganization. I love this child more than anything in the world, and I don't want to make her cry, but I'm near tears myself thinking about going to bed every night. Sometimes I think, "What's the point? I'll just be up in an hour anyway." My husband keeps turning to me for answers, and I'm to the point

where I nearly yell at him, "If I knew the answers, wouldn't Kyra be sleeping?!"

At this point in my own research, I began thinking that other parents going through the frequent night-waking ordeal would have ideas to share. I found a multitude of parents facing the nightly crying versus grin-and-bear-it decision. And there, in the bits and pieces of conversations that quoted personal experience, articles, books, and other sources, along with my own experimentations with my little Coleton, I began to find solutions. There, in personal experience, and in the interpersonal exchanges between parents who have tried every conceivable method, I began to find ideas that did not sentence a baby to hours of nightly crying. I found the solutions that offered more peaceful paths to the rest so desperately needed by the whole family.

I researched the scientific reasons that babies wake up at night and dissected truth from fallacy. I picked apart the myriad solutions I'd read about, immersed myself in whatever I could find on the subject, and kept in regular contact with other sleep-deprived parents. Slowly, from the middle ground between the misery of the cry-it-out method and the quiet fatigue of all-night parenting, rose a plan—a gentle, nurturing plan to help babies sleep.

I Know Because I've Been There

Most books on babies and sleep are written by experts who—while well-versed in the technical and physiological aspects of sleep—simply and obviously don't have a personal understanding of the agony of being kept up all night—night after night—by their babies or the heartache of hearing their little ones cry for them in the darkness. In contrast, I've experienced the foggy existence of sleepless nights. And having four unique children has afforded me the insight that, while it is *possible* for a very young baby to sleep all night, it is certainly the exception.

These "expert" books are typically complicated, difficult to read, and woefully short on solutions. I waded through stacks of books bursting with information about human sleep, but all lacked specific solutions to the sleeping-through-the-night-without-crying-it-out dilemma. Sure, the reader learns the mechanics, but is still left asking one basic question. *How do you teach your baby to sleep—without tears?*

I've presented the answers in a friendly, easy-to-follow format so that even in your sleep-desperate state, you can find your solutions easily and quickly.

To show you how things were going for me when I began working on the concepts herein, this was Coleton's actual night-waking schedule, logged on tiny bits of paper one very sleepless night, a long time ago.

Coleton's Night Wakings

Twelve-months-old

8:45 P.M. Lie in bed and nurse, still awake

9:00 Up again to read with David and Vanessa

9:20 To bed, lie down, and nurse to sleep

9:40 Finally! Asleep

11:00 Nurse for 10 minutes

12:46 A.M. Nurse for 5 minutes

1:55 Nurse for 10 minutes

3:38 Change diaper, nurse for 25 minutes

4:50 Nurse for 10 minutes

5:27 Nurse for 15 minutes

6:31 Nurse for 15 minutes
7:02 Nurse for 20 minutes
7:48 Up. Nurse, then up for the day
Number of night wakings: 8
Longest sleep stretch: 1½ hours
Total hours of nighttime sleep: 8¼ hours
Naps: One restless nap for ¾ hour
Total hours of sleep: 9 hours

And I did *this* for twelve months! (Even as a mother of four I learned that experience is of limited value when each individual child presents their unique brand of sleep resistance, and you are limited by the knowledge you have at that point in time.) So, you see? If you are there now, you really do have my heartfelt sympathy, because I have been there too. And I can get you out of that sleepless place, just as I did for my baby and myself. That's a promise.

Picking my way though ideas and options, experimenting and applying what I had learned, this is the improvement I experienced after creating and using these sleep solutions.

Coleton's Night Wakings

7:50 P.M. Coleton lays his head on my lap and *asks* to go "night night."
8:00 To bed. Lie down to nurse
8:18 Asleep
6:13 A.M. Nurse for 20 minutes
7:38 Up for the day
Number of night wakings: 1 (Improved from 8)
Longest sleep stretch: 10 hours (Improved from 1½)
Total hours of nighttime sleep: 11 hours (improved from 8¼)

Naps: One peaceful nap, two hours long (improved from ¾ hour)
Total hours of sleep: 13 hours (improved from 9 hours)
Amount of crying involved: ZERO

Coleton *finally* followed in his sister's footsteps and began sleeping ten hours straight without a peep. (At first, I would wake up every few hours worried. I'd place my hands on his little body to feel for breathing. Eventually I realized he was just peacefully, quietly sleeping.)

Keep in mind that, during that time, I was actively researching and experimenting with ideas. You have the benefit of following a very tidy plan, so you should have quicker, easier success. Also, certainly, Coleton was different from his sister Vanessa, who at an extremely young age, dove for her crib and woke happily ten hours later. Babies are as different from each other as we adults who raise them. But compare this log to where we started. Even though it took some time to get us to this point, I was ecstatic over our results.

Here's a footnote that will please many of you. Throughout this entire process, my baby continued to breastfeed and sleep with me. Through my own experience and working with other mothers, I realized that bed-sharing–breastfeeding babies *can* sleep all night next to Mommy without waking to nurse, contrary to popular thinking. If you are determined to continue breastfeeding and bed-sharing, you might be able to do so and get better sleep, too!

And Then I Was There Again . . .

In the years since we first released *The No-Cry Sleep Solution* I've been awestruck by knowing that I've helped millions of parents and babies get better sleep. I've been overwhelmed by knowing that parents have read this book in twenty-seven different languages. (You see? Sleepless parents looking for gentle solutions live all over the world.)

I have received tens of thousands of letters from tired parents. Parents who write long, desperate letters, because they would never, ever let their babies cry-it-out; but they are extremely, frustratingly, and sometimes dangerously sleep deprived. I've learned so much about sleep issues by helping these families uncover their stumbling blocks and helping their children (and them) to sleep better. I've helped babies and parents gently solve their sleep problems for over fifteen years.

And then . . . A New Baby in My Family!

My personal experience with babies and sleep expanded: my firstborn daughter, Angela had her first baby—my first grandchild! My daughter is a person who does not function well without sleep, so while she was passionately looking forward to her new baby, she was dreading the newborn stage, as she knew to expect many sleepless nights ahead. She talked to me in detail about newborn sleep. Several months before her baby was even born she began peppering me with questions! She paid close attention to all that I taught her, and when her baby arrived she applied the sleep tips with gusto.

We were delighted and amazed by the results just four weeks after our precious little Hunter was born! Somehow Angela was able to understand her newborn baby's unique brand of communication. She was able to tell when he was tired, when he was hungry, and when he just needed to be held. Things in the sleep department began to flow in an easy pattern starting about a week after Hunter's birth. She followed her newborn's lead, which brought them to a beautiful place where Baby, Mama, and Daddy were all getting fabulous sleep and spending happy, not-too-sleep-deprived days together!

My experiences with my little jewel, Hunter, enabled me to expand what I knew about newborn sleep, and allowed me to refine many of the ideas specifically geared toward those precious first months.

Hunter has had his ups and downs in the sleep department, just like any baby does. Things like teething, mastering new milestones, or illness naturally create little hiccups in his sleep patterns, but overall, it's been fantastic. Just for fun, here's Hunter's actual sleep log at thirteen-months-old:

Hunter's Sleep Log

13-months-old

7:15 P.M. Asleep
3:20 A.M. Diaper change, nurse, bed-share with Mommy
7:05 Up for the day—eyes open and happy, no crying to sleep for this baby, ever!

Number of night wakings: 1
Longest sleep stretch: 8 hours

Total hours of nighttime sleep: Almost 12 hours
Daytime naps: One nap in bed for 1½ hours
One in-sling snooze for about 45 minutes
Total hours of sleep: 14 hours

My Test Families

Back at the start of my sleep journey, once I had found success with Coleton, I searched out other families who were struggling with their baby's night wakings. I gathered a group of sixty parents who were enthusiastic about trying my sleep ideas. This test group is a varied and interesting bunch! When we first met, their babies ranged in age from two-months to twenty-seven-months. One even had a five-year-old with sleep problems. Several parents were there with a first baby, some had babies with older siblings, and one family had twins. Some of the parents worked outside the home; some worked only at home. Some bottle-fed, some breast-fed. Some bed-shared, some put their babies to sleep in a crib, and some did a little of both. Some were couples, and some were single. My test families were all very different from one another—yet they were all exactly the same in one important way: when we first met they were all struggling with sleepless nights.

These parents dutifully completed sleep logs every ten days and emailed me on a regular basis to keep me informed of their progress. (Don't worry! You won't have to do a log every ten days, this was just during the test process.) They asked questions (boy, did they ask questions!), and as we worked through my sleep plan, they provided the information and feedback that helped me refine the ideas.

Proof! It Works!

At the start of our work together, none of the sixty babies were sleeping through the night, according to the medical definition of the phrase, which is when a baby sleeps for a stretch of five or more hours without waking.

As the test families followed ideas in *The No-Cry Sleep Solution*:

- By day ten, 42 percent of the babies were sleeping through the night.
- By day twenty, 53 percent were sleeping through the night.
- By day sixty, 92 percent were sleeping through the night.

Once these babies reached the five-hour milestone, they continued on with more sleep success, some achieving sleep stretches of nine to thirteen hours.

More Sleep Books, More Test Parents

After writing *The No-Cry Sleep Solution* I continued researching and exploring the area of gentle sleep and added three more No-Cry Sleep books to the collection (for toddlers and preschoolers, for newborns, and a book specifically about naps). For each new book I again gathered a new group of test parents—as many as 245 families for each book! The information and ideas shared in these groups have allowed me to add new and important ideas throughout this updated and revised reprint that you have in your hands right now! So you can thank the hundreds of test families who have suffered sleep challenges before you for leading the way to easier, more effective gentle sleep solutions.

How Long Will It Take for Your Baby to Sleep?

Please keep in mind that making this transformation takes time. No crying, but no rushing either. I wish you *could* have results in one day—I certainly can't promise that—but I can promise that things *will* improve as you follow the suggestions.

The irrefutable truth is that we cannot change a comfortable, loving-to-sleep (but waking-up-all-night) history to a go-to-sleep-and-stay-asleep-on-your-own routine without one of two things: crying or time. Personally, I choose time. And this means *patience* and might just represent your first opportunity to teach that particular virtue to your child.

Parents have asked for my help because their *five-year-old* is still waking up at night. Take heart, and keep things in perspective. My new sleep plan will *not* take five years to produce the desired effect!

The Test Families' Experiences

It may help to know what other parents have experienced. The following is what a few of the test parents had to say.

Lisa, a mother of two girls, ages one and five—both with sleep problems—said in her first letter to me:

> I co-slept with Jen, our five-year-old, until she was about a year old, at which time we tried to move her to her own bed. Since that time, she comes into our room EVERY night. Yes, every night for the past four years! Our baby Elizabeth . . . well, at age one she is still getting up three to five times a night. I feel extreme anxiety. During the

night, I hear the minutes ticking away on the clock that sits on my nightstand, waiting for one or the other to call for me, and with each minute everything seems to intensify. I often just break down and cry. As I sit here this morning with my coffee next to me, things don't seem quite SO bleak, but I have to admit that I still feel like crying. I just can't do this anymore. HELP.

Five weeks later I received this email from her:

I know it's not time for another log for us, but I just had to tell you what's been going on. Beth has been going to sleep at 8:30 and waking only ONCE! And getting up at 7:30! I can't believe it!

Jennifer has also been in HER OWN ROOM *ALL* night for ten days in a row now! She's so proud of herself, and I am so proud of her too!

IT'S WORKING! IT'S WORKING! IT'S WORKING!

Kim, the single mother of thirteen-month-old Mathieau, had this to say when we first started to work on her baby's sleep habits:

Well, things aren't going according to my plan at all. I tried to get him down at 7:30—I tried rocking him, nursing him, putting him in his crib, patting his back, rocking again, and nursing again, and he finally gave out at 8:45. I honestly don't know what the problem was tonight. I just hope it won't continue to be like this. I want so badly for this to work, I'm very frustrated.

Three weeks later, Kim had this to say:

Hi! I know I emailed you a couple of days ago about Mathieau sleeping through the night, but I just had to share this with you. Mathieau has slept through the night three—yes, count them, three—nights in a row. Can you believe it? I actually feel like a functional mommy now. He let me sleep in this morning too. He woke around 6:30 this morning to nurse and went back to sleep until 9. I had so much energy today. And even more, the baby-sitter has finally been able to get him to nap, too! Today when I picked him up he was still asleep—he had been sleeping for almost two hours! I am so excited that your ideas are actually working for us. I never expected to see this kind of result so quickly. We have made some MAJOR progress. You are definitely on to something here and you are going to be changing many people's lives.

The mother of a three-month-old, Christine, expressed these feelings when we first spoke:

Ryan's night wakings are becoming very stressful on our family. My husband can no longer sleep in bed with us, so he has grudgingly moved to the guest room. I am petrified I won't be able to function when I go back to work if I am going to continue to be up with him all night like this. I tried to let him cry it out, but it was a nightmare to see my normally happy, peaceful little baby crying so hard and sweating and looking so afraid and alone. I really hope you can help us.

Her log, just forty-five days later, says it all.

7:30 P.M. Asleep
6:00 A.M. Feed
7:30 Up for the day
Number of night wakings: 1 (improved from 10)
Longest sleep stretch: 10½ blissful, wonderful hours (improved from 3)
Total hours of nighttime sleep: 10½

Emily, mother of twelve-month-old Alex, included this information in her first message to me:

Alex sleeps with his mouth on my breast and his body horizontally across mine. He sometimes will sleep next to me, but only until he wakes up again, which is sometimes only five minutes later, and then it is back on top of me.

Alex's triumphant mother sent me this message after thirty days following *The No-Cry Sleep Solution*:

This will be my final log now that my little Alex is sleeping wonderfully. He is asleep by 8:00 P.M., and then I set him in our bed while I usually get up and shower or clean up. (Of course, we have mesh guardrails and we watch him carefully.) Alex may wake up once during the night to nurse, but it only takes him seconds to fall back asleep. I think he may wake up several other times during the night, but he doesn't need my assistance to go back to sleep. He wakes around 7:30 A.M. feeling happy and refreshed.

I can't believe this is the same baby as before. The difference in his sleep habits is truly amazing.

And this from Marsha, another mother of a chest-sleeping baby:

Last night Kailee went to bed at 8:30. She woke up a few times between 8 and 10 but quickly settled herself. I didn't hear from her again until 8:00 A.M.! I am sure you understand that this is complete and total heaven. Kailee has gone from needing to sleep on my chest all night and waking up to nurse eight to ten times a night to sleeping 11–12½ hours straight through. I never thought I would see the day when a baby of mine would sleep through the night. You are a hero in our house. I definitely wish you had been doing this study when my first daughter was a baby.

Remember the mother I quoted earlier who said, "I am truly distressed, as the lack of sleep is starting to affect all aspects of my life"? Two months after Leesa started following my plan, she wrote, "For the last week Kyra has been waking only ONCE, at 3:30 A.M., to nurse! Heeeheeeheeee! I'm darn near giddy on sleep!"

More quotes from the test mommies appear throughout this book in sections called Mother-Speak. Pictures of their sweet, sleeping babies are also sprinkled throughout this book.

Use This Book However It Is Helpful to You

The good news is that you, my reader and new friend, need be involved in this process only to the extent that it is helpful to you. I will ask you to do nothing that is uncomfortable for you or anything but gentle for your baby. Use only those ideas that appeal to you; even using a few of them can help you and your baby sleep better.

My goal is to help you *and* your baby sleep all night—without *either* of you crying along the way.

> **Mother-Speak**
> "I understand that it will take a while to see positive results. But after seven months of total sleep deprivation and exhaustion, just knowing that I'll be sleeping in another month or so seems like salvation."
> **Tammy, mother of seven-month-old Brooklyn**

You Can Sleep, Too

There are no good reasons for you to live as a sleep-deprived martyr. There *are* ways to get your baby to sleep without resorting to all-night cryathons. Action is key—action that will strengthen you and motivate you as you move through these next few weeks. So give the No-Cry Sleep Solution a try and plan on seeing results. You may not go straight from waking up every hour to sleeping ten consecutive hours, but you *will* go from waking every hour to every three . . . to every four hours . . . to, eventually, that all-night milestone, and more.

Shortly after which *you* will resume waking every hour, waiting for the car to pull into the driveway, keys to plop on the kitchen table, and footsteps to resound on the stairs up to your teenager's room. It really does go so fast.

Please be *patient* as you move through the steps. This is so very important. When your baby is unhappy or starts to cry (I said "starts" to cry, not wails for ten minutes!), go ahead and pick them up, rock, nurse, or whatever your heart tells you to do to soothe your sweet baby. Every day will move you one step closer to your goal, and knowing that, you can be more loving and patient.

Remember, too, that an apparent inability to fall asleep on their own is not a baby's fault. They've gotten used to doing things a certain way since their day of birth and would be perfectly happy to keep things as they are. The goal is to help your child feel loved and secure while you help them find ways to fall asleep—and stay asleep—on their own.

In summary, I don't believe a baby should be left alone to cry to sleep. Or even left to cry as you pop in every ten minutes to murmur comforting words without reaching out to touch your cherished baby. But I also know that you can—gently and lovingly—help your baby to sleep *peacefully* all night long.

Part I

Ten Steps to Helping Your Baby Sleep All Night

This section of the book will cover the steps to follow as you create your own sleep solution. You may want to use this page as a checklist as you go through the steps:

☐ Step Nine: Follow Your Plan Until You Are Happy with Your Baby's Sleep (page 99)

☐ Step Ten: Revisit and Revise Your Sleep Plan Over Time as Needed (page 111)

1

Do a Safety Check

You haven't had quality sleep since your new baby entered your life, so you may feel that nothing is more important right now than getting a full night's sleep. But there is indeed something much more important than sleep: your baby's safety. So it's critical that we start there.

In their quest for a few more minutes of shut-eye, well-intentioned but sleep-deprived parents make mistakes. You need to know a lot when it comes to your baby's safety. In Part IV, you'll find safety information and checklists to guide you as you create the safest sleep situation for your baby. So please take the time time to review the information that begins on page 343.

No matter how tired you are, no matter how tempting the situation seems, please be certain that you put your baby's safety above all else.

2

Learn Basic Sleep Facts

M any books about babies and sleep suggest that a parent read pages of complicated facts about human sleep before making any changes. When your eyelids threaten to droop before the first paragraph is read, this becomes an exercise in futility. The facts aren't learned, the plan doesn't get made, the problem doesn't get solved, and one more parent is resigned to another year or two or three of sleep deprivation.

So here, I'll give you just the information you need, short and concise, with a few sleep facts that are important to know. This way, you can get on to the real reason you're reading this book: to devise and implement the right sleep plan for you and your baby.

How Do We Sleep?

We fall asleep, we sleep all night, and then we wake up in the morning. Right? Wrong! During the night, we move through sleep cycles, riding them up and down like waves. We cycle through light sleep to deep sleep to dreaming all through the night. In between these stages, we briefly come to the surface, without awakening fully. We may fluff a pillow, straighten a blanket, or roll over, but generally we fade right back into sleep with nary a memory of the episode.

> All human beings wake up during the night in between the various stages of their sleep cycle.

Our sleep is regulated by an internal body clock scientists have dubbed the *biological clock* or *circadian rhythm*. And they have discovered that, strangely, this clock is set on a twenty-five-hour day—meaning we must continuously reset it. We do this mainly with our sleep-wake routines and exposure to light and darkness.

This biological clock also primes us for sleep or wakefulness at specific times of day. This is the cause of jet lag as well as the sleep problems that plague shift workers. This is also why it's often difficult to awaken on Monday morning—sleeping in and going to bed late during the weekend disrupts established rhythms, and we must reset our internal clocks, starting with the moment the alarm rings on Monday morning.

Anika, ten-days-old

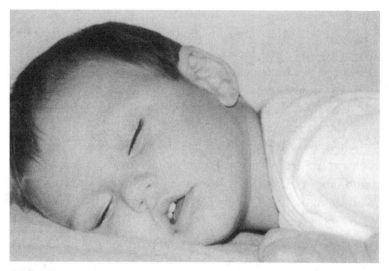

Gavin, ten-months-old

This circadian rhythm affects how alert we feel during various parts of the day. The brain seeks a state of biochemical balance between sleep and wakefulness, and when the scale shifts toward sleep, we feel tired. The sleep-wake patterns change as life stages progress. A baby's pattern is not the same as an older child's, and a child's is different from an adult's.

How Do Babies Sleep?

A baby is born with an immature circadian rhythm. A newborn baby's sleep-wake cycles are spread throughout day and night, only gradually settling into a pattern of defined naps and night-time sleep.

A baby's biological clock begins maturing at about six to nine weeks of age and does not work smoothly until about four to five months. At about nine to ten months, a baby's sleep periods consolidate so that they wake up and go to sleep at about the same times every day, and their sleep spans are longer.

Because the biological clock is the primary regulator of daily sleep and wakefulness patterns, it is easy to see why a baby does not sleep through the night—and why this pattern so adversely affects new parents!

Babies move through the same sleep cycles as adults do, but their cycles are shorter and more numerous. Babies also spend much more time in light sleep than adults do, and they have many more of those in-between stages of brief awakenings.

Reasons Why a Baby Sleeps Like a Baby

The first reason that babies wake so often is developmental. A baby's sleep pattern facilitates brain growth and physical devel-

Maddison, three-years-old and Paige, nine-days-old

opment. Babies grow at an astronomical rate during the first two years of life, and their sleep patterns reflect biological needs that differ vastly from those of adults.

The second reason why a baby sleeps like a baby is survival. They spend much of their time in lighter sleep. This is most likely so that they can easily awaken in uncomfortable or threat-ening situations: hunger, wetness, discomfort, or pain. In fact, acclaimed pediatrician Dr. William Sears, in *The Baby Book* (Little, Brown and Company) says, "Encouraging a baby to sleep too deeply, too soon, may not be in the best survival or devel-opmental interests of the baby."

All the stages of sleep are important for your baby's growth and development. As a baby matures, so will their sleep cycle.

Key Point
Attaining sleep maturity is a *biological* process.

A Baby's Sleep Cycle

Understanding that babies naturally and necessarily follow a par-ticular sleep cycle is crucial to understanding their problems with falling asleep and staying asleep. A typical baby's nighttime sleep cycle looks something like this:

Drowsy; falling asleep
Light sleep
Deep sleep for about an hour
Brief awakening
Deep sleep for about one to two hours
Light sleep
Brief awakening

Rapid eye movement (REM); dreaming sleep
Brief awakening
Light sleep
Brief awakening
REM (dreaming sleep)
Brief awakening
Toward morning: another period of deep sleep
Brief awakening
REM (dreaming sleep)
Brief awakening
Light sleep
Awake for the day

The Likely Culprit of Your Baby's Sleep Troubles? Waking Up on the Kitchen Floor!

Now you know that sleep is controlled by a biological process and that brief awakenings (night wakings) are a normal part of human sleep, regardless of age. All babies experience these. The difference with babies, who require nighttime care every hour or two, is that they are involving the parent in all these brief awakening periods. This realization was the lightbulb moment in my own research—and seems so obvious, now that I understand sleep cycles and their psychology.

Imagine this. You fall asleep in your nice, warm, comfy bed with your favorite pillow and your soft blanket. When your first brief waking occurs, you may change position, pull the covers up, and then fall right back to sleep without ever remembering this happening.

What if you woke up to find yourself sleeping on the kitchen floor without blankets or a pillow?

> **Point to Remember**
>
> Typically, when frequent night-waking babies wake up and start to cry, they are not hungry or thirsty or wet or even lonely; they're just plain tired, as desperate for sleep, perhaps, as their parents but, unlike them, clueless as to how to fall back asleep!

Could you simply turn over and go back to sleep? I know *I* couldn't! You would probably wake up startled, worry about how you got there, fret a bit, go back up to bed, get comfortable, and eventually fall asleep—but not too deeply, because you would worry about winding up back on the floor again. This is how it is for a baby who is nursed, rocked, bottle-fed, or otherwise parented to sleep. They fall asleep rocking, nursing, sucking a pacifier, and so forth and wake up to wonder, "What happened? Where am I? Where's Mommy and Daddy? I want things the way they were when I fell asleep! Wahhh!"

Sleep Associations

Babies make a sleep association, in that they associate certain things with falling sleep and believe they *need* these things to fall asleep. My baby, Coleton, spent much of his first few months in my arms or on my lap, his little head bobbing to the tune of my computer keyboard. From the very moment he was born, he slept beside me, nursing to sleep for every nap and every bedtime. By the time I looked up, he was twelve-months-old, firmly and totally entrenched in a breastfeeding-to-sleep association.

This sleep association philosophy is explained in nearly every book on babies and sleep. When the association is described, no gentle solutions are ever given. It is with the intent of "breaking" this association that the cry-it-out process is recommended. In my opinion—one you probably share, since you've chosen this book—this is a very harsh and insensitive way to teach a baby a new association, particularly when they've learned to associate sleep with a loving ritual such as breastfeeding or being held and rocked in a parent's arms while enjoying a warm bottle. (And what is the new association? "Crying alone in my crib in the dark is the way I fall asleep"? Not a very pleasant alternative.)

What Is a Sleep Problem and Does Your Baby Have One?

During the first year of life, a baby wakes up frequently during the night. About 47 percent of toddlers wake at least once per night and need an adult's help to return to sleep. As you have now learned, night waking is not a problem. It is a biological fact. The problem lies in our preconceptions about how a baby should sleep and in our own need for an uninterrupted night's sleep.

Regarding naps, it is very common for babies and toddlers to nap on an erratic schedule and to require a parent's help to fall asleep. This is biologically normal, but situationally challenging.

Sleep problems arise because we parents want and need long stretches of sleep to function at our best in our busy lives. We need our children to nap for their own health and for our sanity, as well. The idea then, is to slowly, respectfully, and carefully nudge our child's natural sleep maturity so that their sleep patterns stabilize into a configuration that works for everyone in the family. We do this by tuning in to our baby's sleep needs, reading our child's sleepy signals, setting up a perfect sleep environment, and creating comfortable routines, so that your baby joyfully wel-

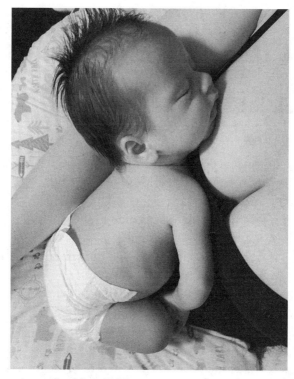

Palmer, one-month-old and Momma

comes sleep, and doesn't need your help to fall asleep for every single sleep-cycle awakening during naps and nighttime sleep.

What is often forgotten is that all families are unique and each parent/child pair has their own comfort level and goals. Before going a step further, I suggest that you examine your situation to make sure that you are seeing things clearly. I've found that during the early years of a child's life, everyone has opinions about how you should be raising your child—particularly when it comes to sleep—and other people's opinions may sometimes cloud your own perceptions of reality. So, take a deep breath, clear out all the cobwebs that other people have placed in your path, and let's first go over what's *not* a problem.

The Sleep Situation That Doesn't Need to Be Fixed

Your child is getting enough sleep, you're getting sufficient sleep, and everyone in your household is happy with how things are going. The problem is that your in-law, your friend or your neighbor is telling you that something in the way you are doing things is wrong and must be changed.

Here's the bottom line: IF everyone in your house is healthy and getting adequate sleep, IF the sleep situation is safe for your child, and IF the people who live in your home are happy with the way things are working out, then NOTHING NEEDS TO BE FIXED, regardless of what anyone else has to say about the "hows" and "wheres" of your family's sleep situation.

If this is the case for you, then the only thing you need to change is your response to unwanted advice about how you are running your own household. You may want to change the subject when the topic of sleep comes up in conversation, or do a little research so that you have more confidence to back up your parenting choices. (See pages 330–333 for more tips to help you handle unwanted advice.)

There's no harm in reading this book and learning more about healthy sleep, as it's likely that there are simple, gentle ways to improve your sleep situation—but don't feel compelled to change anything that is already comfortable and working for you.

Sleep Situations That Do Need to Be Fixed

Let's look at the other side of the coin now. Perhaps the sleeping situation in your house isn't good. Perhaps what used to work doesn't work any longer. Or it's never felt right, but you don't know how to change things. Or possibly your child isn't getting quality sleep and is demonstrating signs of overtiredness. Or maybe it's your sleep that has been disrupted far too long, and you yearn for your own uninterrupted night's sleep. In any of these situations, your entire family will benefit if you'll take a month or so to create and follow a more deliberate sleep plan for your child.

In these cases, the reward for your effort is huge: A child who is happier, healthier, calmer, and better able to learn and enjoy life. And, possibly just as important, a parent—you—who can truly enjoy the daily process of raising a content, well-rested child.

How Much Sleep Does Your Baby Need?

The actual number of hours that your child sleeps is an incredibly important factor for health and well-being, not just for today, but for the future as well. Sleep studies demonstrate that even a daily one-hour shortage in appropriate sleep time could compromise a child's alertness and brain functioning, and can even lead to depression and anxiety disorders later in life. Every child is unique and has their own "personal best" amount of sleep. Your child's behavior, mood, and health can give you an indication if they are getting the right amount of sleep. If you suspect that your child may not be sleeping enough, and if your child is not getting close to the amount of sleep on the following chart, then your child may be chronically overtired—and this will directly affect behavior, mood, health, learning, and growth.

Drew, two-days-old

The Happily Awake Span

The length of time that your child is awake from one sleep period to the next will also have a powerful impact on temperament and behavior, so it is one more important consideration, and earns a prominent place on the chart. As your child progresses through the day, biology demands a nap for regrouping. Without this break a child becomes overtired, wired, and cranky. You'll see on the chart that the span of awake time is very, very short for a newborn baby and this gradually increases over time.

Calculate Your Child's Best Sleep Hours

The chart is an important guide to your child's sleep hours. All children are different, of course, and a few truly do need less (or

Table 2.1 Average hours of daytime and nighttime sleep for babies

Age	Number of Naps	Total Hours of Naptime Sleep	Endurable Awake Hours Between Sleep Periods	Total Hours of Nighttime Sleep*	Total Hours of Nap and Night Sleep**
Newborn***			45 minutes–2		
1 month	3–5	6–7	1–3	8½–10	15–16
3 months	3–4	5–6	1–3	10–11	15
6 months	2–3	3–4	2–3	0–11	14–15
9 months	2	2½–4	2–4	11–12	14
12 months	1–2	2–3	3–5	11½–12	13½–14
18 months	1–2	2–3	4–6	1¼–12	13–14
2 years	1	1½–3	4–6½	11–12	13–13½
3 years	1	1–3	6–8	11–11½	12–13
4 years	0–1	0–2	6–12	11–11½	11½–12½
5 years	0–1	0–2	6–12	11	11–12
6 years	0–1	0–2	6–13	10½–11	10–11
10 years	0–1	0–2****	8–14	10	10
17 years	0–1	0–3****	8–16	8½–10	8½–10
Adult	0–1	0–1½****	8–16	7–9	7–9

*These are averages and do not necessarily represent unbroken stretches of sleep, since brief awaking between sleep cycles is normal.
**The hours shown don't always add up, because when children take longer naps, they may sleep fewer hours at night and vice versa.
***Newborns sleep fi fteen to eighteen hours, distributed over four to seven sleep periods. Premature or sick babies may sleep more hours divided into more sleep periods.
****Older children, teenagers, and adults often nap to catch up on a shortage of nighttime hours.

more) sleep than shown here, but the majority of children have sleep needs that fall within the range shown. Use these numbers as a starting point, and then watch your child for signs of tiredness. A frequently fussy baby is telling you that more sleep is needed, while a happy, calm baby is likely getting the right amount of sleep hours, even if it's less than shown here. I've included all age groups to let you see where sleep hours are headed, to help if you have older children, and so that you can check on your own sleep hours as well.

> **Mother-Speak**
>
> "This describes Melissa to a 'T.' When she's overtired she gets really whiny and clingy and she fights sleep like it is the ultimate enemy! Yet, if she doesn't get a nap, she actually ends up sleeping less at night, and having more night wakings."
>
> **Becky, mother of thirteen-month-old Melissa**

What About Nighttime Feedings?

We have all heard about those three-month-old babies who sleep ten to twelve straight hours every night, without waking to eat. Why these babies sleep so soundly is a mystery. But, when we hear about these amazing babies, we assume *all* babies can and should do this, and we become very discouraged when our five-month-old, eight-month-old, or twelve-month-old is *still* waking up twice a night for feeding.

To my surprise, sleep specialists—even the toughest cry-it-out advocates—agree that up to twelve months of age, *some* children truly *are* hungry after sleeping for about four hours. They recommend that if your child wakes up hungry, you should promptly respond with a feeding.

> **Mother-Speak**
>
> "Sometimes when Carrson would wake up in the night I'd actually hear his tummy growling."
>
> **Pia, mother of eight-month-old Carrson**

Experts also agree that to grow and thrive, a baby may not only want but may also *need* one or two night feedings up to about nine months of age. Experts say that even an eighteen-month-old child may need a before-bed feeding to set aside his hunger until morning. Of course, it can be difficult to know if your baby is hungry or just looking to use nursing or a bottle for comfort. As you follow the steps in this book, your baby will begin to wake up less often just for comfort and your company, and it will become more obvious when your child is waking up due to hunger.

As a baby's system matures they will be able to go for longer periods at night without eating. This is a biological process. Up until that time, research shows that feeding a baby solid food at night doesn't help create longer sleep periods, although some mothers do swear that it makes a difference with their babies. If your doctor gives you the go-ahead to feed your baby solids, you can experiment with this. Don't rush it, though. Babies who start

> **Mother-Speak**
>
> "When Emily was able to understand my questions I would ask her 'Are you hungry?' If she said yes, I would take her downstairs to the kitchen for a snack. This was short-lived because she learned she'd rather stay in bed."
>
> **Christine, mother of eighteen-month-old Emily**

solids too early tend to develop more food allergies, so it's not wise to start too soon.

So it stands to reason that if your baby has slept about four hours, wakes, and appears hungry, you should consider feeding them. (This is especially important if your baby is younger than four-months-old.) Maybe your baby will then sleep another four hours instead of waking frequently from hunger! Also, many babies go through growth spurts when they are eating more during the day, and they may eat more at night, too.

What Are Realistic Expectations?

Most babies awaken two to three times a night up to six months, and once or twice a night up to one year; some awaken once a night from one- to two-years-old, and about a third continue with one night waking as preschoolers. Remember that brief awakenings happen to all human beings, and the "night waking" we are referring to is when a child needs your help to fall back to sleep. A baby is considered to be sleeping through the night when they sleep five consecutive hours, without calling for your help. While this may not be *your* definition of sleeping through the night, it is the reasonable yardstick by which we measure Baby's sleep. That's five hours—not the eight, ten, or twelve hours we may wish for! The difficult aspect of this is that if you put your baby down to sleep at 7:00 P.M., you probably then go about catching up on your daily tasks. Just about the time you head for bed, your baby has already slept four or five hours and may be ready for your attention.

The good news is that, if your baby is biologically ready, you can encourage progress toward that five-hour milestone; once your baby reaches it, you can take steps to lengthen this night-time stretch. This book will tell you how.

Braeden, two-months-old

What Is the *Right* Way to Teach a Baby to Sleep?

William C. Dement, M.D., Ph.D., considered the world's leading authority on sleep, sleep deprivation, and sleep disorders, and founder of the world's first sleep disorder center at Stanford University, explains in *The Promise of Sleep* (Dell):

> No scientific experiments have been done on how best to train an infant to sleep, but I can make a few conjectures. I doubt that a regular pattern of sleeping and being awake can ever be imposed on infants immediately after birth or that anyone should even try. Their biological clocks seem to need to mature before they can keep track

of the time of day. But the same kinds of cues that work for us should work on infants' clocks as they are maturing.

Once you understand how much sleep your child needs, the most important strategy for improving his or her sleep is to set a daily routine and stick to it. Between the ages of five months and five years, the social cues imposed by parents become the primary factor in children's sleep patterns.

According to Dr. Dement, setting a routine and developing healthy bedtime cues and nighttime associations will allow your baby to drift off to sleep. *The No-Cry Sleep Solution* will help you create such a routine, customized for your baby and your family.

Now that you have learned some important basic sleep facts, you can use this knowledge as a foundation for developing your sleep plan. The first step, as outlined in the next chapter, will be to create sleep logs that will give you a clear picture of how your baby is sleeping now. Once you identify the issues that are preventing your baby from sleeping, we will move along to the solutions for helping your baby sleep—peacefully and happily—without your constant nighttime attention. And *without* "crying it out."

3

Assess Your Situation and Create Your Initial Sleep Logs

A helpful first step to improved sleep is to get an accurate picture of your baby's current sleep pattern. Once you determine exactly how your baby is sleeping now, you'll be able to
decide which ideas best apply to your situation. You'll be able to
track your success and make adjustments based on what you
learn.

You can, of course, simply take time to think about your situation and talk it over with your parenting partner or other people close to you and your child. However, casual conversation
often doesn't often pinpoint your real issues, so I've created a
few logs and questions to guide you through this process. You
don't have to complete the logs, or fill out the questionnaires,
but you might find that doing an initial assessment and following
up in a few weeks to a month to be very helpful in speeding you
along on your journey to better sleep.

If you are going to do an assessment and logs, you'll need to
pick a day and night to log what is really happening with your
baby's sleep. There are blank forms for your use at the end of this
chapter.

Filling out the logs and answering a few questions is a very
simple thing to do and can provide you with more clearly defined
goals, but if the idea of it overwhelms you, then just skip this
entire part and head right to the solutions beginning on page 61.

I certainly don't want to create any more stress over your sleep situation! You can always come back here later, if you wish.

Let's Get Started!

Begin by choosing a day to do your initial sleep logs. You will do these logs only one time—and then you'll do a follow-up in ten to thirty days, when you feel ready to assess your progress.

The first step will be to jot down information about your baby's naps in the nap log. Knowing exactly how long it takes your baby to fall asleep, where, when, and how sleep is happening, as well as how long the naps typically last, will all be important information. Since naptime sleep has a great impact on nighttime sleep, this nap data will be very helpful as you determine what changes you'll need to make in your baby's sleep routines. Here was my nap log for Coleton:

Coleton's Nap Log

12-months-old

Time baby fell asleep	How baby fell asleep	Where baby fell asleep	Where baby slept	How long?
1:20	Nursed for 40 minutes	In bed with me	In bed alone	48 minutes

You will find a form for your own nap log on page 56.

On the same day that you complete your nap log you will also do your prebedtime routine log. This information will help you see whether your actions in the evening are helpful in settling your baby for bed or whether they are hindering your baby's ability to settle down for a good night's sleep. Beginning about an

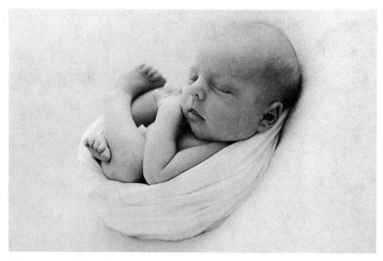

Winter, ten-days-old

hour or two before bedtime, write down everything you do in the prebedtime routine log on page 57.

At each step you will note the time, what activities your baby is engaged in, and the levels of three things:

1. Activity: active, moderate, or calm
2. Noise: loud, moderate, or quiet
3. Light: bright, dim, or dark

Your log will help you take a fresh look at your nighttime routine (or lack thereof!). On the following page you'll see my first prebedtime routine log for Coleton. You may find, like I did, that your evening activities don't consist of what you would call a calm, quiet, settling routine for your baby! Later in this book we'll work together to create a calming presleep routine, but for now, just take a look at what's happening in your house.

Here's what mine looked like in our busy four-child household:

Coleton's Prebedtime Routine Log

12-months-old

Time	What we did	Activity level	Noise level	Light level
6:40	Home from shopping; unload car	Active	Loud	Bright
7:00	Change into pajamas; nurse	Calm	Quiet	Dim
7:45	Play in Angela's room; listen to her new CD; sort her nail polish collection	Moderate	Loud	Bright
8:00	Play airplane and tickle with Daddy	Exceptionally active!	Very loud	Bright
8:30	Watch David's and Vanessa's play: *Ninja Man and the FBI in the Rooftop Battle*	Active	Exuberantly loud	Bright
8:45	Lie in bed and nurse	Calm	Quiet	Dark
9:00	Up again to read with David and Vanessa	Calm	Moderate	Dim
9:20	Back in bed, lie down, nurse to sleep	Calm	Quiet	Dark
9:40	Asleep			

After you have written down your prebedtime activities, log your baby's awakenings for the night. The easiest way is to put a pile of scrap paper and a pencil next to your bed (not a pen, since in the dark a pencil is more reliable). I'd also avoid using your phone as the screen light can be alerting for both you and your baby. Place these where you can easily reach them when you wake up during the night. Make sure you can see a clock from where you awaken. Each time your baby wakes up, write down the time. Note how you were awoken (by a snort, cry, movement). Make a quick note of what you do then—for instance, if you change the baby, write that down. If you are bed-sharing and get out of bed, write that down. If you nurse or give a bottle or pacifier, write that down, too. Make a note of how long your baby is awake, or what time your little one falls back to sleep. Don't worry about good penmanship or details.

In the morning, immediately transfer your notes to your night-waking log on page 58 (or create your own, either on paper or in your phone or computer) so that they make sense. Do this as soon as possible after waking so that everything is fresh in your mind.

Here was my first log:

Coleton's Night-Waking Log
12-months-old

Time	How baby woke me up	How long awake; what we did	Time baby fell back to sleep	How baby fell back to sleep	How long of a sleep stretch since fell asleep*
9:40	Fell asleep nursing				
11:00	Sniff and snort	10 minutes; nursed	11:10	Nursing	9:40–11:00 1½ hours
12:46	Whimper	5 minutes; nursed	12:51	Nursing	11:10–12:46 1½ hours
1:55	Sniff and snort	10 minutes; nursed	2:05	Nursing	12:51–1:55 1 hour
3:38	Whimper (wet diaper)	25 minutes; changed diaper; nursed	4:03	Nursing	2:05–3:38 1½ hours
4:50	Sniff and snort	10 minutes; nursed	5:00	Nursing	4:03–4:50 ¾ hour
5:27	Movement	15 minutes; nursed	5:42	Nursing	5:00–5:27 ½ hour
6:31	Movement	15 minutes; nursed	6:46	Nursing	5:42–6:31 ¾ hour
7:02	Movement, noise making	20 minutes; nursed	7:22	Nursing	6:46–7:02 ¼ hour
7:48	Movement, noise making	Up for the day			7:22–7:48 ½ hour

*I chose to round my times to the quarter hour. If you wish, you can use exact times, such as 1 hour 27 minutes. The overall difference is minimal, so you can choose whichever way is most comfortable for you.

At the bottom of your night-waking log you'll find a place to write down a summary of the information in your log. This summary will help you quickly see how your new efforts are affecting your baby's sleep as you try out the ideas presented in this book. This is what my summary looked like:

Asleep time: 9:40 P.M.
Awake time: 7:48 A.M.
Total number of awakenings: 8
Longest sleep span: 1½ hours
Total hours of sleep: 8¼ hours

When you have filled out your three logs, answer the sleep questions that follow the logs. If this is not your own book, you can photocopy the log pages or simply write the information on blank sheets of paper or on a log you keep in your phone or computer. (You can find blank logs on my website nocrysolution.com.)

When you have completed this groundwork, move on to Chapter 4.

Wonderful ideas, and blissful sleep, lie just ahead. I promise!

Nap Log

Baby's Name: _____

Age: _____

Date: _____

Time baby fell asleep	How baby fell asleep	Where baby fell asleep	Where baby slept	How long?

1. Review Table 2.1 on page 43:
   How many naps *should* your baby be getting? _____
   How many naps is your baby getting *now*? _____
   How many hours *should* your baby be napping? _____
   How many hours is your baby napping *now*? _____
2. Do you have a formal nap routine? _____
3. Are your baby's naptimes/lengths consistent every day? _____

Prebedtime Routine Log

Baby's Name: _____

Age: _____

Date: _____

Key:
Activity: active, moderate, or calm
Noise: loud, moderate, or quiet
Light: bright, dim, or dark

Time	What we did	Activity level	Noise level	Light level

1. Do you have a formal, consistent bedtime routine? _____
2. Is the hour prior to bedtime mostly peaceful, quiet, and dimly lit? _____
3. Does your bedtime routine help both you and your baby relax and get sleepy? _____
4. Any other observations about your current bedtime routine? _____

_____

_____

Night-Waking Log

Baby's Name: _____

Age: _____

Date: _____

Time	How baby woke me up	How long awake; what we did	Time baby fell back to sleep	How baby fell back to sleep	How long of a sleep stretch since fell asleep

Asleep time: _____

Awake time: _____

Total number of awakenings: _____

Longest sleep span: _____

Total hours of sleep: _____

Sleep Questions

1. Review Table 2.1 on page 43:

   How many hours of nighttime sleep *should* your baby be getting? _____

   How many hours of nighttime sleep is your baby getting *now*? _____

   How many total hours of nighttime and naptime sleep *should* your baby be getting? _____

   How many total hours of nighttime and naptime sleep is your baby getting *now*? _____

   How do the suggested hours of sleep compare to your baby's actual hours of sleep?

   Gets _____ hours too little sleep

   Gets _____ hours too much sleep

2. Is your baby's bedtime consistent (within ½ hour) every night? _____

3. Do you "help" your baby to go back to sleep every time, or nearly every time he or she awakens? _____

   How do you do this? _____

4. What have you learned about your baby's sleep by doing this log?

   _____

   _____

   _____

   _____

4

Review and Choose
Sleep Solutions

Once you have done a safety check, learned about basic sleep facts, and completed your initial sleep logs, you are ready to proceed. You will create your baby's customized sleep plan based on the ideas from Part II: The Sleep Solutions. I would strongly suggest that you use all of the suggestions that you think make sense for you and your baby. Stick with them long enough to make an impact—at least two or three weeks. One or two nights isn't enough to judge an idea's value. This is *not* a quick-fix plan, but it *is* a plan that will work. It *is* a plan that will enable you to help your baby sleep better. You just need to choose your solutions, organize your plan, make a commitment, and stick with it.

The ideas in Part II are separated into two sections. The first is especially for newborns (page 121), the second is tailored to babies who are more than four-months-old (page 172). The underlying concepts are clearly described in both sections.

Organize Your Solutions

Read through all the ideas and note those you think could help your baby sleep better. Then, transfer the information to the personal sleep plan, which begins on page 63. This will consolidate all your ideas in one place for easier reference, and keep them

Elara and Olivia, eleven-days-old

organized so that you don't forget important tips. Prepared with your solutions, you can then begin to follow your personal plan. (Go ahead and start using a few of the ideas along the way if you'd like. The sooner you get started, the better!)

5

Create Your Personal Sleep Plan

To move on to this step, first study the ideas in Part II (as directed in Chapter Four) and note those solutions that sound reasonable for your family. Now you can organize your plan and get started on the path to better sleep!

If you are a person who keeps a calendar or to-do list, this section will feel like a comfortable way to keep track of your solutions. However, if you aren't a list-maker you might see this as too much work. I'd recommend that you still fill in the blanks—even if you never look back at them again. It may help you refine your plan in your mind. There are no absolute rules here, so if you'd rather just run free with some ideas and not write anything down, then go for it! Skip right on ahead to Part II. You'll still see sleep improvement, and you can always come back here in a month or so if things aren't progressing as you'd like.

For those of you who like the idea of organizing your plan in writing, you can jot down the solutions you picked to the following section so that all your ideas will be summarized in one place. If you have a newborn, your form begins on page 64. If your baby is more than four-months-old, your form begins on page 69. Once you have created your personal plan you may want to copy the pages and post them in a prominent place, such as on your phone, tablet, computer, refrigerator, or even taped to your bathroom mirror. They will act as a daily reminder of the solutions you will be implementing. During the process, it will be helpful to refer back to the book when you need a refresher on any of the solutions.

This book is in two parts—this section of forms and directions, and Part II—the solutions. So, here we go! Review the solutions and use the forms that follow to create your own personal sleep plan.

My Personal Sleep Plan for My Newborn Baby

Review the referenced pages for each key and check off those items that fit your personal goals. You likely won't check off every box, so aim to follow the solutions that match up best to you and your baby.

KEY 1: Your Top Priority: Get to Know Your New Baby (page 128)

☐ I'll focus on my baby as my #1 priority and let go of any guilt about other things not getting accomplished. I'll review and prioritize other tasks accordingly.

☐ I'll observe how my baby communicates with body language and sounds. My baby appears to show these signs (update this as you learn):

Hunger: _____

Tiredness: _____

Discomfort: _____

A need to be held: _____

KEY 2: Have Realistic Expectations (page 130)

☐ I accept that night-waking is normal newborn behavior.

☐ I'll create cozy, comfortable feeding places and a plan for night care.

☐ I'll create night-feeding and bed-sharing environments that meet all the safety rules from Part V.

KEY 3: Learn to Read Your Baby's Sleepy Signals (page 134)

☐ I'll watch for my child's unique sleepy signs, and put my baby down to sleep, with rocking, nursing, or swaddling, immediately when tired.

☐ My baby's main sleepy signs are:

_____

_____

KEY 4: Respect the Span of "Happily Awake Time" (page 136)

☐ Most newborns can only handle 45 minutes to two hours of wakefulness. My baby needs to sleep after being awake for about _____ minutes. I'll watch the clock or set a quiet alarm to remind me it's near sleep time and then watch my baby for sleepy signs.

KEY 5: Differentiate Between Sleeping Noises and Awake Noises (page 138)

☐ Babies grunt, groan, coo, whimper, and even cry during sleep. When my baby makes noises, I will watch and listen to determine if my child is actually awake.

KEY 6: Use the Soothing Sounds of Pink-Hued White Noise (page 141)

☐ I'll use quiet white noise whenever my little one is showing signs of tiredness and ready to sleep—for naps and nighttime sleep.

KEY 7: Set Your Baby's Biological Clock (page 143)

☐ I'll review the tips on pages 143–144 and use the following DAYTIME solutions:

_____

_____

_____

☐ I'll review the tips on page 144 and use the following NIGHTTIME solutions:

_____

_____

KEY 8: Ensure Adequate Daily Naps (page 145)

☐ Per the Sleep Chart on page 43:

My baby needs _____ naps per day, for a total of about
_____ hours of naptime sleep.

☐ I'll watch my baby for signs of tiredness and make sure to
allow ample naptime.

KEY 9: Understand and Respect Your Baby's Sucking Reflex (page 147)

☐ I'll make certain my baby is getting ample time to suck
(either breast, bottle, or pacifier).

☐ After the first few months of age, I'll sometimes let my
baby suck until sleepy, but not totally limp-asleep.

KEY 10: Help Your Baby Make Friends with the Bassinet (page 153)

☐ I'll allow my baby to get used to sleeping alone at least
some of the time. I'll aim for the following to occur in the
bassinet or crib:

Naps (at least once per day):

_____

Night-waking (at least one sleep cycle period):

_____

KEY 11: Swaddle Your Baby at the Right Times in the Right Way (page 158)

☐ I'll purchase a safe and age-appropriate swaddle blanket or sleeper.

☐ I'll review all the do's, don'ts and safety rules for swaddling.

KEY 12: Give Your Baby Opportunities to Fall Asleep Unaided (page 161)

☐ I'll place my baby in the crib, cradle, or cradle-swing when comfortable and drowsy some of the time. I'll do this _____ times for naps, typically at these times of day:

_____

and for _____ night-wakings, typically:

☐ first awakening   ☐ midnight   ☐ early morning

☐ I'll set up a cozy sleep place to aid with falling asleep, using the tips on pages 163–165.

KEY 13: Provide Motion for Peaceful Sleep (page 165)

☐ I'll hold my baby in my arms or a soft carrier frequently throughout the day.

☐ I'll use a swing, glider, or rocking cradle for some naps. I'll review all the safety information for the device.

KEY 14: Develop a Hint of a Bedtime Routine
(page 168)

☐   I'll create and follow a simple bedtime routine using these
factors from page 169:

_____

_____

_____

KEY 15: Live by the *No-Cry Philosophy* and Enjoy Your
Happy Family (page 169)

☐   I'll be kind to my baby and myself. I'll be a thoughtful,
compassionate parent and keep the following factors
in mind:

_____

_____

_____

My Personal Sleep Plan for My Baby (Four-Months- to Two-Years-Old)

☐   I will get myself ready.

- I am committed to doing things that will help my baby
sleep better. I don't want my baby to cry, so I am willing to
be patient and make changes day by day. I'll follow my
plan and soon we will both be sleeping well.

☐ I will learn to read my baby's tired signs and put them to bed as soon as I see the signs.

• I know my baby is tired when these things happen: (see list on page 136)

_____

_____

_____

_____

_____

_____

☐ I will identify my baby's happily awake span (see chart page 43) and use this span plus signs of tiredness to identify time for sleep:

• My baby can stay happily awake for _____ hours _____ minutes

☐ I will create and follow a bedtime routine.

• This is our nightly routine:

Approximate time	Activity

☐ I will establish an early bedtime.

• My baby's new bedtime is: _____

• We begin our bedtime routine at: _____

☐ I will follow a flexible yet predictable daytime routine.

• This is a rough outline of our typical day (write in your planned awake time, naps, meal times, bedtime, and anything else that helps you organize your day). This is not a rigid schedule, it is a flexible guideline. It will slightly change day-to-day and can help set your baby's biological clock.

Approximate time	Activity

☐ I will make sure that my baby takes regular naps.

• According to the chart on page 43 my baby needs:

_____ naps for a total of _____ naptime hours.

• Times for my baby's naps are: _____
(Adjust this time daily based on tired signs and awake hours.)

- I will watch my baby carefully for signs of tiredness: decreased activity, quieting down, losing interest, rubbing eyes, looking glazed, fussing, yawning; and I will put my baby down for a nap at those times, or when the happily awake span has been reached.

- The ways I will encourage naps are: _____

  _____

☐ I will help my baby learn how to fall asleep without help: (Idea One)

- I will spend daily quiet time letting my baby play in bed.

☐ I will help my baby learn how to fall asleep without help: (Idea Two)

- I will encourage my baby to fall asleep for naps in these various places and ways: _____

  _____

  _____

☐ I will introduce a lovey.

- I will keep a lovey with us when we snuggle and when I put my baby to bed.

☐ I will make night sleeping different from daytime naps.

- I will keep our nighttime quiet, dark, and peaceful.

☐ I will develop key words as a sleep cue.

- Our key words are: _____

☐ I will use white noise or music as sleep cues.

- Our white noise or music sounds are: _____

_____

_____

☐ I will change my baby's sucking to sleep association.

- I'll use Pantley's Gentle Removal Plan:

☐ At least _____ times during daytime naps.

☐ The first falling asleep of the night.

☐ At least _____ time(s) during the night.

- Other things I will do: _____

_____

_____

_____

☐ I will help my baby fall back to sleep while continuing to bed-share.

- I won't respond too quickly; I'll wait for true "awake sounds" and not respond to "sleeping noises."

- I'll shorten the duration of my nighttime help routine (nursing, rocking, or offering a bottle or pacifier).

- I'll use the gentle removal plan as often as I can.

- I'll scoot away from my baby after they fall asleep.

- I'll use white noise to aid in falling back to sleep.

- I'll try to use key words and pat or massage my baby back to sleep.

☐ I will help my baby fall back to sleep and move them to their own bed. I'll be patient and make the change over a period of several weeks.

- These are the things we will do: _____

_____

_____

_____

☐ I will have my partner help my baby fall back to sleep.

- These are the things we will do: _____

_____

_____

- My helper will tend to my baby upon waking, by doing these things: _____

  _____

  _____

- My helper will transfer my baby to me if either my baby or the helper gets upset, and then I will do these things: _____

  _____

  _____

☐ I will help my baby fall back to sleep step-by-step.

- This is my plan to shorten the duration and type of my nighttime help routine in these steps over a period of several weeks:

  Phase One _____

  _____

  _____

  Phase Two _____

  _____

  _____

  Phase Three _____

  _____

  _____

Phase Four _____

_____

_____

Phase Five _____

_____

_____

Phase Six _____

_____

_____

☐ I will write a bedtime book and read it to my baby every night before bed.

☐ I will create a bedtime poster that shows our routine and follow it nightly.

☐ I will be patient, I will be consistent, and soon we will all be sleeping.

• I *will* have sleep success if I am persistent, consistent, and patient. I need to just relax, follow my plan, and do occasional logs to gauge our success. After I do each log, I will analyze my success and make any revisions to my plan. Soon my baby and I will both be sleeping.

6

Follow Your Plan for Ten to Thirty Days

Now that you have created your own personal sleep plan, it's time to officially begin the process of helping your baby to sleep all night—and to nap better, as well. How quickly you see sleep success will depend on how accurately the solutions you picked match your situation, and how persistently you follow your plan. I strongly recommend that you make your baby's sleep a priority in your family for the next month or two. This means discussing your sleep plan with everyone who shares in the care of your child so that everyone is on the same page. It might also mean avoiding going out during scheduled naptimes or your planned prebed routine and bedtime.

I know that staying true to your plan can be a challenge. With four children in our family, we sometimes seemed to live on the road. Between school and after-school events, sports activities, birthday parties, and everything else, we were always on the go. When I was working on Coleton's sleep routines, I organized our days around his sleep times as much as possible. I made good use of car pools, called in favors, asked Grandma for help, and did anything else I could do so that Coleton would be home for his naps and bedtime routine. Once he began sleeping ten or more hours at night and taking a regular two-hour nap, I was able to relax and be more flexible. Once his sleep was consistent, we could extend his nap or bedtime by an hour or two, and he

Matthew, eleven-months-old, and Mike

would just go right to sleep when we did get home and often sleep later in the morning. Likewise, you won't be tied to your baby's nap and bedtime schedule forever, but the more consistent you can be right now, the sooner you will see sleep success.

What If You Can't Do It All?

You may start out motivated to follow your plan entirely, and then your efforts may be disrupted. Illness, vacations, visitors, sleep regressions, new milestones, and teething are just a few examples. You may find yourself giving up in the middle of the night, and berating yourself in the morning for abandoning your plan. It can be frustrating when these things happen. But hear me now: Life happens and distractions occur! Even if you only follow part of your plan, and even if you can't be 100 percent consistent, you will still see sleep improvement. Even a few changes in your routines and habits can bring better sleep. And when things settle down around your house, you'll have a running start to really focus on your sleep plan and get your baby sleeping all night.

The Road to Success Is Really More Like a Dance

Most of you will find that attaining sleep success will not be a straight, easy road, even if you follow your plan perfectly. Instead, you will find that it's more like a dance: two steps forward, one step back, and even a few sidesteps in between.

I experienced this with Coleton. We'd had our very best night up until that point: He'd fallen asleep on his own and *stayed* asleep for seven hours. I was thrilled! A new level of success! But my party was short-lived. The very next night, he would not even *attempt* to go to sleep by himself; he nursed nearly constantly, and fussed in between sessions. Then he woke frequently, whining, "Mama, Mama" until I would nurse him again. I noticed this same pattern emerge with a number of my test families, I would get an email filled with joy, and a day or two later another message from the distressed parent asking, "What happened? We were up all night!"

Indeed, what happens? The variables are limitless. The baby gets sick, *you* get sick, he's teething, she missed a nap, he starts to crawl, you have company from out of town, or the moon is full. You may be able to pinpoint the reason, or maybe you'll be scratching your head wondering why your baby had such a rough night. And then

Nico, two-weeks-old, and Daddy

the next night, your baby has the best night's sleep ever. Just more proof that babies are anything but predictable.

The good news is that, when you follow your sleep plan, this complicated dance does end up where you want to go. That's why doing a few logs along the way can be reassuring. When you have visible proof of successful improvements, you can live with these annoying "sidesteps."

Maybe twenty, thirty, or even sixty days will pass before you achieve what you call a really good night's sleep—but in the big picture, a few months is nothing but a blink. That's another gift my four children have given me: perspective. I have a thirty-year-old daughter now, and she has her own child. I know how quickly childhood passes. Too quickly, as I know you're sure to find. It seems as if I held my firstborn Angela in my arms just yesterday, but now I'm rocking her child to sleep.

So, here you go. Good luck with your sleep plan, and (soon) sweet dreams!

7

Do Follow-up Logs and Review Your Plan in Ten to Thirty Days

Now that you've followed your sleep plan for ten to thirty days, you may want to do a second set of sleep logs, analyze your success, and make any necessary changes to your plan. In fact, you can do this every ten to thirty days that you follow your sleep plan (Chapters 9 and 10) up until you achieve the sleep results that you are comfortable with.

It's perfectly fine to log at whatever interval best suits you. I do suggest that you wait *at least* ten days between your logs, however, to give you and your baby ample time to adjust to your changes in routine. If you log more frequently than this, you may just frustrate yourself by focusing too hard on your desire for sleep and by looking for too much success too quickly (like hopping on the scale every day when you're on a diet).

Using the following forms, create new sets of logs; be sure to read the instructions, and answer the questions. Read the information in the sections following each log and in the next chapter, which will help you analyze your progress.

Follow-up Nap Log

Baby's Name: _____

Age: _____

Date: _____

How many days have you been following your plan? _____

Time baby fell asleep	How baby fell asleep	Where baby fell asleep	Where baby slept	How long?

1. Review the sleep hours chart on page 43:
   How many naps should your baby be getting? _____
   How many naps is your baby getting *now*? _____
   How many hours should your baby be napping? _____
   How many hours is your baby napping *now*? _____
2. Do you have a formal nap routine? _____
3. Are you watching for sleepy signs and putting your baby down for a nap as soon as you notice signs of tiredness? _____
4. Are your baby's naptimes/lengths consistent every day? _____

Follow-up Prebedtime Routine Log

Baby's Name: _____

Age: _____

Date: _____

How many days have you been following your plan? _____

Key:
Activity: active, moderate, or calm
Noise: loud, moderate, or quiet
Light: bright, dim, or dark

Time	What we did	Activity level	Noise level	Light level

1. For the past ten days, approximately how many days did you follow your formal bedtime routine? _____

2. Is the hour prior to bedtime mostly peaceful, quiet, and dimly lit? _____

3. Does your bedtime routine help your baby wind down and prepare for sleep? _____

4. Is your nightly routine consistent, acting as a bedtime cue for your baby? _____

5. Is your bedtime routine relaxing and enjoyable for you? _____

Follow-up Night-Waking Log

Baby's Name: _____

Age: _____

Date: _____

How many days have you been following your plan? _____

Time	How baby woke me up	How long awake; what we did	Time baby fell back to sleep	How baby fell back to sleep	How long of a sleep stretch since fell asleep

Asleep time: _____

Awake time: _____

Total number of awakenings: _____

Longest sleep span: _____

Total hours of sleep: _____

8

Analyze and Celebrate Your Achievements and Evaluate Your Sleep Plan

It's time to think about what's happened since you began following your sleep plan. It's also the time to tweak your plan and make any changes that you've learned are necessary to help your baby sleep better. Because we can't sit down over a cup of tea and talk about your baby (wouldn't that be nice!), I've created this chapter to help you figure out which parts of your plan are working, and which ones need to be changed. Start by using the information from your logs in Chapter 7 to complete the comparison chart that follows. Fill in the times from both logs and the amount of change.

	First log	Second log	Amount of change
Number of naps			
Length of naps			
Bedtime: Asleep time			
Awake time			
Number of awakenings			
Longest sleep span			
Total hours of sleep			

Now take a few minutes to answer the following questions that will help you analyze your efforts. If you can, talk over the information with your spouse, your parenting partner, or another parent who is working on their own sleep plan. You may even want to search out a like-minded group of parents and create a support group—either in person or via email, text, or social media. The support of other parents who are going through the same things that you are right now can be very helpful and enlightening.

Evaluate Your Sleep Plan

How closely did you follow your plan?

☐ I have been following all parts of my plan exactly.

☐ I followed some parts of my plan, but not everything.

☐ I started out great, but reverted back to my old patterns.

☐ Plan? What plan? (Oops, better start over with Step One!)

Have you seen positive changes in at least one area (for example: a fifteen-minute increase in naptime or sleep span; an earlier bedtime; a reduction in the number of night wakings)? _____

Which areas show the most change? _____

Why do you think that's true? (What have you done to influence this?) _____
_____
_____
_____

Which areas show the least change? _____

Why do you think that's true? (What have you done to influence this?) _____
_____
_____
_____

What have you learned about your baby's sleep habits? ____
_____
_____
_____
_____
_____
_____

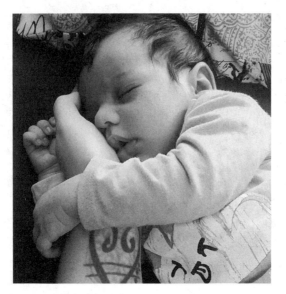

Jai Gale, three-months-old

Which parts of your plan seem to be having the best influence on your baby's sleep? _____
_____
_____
_____

What changes do you think you now need to make? _____
_____
_____
_____

How are you going to make these changes? _____
_____
_____
_____

The following sections are divided into three parts. Find the one that matches your level of success and read through the information. You may also want to read through the other sections for additional insight and ideas. Choose from these options:

If Your Baby Is Now Sleeping Through the Night (Five or More Consecutive Hours)

Congratulations! I'm truly thrilled that you have seen such great sleep success so quickly. I suspect that you have more energy and are feeling happier even though your sleep has improved for just a few days. It's amazing how a little sleep can have such a peaceful impact on your life, isn't it?

We need to address a few issues now that you've seen some success. First, this is only the beginning! Now that your baby can sleep five or more hours straight, you likely will see that span increasing little by little, night by night. You can help this along by continuing to follow your plan.

It's important to stick with your plan because your baby's sleep pattern is newly changed. If you revert back to your old ways, it's likely that your baby will, too; after all the work you've done, that would be very frustrating. Stay with your plan for a while (at least a few weeks or even a month) to make sure that the changes "stick."

Remember that babies' sleep patterns fluctuate. Don't be discouraged by an occasional night, or even a week, of sleep disruptions. All kinds of things can affect your baby's sleep: teething, sickness, vacations, visitors, growth spurts, or simply disruptions to your daily routine. Consistently stick to your plan, and over the next few months you will see your baby's sleep stabilize into a very comfortable pattern that is less and less affected by daily disruptions.

You may find that even though your baby is now sleeping longer spans, you are continuing to wake up throughout the night. This can be the icing on the cake of frustration! If this is the case for you, you will find lots of ideas in Part IV.

If you are a breastfeeding mother, this sudden decrease in your baby's night wakings may cause you some discomfort because of engorgement. You can find solutions on pages 327–329.

Please give yourself a pat on the back and give your baby a big hug. You did it! You've reached a major sleep milestone! Now it's important to continue following your sleep plan, as babies are notorious for abandoning their great sleep if you fail to follow the solutions that have brought you to this point.

If You Have Seen *Some* Success

Congratulations! Even if your baby isn't sleeping *all* night, I'm sure you're feeling much better about your baby's sleep—and yours! Take some time to think about what has happened since you've started using your sleep plan. Determine which ideas seem to be working best, and continue with those. Decide if any of the ideas aren't helping, and modify them or stop using them altogether. Once you have done this, proceed with your revised plan for ten or more days; then, do another log and analysis.

Read though the next section to determine if there are any hidden issues standing in the way of more rapid sleep success.

If You Haven't Seen Any Positive Changes

I understand how difficult this is, and I wish I could give you a hug. I know you are feeling very frustrated right now. But take

Ahsha, one-month-old

heart. A number of my test parents didn't see any changes at first, but once they evaluated what had occurred, reviewed the ideas, and modified their actions they began to see significant improvements. I'll try to help you figure out why the plan isn't working for you just yet.

Let's start by having you consider the possible issues that can block your success.

Have You Followed the Steps?

This book is set up very simply and lays out the approach step by step, in a specific and well-defined order. Is it possible that, in your desperation for sleep, you skipped some important information? As an example, Chapter 2 explains how your baby sleeps; without benefit of this information, you won't understand the logic behind each idea. You may have made customized changes and unknowingly defeated the purpose of the suggestion. I suggest that you read over the first few sections of this book and begin anew. Don't get discouraged. Many parents have had to restart the plan, and they have gone on to fabulous sleep success, as you will, too.

If you realize that you've been skipping steps, go back to the beginning and fill in your gaps. Refine your plan, and let's get your baby sleeping!

Have You Chosen the Right Plan?

It is possible that you chose the wrong steps in your plan. Review Part II (pages 121–268), and evaluate whether you've selected the most appropriate ideas for you and your baby. Once you've figured out which plan you should be following, renew your commitment.

Before now, you were living with your sleep disruptions without understanding them. Now that you've been thinking differently about your baby's sleep, you should be able to look clearly at what's preventing sleep. Once you identify those issues, you can move forward with a successful sleep plan.

Are You Being Patient?

I know. You're tired. You want to sleep. Tonight.

Take a deep breath. You can do this. It won't take forever. If you focus on what's going wrong instead of what's going right, you'll just make yourself miserable, like this anxious test mommy did:

Mother-Speak

"It's amazing (and depressing) how consistent her waking-up pattern is—she's up every 1.75 hours. I find the sleeping process to be a lot more frustrating for me now that I am actually *trying* to fix it. It was easier on me mentally when I had just given up and accepted her constant night wakings."

Kelly, mother of eighteen-month-old Savannah

You may have heard about the amazing "two-day results" someone had with a cry-it-out program, and you hoped to see the same kind of quick change in your baby—without the crying part, of course. Except that it's been weeks, and you've seen little or no improvement. Things may even seem worse than before.

Remember that back when we first met—in the Introduction—I explained that cry-it-out sleep training is rarely the quick answer that it seems. Check back with your friend in six months and you'll likely hear about repeated and ongoing challenges. I promised that I could get your baby to sleep through the night. I didn't promise a speedy miracle. Also, it is likely that your sleep issues will be more frustrating for you now that you are trying to solve the problem. Before today, it was easier to play ostrich—not willing to acknowledge the true frequency of your baby's night wakings, or how negatively they were affecting your life. Now that you're working on getting your baby to sleep longer, you'll be very focused on this part of your life and therefore much more aware of your own lack of sleep.

I'm sure that your baby isn't so very different from all the others who have found success with this method. Take a quiet moment, review all the ideas, and analyze your sleep plan. I'm willing to bet that the next few weeks will bring you closer to the results you are hoping for.

Have You Fully Committed to Your Plan?

Sometimes parents begin the plan with a half-hearted attempt and hope to see miraculous changes. They review the sleep ideas, choose one or two that seem easy or quick, and then find themselves a month later with no change in their baby's sleep pattern. Not until they *truly* commit to their plan do they see sleep success. Only you can determine if you have created a purposeful plan, given it honest effort, and followed it faithfully.

Mother-Speak

"I realized that we were only partially following our plan. I guess we were hoping that changes would just magically happen. My husband and I talked today and agreed: no more casually following the ideas. Today we get serious."

Neela, mother of eighteen-month-old Abhishek

Have You Had Success, but You Don't Realize It?

You may be searching for absolute sleep success—those blissful eight straight hours without waking up, and you're missing the fact that your baby *is* sleeping better than before. Maybe you've

Mother-Speak

"A few times I sent my log to you feeling like a big failure, but then you would respond with congratulations over our improvement. Your comments would prompt me to look closer at our logs, and I would see that good things were definitely happening!"

Christine, mother of eighteen-month-old Emily

logged two extra night wakings, and you're feeling disappointed. But wait! If your baby has slept more hours overall, then the number of wakings may not represent bad news at all! In other words, six wakings during a period of ten hours is a great improvement over five wakings during a period of eight hours. Or perhaps your baby's bedtime is an hour earlier than it was before. Or you're now taking only twenty minutes to put her to bed instead of an hour. Or each time she awakens at night she's only up for a few minutes, far less than she was keeping you up before. Take another look at your logs and compare them. Are you really having success, but you didn't see it at first?

Have You Faced Setbacks or Unusual Situations?

If you have been struggling with your sleep plan because of teething, sickness, vacation, growth spurts, or any other disruptions in your family routine, you will find your progress slower than it would have been had all these things not interfered with your baby's naps and nighttime sleep.

Such is the life of a parent! If you were ever bored before a baby entered your life, this new little person has erased the word

---

Mother-Speak

"When I first started with my plan, everything was going really well. But it seems that whenever I think we're making progress, things backfire. First the holidays hit, then he got a bad cold. Now he's teething, and it's waking him up every two or three hours again. I think he had a growth spurt in between, too. I told him I was going to sell him to the neighbors this morning, and we both laughed so hard."

Susan, mother of ten-month-old Luke

from your vocabulary. Setbacks are an inevitable issue as you work your way through your sleep plan. Just keep moving forward. Despite all the interruptions, you *can* make progress. And when things settle down, you're likely to see that success is right around the corner.

Persistence and consistency are the keys. Do your best to stick to your plan despite the setbacks. Even if you can't manage every step, the ones that you do adhere to will create positive changes for you.

Typically, when life settles down, a baby's sleep pattern will too. Here's a quote from the same mother a few weeks later:

Mother-Speak

"Finally his teeth have erupted, his congestion has ceased, and he is feeling much better. Here is last night's log—back to normal! This was Luke's first time sleeping more than six hours straight in about three weeks. I can't tell you how pleased I am. I guess the neighbors don't get him after all."

Susan, mother of ten-month-old Luke

Are There Medical or Developmental Issues That Are Interfering with Your Baby's Sleep?

There may be more to your baby's inability to sleep than just habits and routines. You may be unaware of a medical or developmental issue that is impairing your baby's ability to sleep well. It's always wise to talk to your doctor if you have any concerns about your baby's health. Part III, Special Situations (pages 269–313) covers the most common problems that keep babies up at night, and includes many tips and solutions for solving them.

9

Follow Your Plan Until You Are Happy with Your Baby's Sleep

At this point in your sleep journey, you may have discovered that you need to change parts of your plan. You may have realized that your baby's sleep habits are different from what you first suspected, and it's time to adjust your strategy. Based on what you've learned, you can add to your original plan, or even eliminate a few ideas. Or, you may have determined that your plan is the right one, and you just need to recommit to spending more time following it.

Now that you've had some time to live with these new ideas you'll begin to understand more of what you've read and how to apply the concepts. You might have had a few "aha!" moments, when something your baby does clicks with something you've read, and you suddenly come to a deeper understanding of the rationale behind the solutions.

Every Baby Is Different; Every Family Is Different

I'm always a bit suspicious of those charts about baby development and milestones that tell you exactly what to expect at

Adrien, seven-years-old and André, seven-months-old

every week of age. Babies are as different from one another as we adults are different from each other, and to assume that all babies do the exact same things at the exact same time is simply not reasonable. As the mother of four children, I *know* that babies develop on extremely different timelines. My children demonstrated the uniqueness of their own development as they all passed the major milestones at very different times. Vanessa was only eighteen-months-old when she used her first sentence, "Cookie Mommy please," while Angela waited to begin talking in full sentences until she was nearly two and a half. David walked at ten months, and ran soon after that, while Coleton was content to crawl and be carried until he was sixteen-months-old. As you already know, Angela didn't sleep through the night until she was two, while Vanessa managed that feat all on her own at six weeks of age. What's most interesting about these comparisons is that, regardless of their early differences, by preschool age all of my children talked and walked perfectly, and they all slept through the night. Today, I have three who are college graduates, one who's a college sophomore, and all four are smart, capable, talkative people and very active athletes. When they first walked or talked is irrelevant. My point here is that children are unique. When it comes to sleep, there are things that you can do to help your baby sleep *better*, but the time when your little one begins to sleep all night, every night will also be affected by their individual temperament and physiology. Therefore, it's best if you don't compare your baby's sleep habits to those of other babies, but rather to their own schedule, week by week and month by month. *Your* success will be found by noting improvements in your individual baby's patterns as you work through your sleep plan.

How Long Is This Going to Take?

Patience, patience. We are dealing with a real live little human being here, not a computer that can be programmed. While it would be pure brilliance if I could invent a one-day-no-cry-sleep-solution, I don't harbor any fantasies that such a plan exists. I suggest that you celebrate every piece of success along your way. Taking a longer nap now? Great! Falling asleep quicker? Wonderful! Sleeping longer stretches at night? Hallelujah! If you can honestly appreciate each little victory along the way you'll feel better about this whole sleep issue. You *are* on the path to all-night sleep. It will happen. Now is the time to recommit to your plan and add another giant scoop of patience. Good luck as you continue on your journey to all-night sleep!

"I've Tried Everything! Nothing Works! Help!"

The ideas in this section are intended for anyone at the end of their rope and truly ready to give up and let their baby cry it out.

For so many different reasons, not every test family I worked with had fabulous, immediate success. A few parents struggled along for weeks until they felt it was completely hopeless. Some were able to reevaluate what was happening, make some plan adjustments, and go on to success. Others struggled still, like these two families:

> "I have nothing good to report. I began two logs for you and failed to complete both. The first one, I got only as far as 10:41 P.M. It was unbelievable! She was up so many times I just couldn't keep up. She slept in our bed and kept waking up. It is crazy. It is enough already. We are beyond exhausted! I don't want to be the one test mommy who fails the program, but it looks like it is headed in that direction. Every day, my husband and I talk about letting her cry it out. We even tried to let her cry for one minute and even got up to two minutes, but neither one of us could go beyond that, so even though we threaten to do it, I don't think that letting her cry herself to sleep is an option. We don't know what to do."

> "I cannot cope anymore. I feel like I am totally losing it. Once again, I have gone from bed to bed all night long. I can hardly function. He is awake now and he's been awake nursing on and off since 4:00 A.M. It's now after six, and every time I pop him off he cries like I am hurting him. It's just ridiculous, and I am beginning to hate nursing! This is horrible. I have been crying. My friends are no help at all. They say, 'See, I told you so. You should never have spoiled him. You should just let him cry, he'll go to sleep.' I know that they're wrong and that I am doing the right things with my baby, but I cannot take this 'no sleeping' much longer."

If you are at this point in *your* life, I'm going to give you three ideas that are drastically different from anything else I have suggested. You are obviously at a dangerous level of extreme emotions, and you don't want to accidentally hurt your baby in the night by shaking or hitting them. These things can happen when you get to your breaking point. (Even the most connected and loving parent can get pushed to anger by severe sleep deprivation.) You also don't want to begin to resent your baby or find your sleeplessness interfering with what should be joyful days with your baby.

As long as your baby is more than four-months-old and has a clean bill of health from your doctor, you can use any of the following three ideas.

Take some time and think about them. Talk the ideas over with your husband, partner, parent, or a friend you can trust. Take a deep breath. (If your baby is younger than four- or five-months-old, please read the section about newborns that begins on page 121 and wait before applying any drastic measures.)

Is it the Baby's Sleep Patterns or Your Own Postpartum Depression Causing Your Struggles?

It's hard for any parent to deal with a baby's sleeplessness, but it can be overwhelming if you have a newborn and are suffering from postpartum depression (PPD). PPD is a medical condition that occurs in the first few months after childbirth. It is caused by biochemical and hormonal changes that happen after pregnancy and delivery.

While PPD affects all women differently, some typical symptoms can help your physician make the diagnosis. You probably are not experiencing everything on the following list, and the degree of symptoms may range from mild to severe, but if a number of these apply to you, you may be suffering from PPD, and should give your doctor a call.

Aurora, ten-days-old

Symptoms of postpartum depression may include but are not limited to:

- Feeling hopeless, worthless, or inadequate
- Frequent crying or tearfulness
- Lack of energy
- Loss of pleasure in activities you normally enjoy
- Difficulty doing typical daily chores
- Loss of appetite
- Feelings of sadness, despair, guilt, panic, or confusion
- Extreme mood swings or feelings of anger or anxiety
- Memory loss
- Overconcern for baby's safety
- Fear of losing control
- Worrying that you may hurt your baby
- A desire to escape from your baby or your family

- Withdrawal from social circles and routines
- Thoughts about hurting yourself

If you suffer from any of these symptoms, particularly thoughts about hurting yourself or your baby, then please call a doctor today. Right now. Your condition requires immediate medical care, and a doctor can help you. If you can't make the call, then please talk to your partner, your mother or father, a sibling, or close friend and ask them to help you arrange for help. Do this for yourself and for your baby. If you can't talk about it, rip this page out or copy it and hand it to someone close to you. It's that important. You do not have to feel this way.

> "In the time it takes you to read this chapter, you could set up an appointment with a doctor. Remember, this is a medical problem and it can be serious; for your sake, for your baby, and for all those who love you, you must make that call. With help, you will regain your life and your perspective."
>
> **Vanessa, mother of Kimmy (12), Tyler (10), Rachel (5), and Zachary (3)**

If you are a healthy parent with a healthy baby over four- or five-months-old, but at the absolute end of your rope due to your baby's sleep patterns, you may want to try one of the following ideas.

Idea Number One: Take a Break

For the next week, or even two, do not fight the night wakings at all. Do whatever works to get your baby back to sleep fastest. Get rid of your bedroom clock, or at least turn it around so that you can't see it. Don't peek at your phone in the middle of the night. Go to bed as early as possible, and stay in bed as late as you can in the morning. Prioritize your life, and don't do anything that can wait a week or two to get done. Take naps when and if you can. Call this your "I'll do anything just to get some sleep" week. Do this for a week or even two, as a breather and then go back to the ideas in this book with a fresh outlook. Or, if just chilling out and going with the flow seems to work for you, do it for a month, and see if your baby will outgrow her night waking issue on her own. I'll be honest and say that it's unlikely to happen that way. But after filling your sleep tank, and paying off some of your mounting sleep debt, you'll feel better and be much more able to approach a sleep plan.

During this time, read Chapter 8 (Analyze and Celebrate Your Achievements and Evaluate Your Plan) especially the section beginning on page 92, and review the ideas for solving special situations in Part III. The information in this section may be able to help you figure out what problems are preventing you from having sleep success.

Idea Number Two: Get Really Serious

Continue to follow the steps in this book with one major change. Get serious! No more "maybes," "kind-ofs," "really shoulds," or "next times." Take some quiet time to reread the first parts of this book, focus, and concentrate. Create a plan for yourself based on what you learn about sleep and what you know about yourself and your baby. Have confidence in the program because it can work for you. Follow every idea religiously.

If your baby spends all or part of the night in bed with you, and continues to wake many times during the night, you may have to move your baby to the crib in order to gain longer sleep stretches. This will require that you get up and down for a few days but should end up with your baby sleeping longer. You will find ways to do this beginning on page 247. Once your baby is sleeping soundly and consistently, you always have the option of bringing her back to your bed if you wish.

Many of the parents who reached the point of utter frustration discovered that they were only following the suggestions partway—hoping success would happen anyway. Following the suggestions half-heartedly might only bring you minor success, if any at all.

Please reread the Introduction, and review the section of solutions found in Part II. Modify your plan as necessary and follow it exactly, and your baby will sleep. Now is a good time to visit my website, blog, or social media for some encouragement.

The majority of parents who follow *The No-Cry Sleep Solution* faithfully see outstanding results eventually. You can do it too.

Idea Number Three: A Temperate Alternative to Letting Your Baby Cry It Out

If you are ready to give up, if you are geared up to toss this book and all my ideas out the window and just let your baby cry it out, then this section is written specifically for you.

Dr. Sears calls the place where you are "the danger zone," and he warns that if your baby's nighttime routine is making you angry, and making you resent your baby, something must change. Again, I'm including the following suggestion because you are at your wits' end. It may work beautifully, or it may just upset you more, but if you truly are going to let your baby cry it out it doesn't mean you have to approach it in a harsh all-or-nothing manner.

If at any point you feel that letting your baby cry at all is making things worse instead of better, go immediately to Idea Number One and take a week to reevaluate what's happening.

This suggestion is more appropriate if your baby is more than one year of age. But if you have a younger baby (older than four months), and you are on the verge of putting your baby in a crib and earplugs in your ears, then this is a better alternative. Here are the steps to a temperate alternative to cry it out.

1. Give your baby extra one-on-one time during the day (especially morning and before bedtime). Increase the amount of time during the day that you cuddle, hold, and carry your baby.

2. Teach your baby the difference between light and dark. (Take her in a bathroom and play a game—lights out: dark! Lights on: light! Read books about opposites. Morning and evening, comment on the time of day as you look out the window.)

3. At bedtime, explain your expectations clearly. For example, you might tell her, "We nurse (or have a bottle) when it's light. We sleep when it's dark." Look for some children's books about bedtime and sleep. Or write your own book (see pages 263–264). Read these books to your child as part of your bedtime routine.

4. When your child wakes up during the night, repeat your expectations. For example, you would say, "Shhhh. Night night. We nurse in the light. We sleep in the dark. It's dark now. We sleep." Pat her or rub her and tell her it's time to go to sleep. Stay calm and peaceful, but don't give in to the actions that have brought you to this point.

5. Because you are changing your regular patterns of behavior, your child will cry, after all, you are going against your child's expectations and drastically changing your actions. Big changes can be confusing, and your child may get very upset and cry. Maybe cry a lot. Be prepared for this and tell yourself, "It's going to be OK. I am only going to do this

for [you fill in how many] nights." (Choose how many nights you are willing to do this.)

6. If you find that even as frustrated as you are with the lack of sleep, you have your own meltdown or just can't let your baby cry in the crib, even with you standing bedside, by all means pick your baby up. You can then hold or rock them, hum to them, rub their back, put your cheek against theirs, anything that helps your baby or you. (If you are breastfeeding and your husband, partner, or another of your baby's caregivers can handle this part, it's often much easier on both Baby and Mommy.)

7. If your baby does not depend on nursing or a bottle, but wakes you repeatedly to be held or rocked, you can use this same idea. Except, keep your baby in the crib, and lean over to pat, rub, or otherwise soothe your baby. (One mother tried this and actually fell asleep on the floor with her hand through the crib slats, patting her baby's bottom—but it worked!)

8. Whisper words of comfort (these are as much to keep you calm as to help your baby know that you are there). "This will all be over in a couple days. I love you. It's OK. Time to sleep." You can even softly hum a lullaby or favorite tune.

9. If you have previously parented your child to sleep, this change might bring about some extreme emotions from both your baby and you. At any point that either you or your baby are too upset, give up the plan for tonight. There is no prize for going the full round if you just can't take it. Go ahead and nurse, give a bottle, or resort to whatever method calms your baby down and helps you both go back to sleep. By this point your baby will be very tired and may fall asleep quickly. There is no reason to push yourself or your baby to the limit. Just try again with the next night waking, or tomorrow night.

10. You may want to choose a time when you stop the process for the night. For example, "I'm going to do this until 3:00 A.M. After that I'm going to just bring her to bed so we can both get some sleep."

11. I know that we both believe that any crying is bad. But if you are at the end of your rope, with no more patience for gradual adjustments, it may be the last resort. You have been a very attached parent, and your baby has been nurtured and loved. Certainly, being well rested and peaceful is important for both of you. Martha and Williams Sears in *The Breastfeeding Book* declare, "Crying and fussing in the arms of a loving parent is not the same as crying it out." So if you feel you must resort to this process, don't beat yourself up over it. Just get through it as quickly as possible, and give your baby lots of daytime love and snuggles.

12. Remember, at any time, even in the middle of the night, it's perfectly OK for you to give up this idea and go back to Idea Number One on page 105.

Point to Remember

Before you embark on any drastic sleep method with your challenging sleeper, make an appointment with your doctor to be sure that your baby is healthy and that a hidden physical problem isn't the cause of sleep woes. There are no absolute rules when it comes to raising a baby, and no guarantees that any particular method will bring a specific result. Families are made up of human beings: children and parents. Each is unique in their personalities, needs, desires, and values. Be true to yourself, your goals, and your beliefs. And above all, be patient and loving with your baby and kind to yourself.

10

Revisit and Revise Your Sleep Plan Over Time as Needed

Now that you've followed your sleep plan for a while, you may want to do another set of sleep logs, analyze your success, and make any necessary changes to your plan. You can also use the information in this chapter every few weeks or once a month until you feel satisfied with how your baby is sleeping.

Using these forms, create your new logs, and again, be sure to read the instructions that follow them. Photocopy the forms to make sure that you have enough to take you through to your ultimate and final sleep success, or create your own in a notebook or on your device (I have blank forms on my website NoCrySolution.com).

Review the information in Chapter 8 as you move through this process.

Keep This Book Handy

Even after your baby sleeps through every night, and naps like a dream, it's not just highly possible, but very likely that you'll still experience setbacks over the next few years. That's normal childhood development. A variety of issues (discussed in Part III), such as ear infections, teething, separation anxiety, illness, and vacations, are likely to disrupt even the best sleeper's schedule.

Nicolas, seven-months-old, with Mami

Don't fret too much about this normal occurrence. Just dig out this book and follow your plan for a week or two to get your baby back on track.

Use the logs and the evaluations on the following pages every few weeks (or once a month) if you find it helpful, until you reach your ultimate sleep success, and then use them at any time in the future when your baby's sleep needs an adjustment.

Nap Log

Baby's Name: _____

Age: _____

Date: _____

How many days have you been following your plan? _____

Time baby fell asleep	How baby fell asleep	Where baby fell asleep	Where baby slept	How long?

1. Review Table 2.1 on page 43, or copy the information from your first log:

   How many naps should your baby be getting? _____

   How many naps is your baby getting *now*? _____

   How many hours should your baby be napping? _____

   How many hours is your baby napping *now*? _____

2. Do you have a formal nap routine? _____

3. Are you watching for sleepy signs and putting your baby down for a nap as soon as you notice those signs of tiredness? _____

4. Are your baby's naptimes/lengths consistent every day? _____

Prebedtime Routine Log

Baby's Name: _____

Age: _____

Date: _____

How many days have you been following your plan? _____

Key:

Activity: active, moderate, or calm

Noise: loud, moderate, or quiet

Light: bright, dim, or dark

Time	What we did	Activity level	Noise level	Light level

1. Since your last log, approximately how many days did you follow your formal bedtime routine? _____

2. Is the hour prior to bedtime mostly peaceful, quiet, and dimly lit? _____

3. Does your bedtime routine help your baby wind down and prepare for sleep? _____

4. Is your nightly routine consistent, acting as a bedtime cue for your baby? _____

5. Is your bedtime routine relaxing and enjoyable for you? _____

Night-Waking Log

Baby's Name: _____

Age: _____

Date: _____

How many days have you been following your plan? _____

Time	How baby woke me up	How long awake; what we did	Time baby fell back to sleep	How baby fell back to sleep	How long of a sleep stretch since fell asleep

Asleep time: _____

Awake time: _____

Total number of awakenings: _____

Longest sleep span: _____

Total hours of sleep: _____

This is a comparison of your logs. Fill in the times and the amount of change:

	First log	Second Log	Amount of change	Third log	Amount of change	Fourth log	Amount of change	Fifth log	Amount of change
Number of naps									
Length of naps									
Bedtime: Asleep time									
Awake time									
Number of awakenings									
Longest sleep span									
Total hours of sleep									

Use this worksheet to examine your experience every time you do a new log:

Since your last log, how closely did you follow your plan?

☐ I followed all parts of my plan exactly.

☐ I followed some parts of my plan, but not everything.

☐ I started out great, but reverted back to my old habits.

☐ Plan? What plan? (Oops, better start over with Step One!)

Have you seen positive changes in at least one area (for example: a fifteen-minute increase in naptime or sleep span; an earlier bedtime; a reduction in the number of night wakings)? _____

Which areas show the most change? _____

Why do you think that's true? (What have you done to influence this?) _____

_____

_____

_____

Which areas show the least change? _____

Why do you think that's true? (What have you done to influence this?) _____

_____

_____

_____

_____

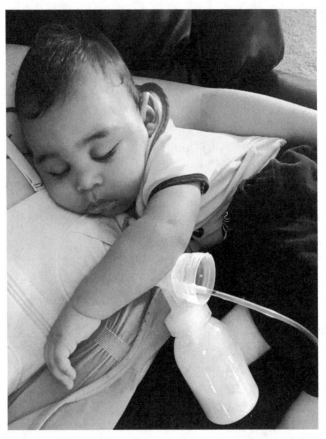

Emory, seven-months-old, and Mama

What have you learned about your baby's sleep habits? ____

_____

_____

_____

_____

_____

Which parts of your plan seem to be having the best influence on your baby's sleep? _____

_____

_____

_____

What changes do you think you now need to make? _____

_____

_____

_____

How are you going to make these changes? _____

_____

_____

_____

Part II

The Sleep Solutions

Part One: Solutions for Newborn Babies— Birth to Four Months

(If your baby is older than four months you can skip to page 172.)

Congratulations on the birth of your new baby. This is a glorious time in your life. Whether this is your first baby or your fifth, you will find this a time of recovery, adjustment, sometimes confusion and frustration, but—most wonderfully—of falling in love.

Even though this may surprise you, newborn babies do not have sleep problems. They arrive fresh from the womb where they slept up to twenty hours per day. Twenty hours! Clearly, newborns know how to sleep! The perception of "problems" arises because their sleep cycles don't match up to ours—normal sleep for them includes waking up every few hours for nourishment, which clearly isn't normal for us! In addition, we can actually create sleep problems for our new babies if we don't understand how their natural sleep process works.

You are very lucky to be reading this book now. The things that you do during the first few months can help everyone in the house sleep better and will also set a pattern for the next year or two or more. You can do this in a gentle, loving way that requires no crying, stress, or rigid rules. Applying some general ideas during these early months can help your baby get all the perfect, natural sleep necessary, plus set the stage for better sleep for the years to follow.

When your baby reaches four months of age (or a bit older if your baby was a preemie or has special needs), you can begin using those ideas for older babies which begin on page 172.

Read, Learn, and Beware of Bad Advice

Absolutely *everyone* has an opinion about how you should raise your baby. Remembering back to when my first child was born, I was amazed at how many people felt compelled to share their advice. One day, when Angela was just a few days old, a friend—

Sumair, nine-days-old, and Mumma

a single, childless friend, I must add—came by to visit and see my baby. She was napping at the time, and we were chatting. Angela awoke with a cry, and I popped up to get her. He laughed and said, "Oh, you don't have to *run* to her. When babies cry, they don't even know where the sound is coming from!" (Where, I wondered, did he learn *that* bit of nonsense?)

The danger to a new parent is that these tidbits of misguided advice (no matter how well-intentioned) can truly have a negative impact on our parenting skills and, by extension, our babies' development, if we are not aware of the facts. The more knowledge you have the less likely that other people will make you doubt your parenting skills.

My mission, and that of other parent educators, is to present the facts as we know them, so you can choose your approach from the proactive strength of knowledge. In other words, if you are well informed, then you protect yourself and your family from the barrage of "shoulds" and "woulds" that don't fit you or your family and that may even have no evidence or supporting facts.

That's the game plan that the interesting conversation with my single, childless friend prompted me to develop. I realized that, had I not been informed and confident on this particular issue, my friend's opinion would have left me confused, worried, and self-doubting. At the very least, he did manage to shock me speechless.

So, your best defense is knowledge. The more you know, the more easily you will develop your own philosophies about child rearing. When you have your facts straight, and when you have a parenting plan, you will be able to respond with confidence to those who are well-meaning but offering incorrect or even dangerous advice.

So, your first step is to get smart! Know *what* you are doing, and know *why* you are doing it. Then, when those amateur experts share their advice, you can smile, say "Oh, really?" and then go about your business, with quiet confidence, in your own way.

There are a number of outstanding books about babies in the marketplace. I suggest that you read a baby book or two and build your store of knowledge. Choose your books wisely; ask for recommendations from friends who share your parenting beliefs, and find authors who have philosophies that match your own way of thinking. As you read, keep in mind that no author will parallel your beliefs 100 percent, so you must learn to take from each one the ideas that work best for your family. In this book, I will help you learn all about babies and sleep. The best place to start, of course, is at the beginning.

The Biology of Newborn Sleep

During the first several months of a baby's life, they simply sleep when they are tired. Their waking-sleeping pattern mainly revolves around their stomach: awake when hungry and asleep when full. You can do very little to force a new baby to sleep when

Chantelle, twelve-days-old

they don't want to! However, there are many things you can unknowingly do that can prevent your baby from easily falling asleep and many factors that can disrupt your newborn's sleep— night and day.

A very important point to understand about newborn babies is that they have very, very tiny tummies. New babies grow rapidly and their diet is liquid. Formula digests quickly, and breast milk digests even more rapidly. Although it would be nice to lay your little bundle down at a predetermined bedtime and not hear a peep from them until morning, even the most naïve among us know that this is not a realistic goal for a tiny baby. Newborns need to be fed every two to four hours—and sometimes more. During those early months, your baby will have tremendous growth spurts that affect not only daytime but nighttime feeding as well, sometimes pushing that two- to four-hour schedule to one to two hours around the clock.

Babies are unpredictable, and a handful of them will make their own rules. Some newborns will sleep four or five hours straight, leaving their parents to worry if they should wake them for a feeding. The answer to this is an unequivocal "maybe." If your baby happens to fall into this pattern you'll need to talk to your doctor and find out if it's OK for your particular baby to stretch time between feedings. This will depend on your baby's size, health, and possibly other factors as well.

Sleeping Through the Night

Mother-Speak

"I remember when Rachel was a newborn, she would suck away happily for most of the day for a week or two at a time. Had I not known that this sometimes happens, and that it is necessary for the wild growth babies sometimes experience, I might have tried to enforce a schedule. Instead, I simply accepted my role in life then: a binky with legs."

Vanessa, mother of two-year-old Rachel

You have probably read or heard that babies start "sleeping through the night" at about two to four months of age. But wait! What you must understand is that, for a new baby, a five-hour stretch (the one I mentioned earlier) is considered a full night. Many (but nowhere near all) babies at this age can sleep an uninterrupted five hours. (Not that they always do.) A far cry from what you may have thought sleeping through the night meant!

Here we pause while the shock sinks in for those of you who have a baby who sleeps through the night but didn't know it.

If your baby is already sleeping through the night, enjoy the heady privilege of bragging rights the next time someone asks

Mother-Speak

"By two-months-old our little Emily was sleeping a seven-hour stretch every night. But instead of developing that into a longer night's sleep, she went in reverse, until she was waking every three to four hours. Luckily, your sleep solutions have helped us fix that!"

Christine, mother of eighteen-month-old Emily

about your baby's sleep. But, if you're thinking of putting this book away now, not so fast. Babies are fickle, and their sleep patterns ebb and flow over the early years.

What's more, while the technical definition of a full night's sleep for a baby may be five hours, most of us adults wouldn't con-

Yasmin, ten-years-old, and Maya, five-days-old

sider that anywhere near enough sleep. Also, some of these sleep-through-the-nighters will suddenly begin waking more frequently, and it's often a full year—or even two—until your little one will settle into a mature, all-night, every-night sleep pattern. However, there are many things you can do to improve your baby's sleep—no matter the age.

> **Point to Remember**
>
> Caring for a newborn is an all-out 24-hour-a-day commitment. Prioritize your life around your baby right now. Relax, stay happy, and soak up this special time, because it passes quickly.

The Fifteen Keys to Amazing Newborn Sleep

The following section is filled with ideas that will help you work with your newborn baby, and that will set you up to encourage a better sleep pattern sooner rather than later. (The information here is a brief summary of the material found in my book *The No-Cry Sleep Solution for Newborns*, so if you desire more details about the first four to five months, then I suggest you check into that book or my website for more information.)

Key 1: Your Top Priority: Get to Know Your New Baby

New babies will tell you what they need—but you need to watch, listen and learn. Your baby is born with a unique personality, and you will soon become the best interpreter for your own baby. But it takes time to figure your baby out! You may feel more love than you've ever felt before in your life, but that doesn't mean you'll know how to interpret your baby's body language and noises right

Callen, ten-days-old

off the bat. The good news is that you will learn quickly. Don't let the outside world prevent you from taking the time you need to learn all you can about your brand-new baby. In the early weeks, avoid having too much company, too many outings, and too many distractions, as these can get in the way of focusing on your baby. Relax your housekeeping standards. Whittle down your to-do list. Remind yourself every day that your number one priority is getting to know your baby.

Your newborn will communicate to you with body language and sounds: hunger, tiredness, discomfort, or a need to be held. Beginning on page 136 you can review the typical signs that babies show to tell you these things. Review the list, and then watch your own baby to learn their unique language. It will be fun when you can figure out what your infant is telling you! The more that you accurately respond to your infant's cues, the happier they will be. If you

Camden, one-week-old, and Dad

can understand what your baby is trying to tell you, then they will cry less, have more peaceful alert moments, and their sleep will be easy, natural, and amazing.

Key 2: Have Realistic Expectations

Newborns sleep a lot, but here's the challenge: Their fifteen to eighteen hours of daily sleep are distributed over four to seven (or more!) brief periods—day and night. These sleep periods can be as short as twenty minutes or as long as five hours. At first, for your newborn, there is no difference between day and night, and no concept of hours, days, or weeks. Your baby simply exists in the moment, so don't expect your little one to grasp the concepts of naptime or bedtime right now.

Tommaso, one-week-old

Newborn babies have teaspoon-sized tummies, and they experience rapid growth. They need to be fed small amounts at a time, every two to four hours—and oftentimes more than that. This frequent feeding is necessary to fuel your newborn's amazing development.

Newborn Sleep Patterns Are Predictable

Your new baby *will not sleep through the night.* Your newborn's naps will not adhere to any specific schedule. You cannot "sleep train" a newborn, and there are no shortcuts to sleep maturity—it takes time and patience. However, newborns *will* fall asleep easier and then sleep better and for longer stretches when you understand and respect their sleep needs. In addition, babies who are getting all the sleep they need, at the times they need it, are much happier and more peaceful.

Make Yourself Comfortable

I've yet to hear a parent tell me that they love getting up through-out the night to tend to an infant's needs. As much as we adore our little bundles, it's tough when you're woken up over and over again, night after night. Because it's a fact that your baby will be waking you up, you may as well make yourself as comfortable as possible.

Accept Night Wakings with Your Newborn

The first step is to learn to relax about night wakings right now. Being stressed or frustrated about having to get up won't change a thing. The situation will improve day by day; and before you know it, your little newborn won't be so little anymore—you'll have a toddler who is walking and talking and getting into every-thing in sight during the day and sleeping peacefully all night. But you're in this newborn-no-sleep stage right now, so do what you can to get through it as comfortably as possible. Here are a few ideas to make these night activities less disruptive for the adults in the house:

- Make your nighttime-feeding place as cozy and comfortable as you can. If you feed your baby while sitting in a chair, I suggest you move your most comfortable chair into the baby's room for now. If you use a rocking chair, make sure it has soft padding on the seat and back. Get yourself a soft footstool, and put a table beside you for your glass of water, a snack, your iPad, Kindle or book, a night-light, and any-thing else that helps these nighttime episodes seem more inviting.
- If you bottle-feed, make sure everything you need is ready and waiting so you don't have to travel to the kitchen. (Wonderful portable bottle stations are available.) Or have your supplies ready to go and formula premade.

- Invest in a nursing pillow or experiment with how to use bed and sofa pillows to support both the baby and you during your feeding sessions. (Do not fall asleep with your baby on one of these cushions, it's extremely unsafe.)
- If you breastfeed in bed, make sure you are very comfortable, and your baby is safe. Many mothers complain of a sore back from nursing in bed. This is usually from arching your back to bring breast to baby. Instead, get yourself in a relaxed and restful position and let your baby fold around you. Babies are remarkably flexible and will tuck into whatever space you allow. Even a big eighteen-month-old can get comfortably curled into the space provided when you lie on your side and bring your knees up (speaking from lots of experience.)
- If you and your baby bed-share, make sure the bed is big enough for everyone to get comfortable. If you're squashed, invest in a bigger or second mattress. (Many bed-sharing families have a king-sized mattress and a single mattress placed on the floor side-by-side. You may not win any design awards, but it's a very helpful arrangement.)
- Arrange your schedule around your baby as much as possible during these early months. Avoid planning evening activities that interfere with your bedtime routine or keep you out too late. Seriously, the world will wait for a few months.

Point to Remember

Relax and slow down. This is a very brief time in your life. Take the pressure off yourself, and you might notice no one else is expecting you to be Super Parent. Put off doing all those less important things in favor of the one most important: taking care of your new baby. It's OK—really.

Key 3: Learn to Read Your Baby's Sleepy Signals

Newborns will show you signs when they're tired. Reading these sleepy signals correctly is critically important, and will affect the results of every other key. If you miss the window of tiredness, your baby will quickly become overtired. An overtired baby is cranky, cries more, and ironically, won't fall asleep easily or for very long. On the flip side, a baby who is not yet tired will reject any efforts to sleep and fuss over your insistence! Dancing between just tired enough and too tired is a fine line, but if you know what to look for, you can find the perfect moment with your baby.

A very common mistake is to misread a baby's signals and respond in just about the opposite way that your baby means for you to. Many people interpret a baby's actions and sounds to mean "I need you to sing louder," or "shake the rattle more," or "keep

Alexander, two-weeks-old

bouncing me," or "try harder to get me to smile,"—when what the baby is desperately trying to say is, "I am tired and I need to sleep—please put me to bed!" If you learn to speak your baby's language, you will enjoy the prize of clear communication and easier sleep.

Take time to review the list of typical signs of fatigue on page 136. Get familiar with your baby's unique sleepy signs, and put your baby down to sleep, with babywearing, rocking, nursing, or swaddling, immediately when they seem tired. Your reward will be blissful, easy sleep.

Watch for Signs of Tiredness

Babies cannot put themselves to sleep, nor can they understand their own sleepy signs. Yet a baby who is encouraged to stay awake when their body is craving sleep is typically unhappy. Over time, this pattern develops into sleep deprivation, which further complicates your baby's developing sleep maturity.

Mother-Speak

"I discovered that I had been putting Carrson to bed completely by the clock, not paying attention to his tiredness. Once I changed this dynamic and kept an eye on both, he fell asleep easier and slept longer."

Pia, mother of eight-month-old Carrson

Most newborns can only handle 45 minutes to two hours of wakefulness. Once a baby becomes overtired, they will become overstimulated and find it harder to fall asleep and stay asleep. Look for that magic moment when the baby is tired, but not overtired.

These are some of the signs of tiredness your baby may show you. Your infant may demonstrate only one sign, or two, or more at the same time:

- A lull in movement and activity
- Quieting down
- Losing interest in people and toys (looking away)
- Looking "glazed," staring off into the distance
- Limp, sagging face and jaw
- Fussing
- Rubbing eyes, ears, or face
- Yawning

The following signs tell you that your baby might be overtired:

- Fretful crying (which can also indicate hunger)
- Arching backward or going rigid (can also indicate pain)
- Flailing, uncoordinated movements of arms and legs
- Chin down, head nodding loosely
- Drooping eyelids, slow blinking, eyelid fluttering
- Dark circles appearing under the eyes; eyes appearing red or bloodshot

Learn to read your baby's sleepy signs and put your little one to bed when that window of opportunity presents itself. This will absolutely help your baby to fall asleep easily and naturally.

Key 4: Respect the Span of "Happily Awake Time"

From the moment your baby wakes up, either in the morning or after a nap, the benefits of the previous sleep session start getting used. Your baby wakes up refreshed, but as time passes, little by little, the energy gained during sleep time is depleted and an urge to return to sleep begins to build. When we catch a baby in that in-between stage and encourage sleep, we allow a "fresh start" after

Saajan, two-months-old

each sleep period. If we push babies past this period, they become fussy, cry more easily, and cannot fully engage with people or the world.

As children age, the length of time that they can stay happily awake increases. Newborns can only stay happily awake for forty-five minutes to an hour or two at a time. At about three months some babies still need a nap every hour or two, but some can be awake for as long as three hours, if they are routinely sleeping well at night and getting good, long naps. By six months most babies can stay awake for two to three hours. However, most newborns—good sleepers and frequent-wakers alike—do best with short awake spans interspersed with plenty of naps.

If your baby has been awake beyond the "happily awake span," you have likely missed some sleepy signals, and your newborn is overtired. An overtired baby will be fussy and find it hard to sleep, yet won't be able to stay happily awake, either. And the more overtired your baby gets the more they will cry, to the point of being unable to turn off frustration long enough to fall asleep, until they eventually wear out. This becomes a pattern that can disrupt sleep, growth, and temperament.

Point to Remember

If you want your baby to be peaceful, cry less, and sleep better, keep one eye on the clock. Perhaps even set a timer or your phone to buzz as a reminder that sleep time should be near—then watch for those tired signs. Don't let your newborn stay awake for too long at a time. The result of watching the "happily awake" time span is a baby who is happy when awake and peaceful when asleep.

Key 5: Differentiate Between Sleeping Noises and Awake Noises

Most newborns are not quiet sleepers. Many babies grunt, groan, coo, whimper, and sometimes even outright cry during sleep. These noises don't always signal awakening, and they don't always require any action on your part. These are "sleeping noises," and your baby is nearly or even totally asleep during these episodes. These are not the cries that mean, "I need you!" They are just normal sleeping sounds. Babies are also active sleepers. They move around, twitch, and shift position many times during sleep.

If you respond too quickly to every little peep or movement you can actually teach your baby to wake up fully and frequently throughout the night, or in the middle of a nap, making it shorter than it should be. And that is the opposite of your goal for great sleep! I remember when my first baby, Angela, was a newborn sleeping in a cradle next to my bed. Her cry awakened me many times, yet she was asleep in my arms before I even made it from cradle to rocking chair to sit down. She was making sleeping noises. In my desire to respond to my baby's every cry, I actually taught her to wake up more often!

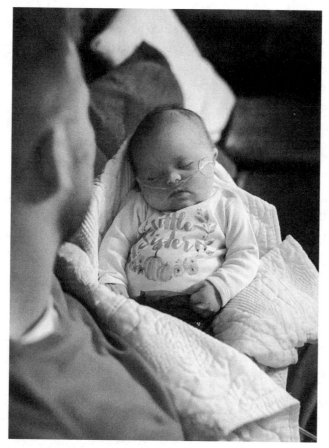

Audriel, two-months-old, and Daddy

Most health care providers recommend that parents shouldn't let a newborn sleep longer than three or four hours without feeding, and the vast majority of babies wake far more frequently than that. (Remember, there are a few exceptional babies who can go longer.) No matter what, your baby will wake up during the night. (See Part I.) The key is to learn when you should pick your baby up for a night feeding and when you can let them go back to sleep on their own.

This key is of primary importance to bed-sharing, breastfeeding mothers. It is instinct to put your baby to the breast anytime they make a peep. However, just because your baby is making noises or moving around *does not mean that they are awake*—so be patient, pretend to be asleep (that should be easy), and respond to your baby only if they really need to nurse.

When your baby is making noises, and you're not sure if your little one is awake or not, but you are feeling ready to pounce—take a pause. If your baby is *really* awake and hungry, you will—*always, of course!*—want to feed your little one as quickly as possible. You'll know right away if this is the case—newborns are built to be able to ask for food, and they can be very vocal about it. However, if your baby is just sleeping noisily—let them do it without your interference.

Point to Remember

Watch closely and listen carefully when your baby moves around and makes noises during sleep. If your baby really is waking up and hungry—feed your newborn quickly. However, if your baby is just making sleeping noises and sleeping movements—let your newborn continue to sleep without your interference.

Key 6: Use the Soothing Sounds of Pink-Hued White Noise

The environment that your baby enjoyed in the womb was filled with a constant symphony of sound, therefore many newborns find a totally quiet room disconcerting. Because of this prenatal history, "white noise" sounds can be soothing to many babies and help them to relax, fall asleep, and stay asleep. White noise is an indistinct background hum, such as the rumble of a motor, the drone of a fan, or the swish of ocean waves.

White noise is also helpful because it blocks out sharp noises (clinking dishes, dogs barking, television sounds, sibling squeals) that can wake your sleeping newborn. It also creates a consistent sleep cue that tells your baby it is time to sleep.

Not all white noise is created equal! Pink noise is a variant of white noise that sounds full, deep, rich, and monotonous. Perfect examples of pink noise are the sounds of a heartbeat, a fan or humidifier, ocean waves, the patter of rainfall, or the rustling of leaves on a tree. In contrast, examples of pure white noise include things like a vacuum cleaner, the static between stations on a radio, and the squeal of a hair dryer, which all are made up of a higher pitch and intensity. As you can see, there are subtle but important differences that make pink noise gentler on the ear, and a better match for aiding sleep.

You can purchase white noise machines or apps, and most contain pink noise options, though they may be not labeled as such. It will be easy to pick out the right noise if you look for steady, lower pitched sounds that feel relaxing and comfortable to your own ear. The noise must be loud enough to be effective, but not so loud as to harm your baby's hearing. Find the perfect volume by putting your own head near where your baby's head will be resting—turn on the noise and listen. The sound should be at the

Everly, three-weeks-old

level of a pleasant background hum, about the volume of rainfall or a bathroom shower. The source of the sound should be placed a distance away from your baby, such as on a dresser across the room, not right in their bed, because that could impact the development of your baby's hearing.

Turn on your baby's white noise whenever your little one is showing signs of tiredness and ready to sleep—for naps and nighttime sleep. It's perfectly fine to leave pink-hued white noise playing at a low volume during the entire nap and all night long if you would like. Turn the white noise off *as soon as your baby is awake* so that it retains its magical sleep-inducing powers and so that your baby can learn about the world and its many different sounds.

Key 7: Set Your Baby's Biological Clock

Many new parents don't believe me when I tell them that a new-born sleeps fifteen to eighteen hours per day. That's a lot of sleep—but for most parents it feels like your baby is only sleeping half that much. The reason that it doesn't feel like that much sleep is because a newborn's sleep is distributed over four to seven (or more) sleep periods—day and night, oftentimes in small chunks. In addition, new parents are exhausted by day's end and looking forward to a good night's sleep, so a baby's waking every few hours can make it seem you're not getting any sleep at all! All this waking up is perfectly normal, I'm afraid, and part of the way that babies are made. The good news is that you can help consolidate those many sleeping periods into longer stretches by helping to set their biological clocks.

Human sleep is regulated by an internal body clock that primes us for wakefulness during the day and sleepiness at night. Babies are born with an undeveloped biological clock that takes many months to mature. While biology will largely dictate the maturity timeline of your baby's biological clock, there are a number of things that you can do to help the cause.

Daytime tips:
- Provide ample, frequent feedings during the day.
- Make your baby's awake times interesting but avoid over-stimulation, particularly in the hour before a nap or bedtime.
- Have a bit of outside time daily, early in the day whenever possible.
- Give your baby several active parts of the day with tummy-time to allow freedom of movement.
- Try to enjoy some daily sunshine (either outside or by a window) when possible.

- Provide plenty of naps according to the "happily awake span" shown on the chart of page 204, in the column for "Endurable Awake Hours."
- Locate naps in the middle of family life instead of a quiet, dark bedroom, as long as your baby naps well in this way.
- Aim for an early bedtime aligned with your baby's signs of tiredness.

Nighttime tips:
- Use a bedtime routine that includes unique actions like a bath, a massage, and a change into pajamas to signal the difference between naptime and bedtime. (You can read more about bedtime routines in Key 14.)
- Keep the house dimly lit and peaceful in the hour before bedtime. Lower the volume of music or the TV.
- Feed your baby at night whenever your child is hungry.
- Keep night feedings dark, quiet, and toy-free.
- If your home is noisy after your baby's bedtime, use white noise to cover up the sounds of the family or neighborhood.
- Maintain darkness throughout the night, and use only a tiny night-light for diaper changes.

Nighttime Bottle-Feeding with Ease

If you are bottle-feeding your baby, make sure that everything you need for night feeding is close at hand and ready to use. Your goal is for your baby to stay in a sleepy mood and nod right back off to sleep. If you have to run to the kitchen to prepare a bottle while your baby fusses or cries, you'll just bring both of you to the point of being wide awake, and what may have been a brief night waking will turn into a long period of wakefulness.

Nighttime Diapers

If your baby is waking every hour or two during the night, you don't have to change their diaper every time. Again, remembering back to when Angela was a newborn and I was a "newmom," I dutifully changed her every hour or two when she woke up. Oftentimes I was changing one dry diaper for a new one. I eventually learned that I was more "tuned in" to the diaper issue than she was!

I suggest that you put your baby in a good-quality nighttime diaper, and when they wake up, do a quick check. Change them only if you have to, and do it as quickly and quietly as you can in the dark. Use a tiny night-light when you change the baby, and avoid any bright lights that can signal daytime. Have your changing supplies organized and close to your baby's bed, and make sure you use a warm cloth to wipe that sleepy bottom—nothing like a cold, wet jolt to wake your baby up fully! (Check into the many available types of baby-wipe warmers, and keep one near your nighttime changing station or wet your washcloth in warm water.)

Key 8: Ensure Adequate Daily Naps

Before birth your baby slept 20 hours a day *or more*. Waking periods were random and for very short periods of time. (Much of what is felt during pregnancy are movements made during sleep.) After birth, newborns begin to consolidate their sleep into more defined sleep segments. They still need a lot of sleep and need to nap up to eight hours each day. (See the Sleep Chart on page 204.) These daytime nap hours are critically important to their health, growth, and happiness. And in addition, ample, quality naps will actually help your baby sleep better at night.

Point to Remember

Sleep begets sleep, when it comes to babies.

Newborns want to sleep when they are tired, just like they did in the womb. But in the womb, the environment was always perfect for sleep. Your baby enjoyed a perfectly controlled temperature, gentle darkness, the soft white-noise thump-thump of your heartbeat, and a fluid cradle that gently rocked their floating body. But suddenly, one day, everything changed. The world outside the womb was an entirely different story. Since your baby cannot control the outside environment, it's up to you to create a perfect napping situation.

Steele, two-months-old, and Mommy

What happens when your baby's needs are not correctly interpreted, and they aren't given a cozy place to snooze? They cry. They fuss. They do not sleep.

You'll remember from Key 4 (page 136) that your newborn can only stay happily awake for a short period of time (forty-five minutes to three hours, depending on age) before needing to sleep again. Keep one eye on the clock and one eye on your baby (watching for signs of tiredness), and when it's time for sleep, create a cozy environment for your baby's naptime.

Newborns aren't very flexible when it comes to their sleep. Missing a nap or pushing a bedtime past your infant's desired sleep times can interfere with sleep, not only for that particular sleep session, but also for the remainder of that day—or even the next one. So, if your newborn is particularly fussy and not sleeping well, consider if yesterday's nap needs were compromised and pay closer attention to sleep today.

Key 9: Understand and Respect Your Baby's Sucking Reflex

Babies are born with an incredibly strong sucking reflex that is possibly their most important instinct. Feeding frequently is the means to their survival, so the need to suck is an unstoppable instinct. In addition, your baby's sucking reflex is also a method of stress release and relaxation. Most babies need the soothing

Point to Remember

If you are breastfeeding your baby, frequent sucking will be important for feeding, relaxing, bonding, and milk production. You can't breastfeed your infant "too much." (And in the early days, the more you nurse, the easier it will become for both of you.)

Adrian, one-month-old, and Mommy

effect of sucking even in between feedings, and this is commonly referred to as comfort nursing.

Feeding requires your baby's complete and focused attention, so it's likely that your baby will fall asleep after expending the energy that feeding requires. It's nearly impossible to prevent babies from becoming drowsy as they suck. It's normal for your newborn to fall asleep while sucking. Embrace this!

When a baby gets *past the newborn stage* and continues to *always* fall asleep sucking, for every nap and every nighttime sleep, they come to associate sucking with falling asleep; over time, there is a very good chance that this habitual routine will make it very hard for them to fall asleep any other way. A large percentage of parents who are struggling with older babies who cannot fall or stay asleep are fighting this natural and powerful sucking-to-sleep association.

To prevent facing this dilemma months from now, once breastfeeding is fully established, and your baby is past the early weeks, healthy, and growing well, you can begin to slowly separate the act of sucking from the act of falling asleep. Your baby will likely become very drowsy when sucking, and that's what you want, but you don't always have to keep your baby attached until they are so fully asleep that the nipple falls from their mouth.

Point to Remember

If you want your baby to be able to fall asleep without your help a few months from now, it is essential that you sometimes let your baby suck on the nipple until they are very sleepy, but not totally limp-limbed-asleep. After the first few weeks of life, about one-third or more of the time, remove your baby from your breast or the bottle when they are drowsy and done feeding, but before they begin the fluttery, on-off pacifying sucking that is non-nutritive but sleep inducing.

It's natural for your baby to require sucking time beyond meal time. This non-nutritive sucking does not have to be totally avoided, because it provides a lovely bonding opportunity for you and your baby and can help establish a healthy milk supply if you are breastfeeding. However, sucking should not be an absolute necessity for sleep. So, some of the time, before your baby is totally limp-limbed and snoring, remove them from the breast or bottle to finish falling asleep without the nipple in their mouth.

Pacifier use and finger-sucking have slightly different rules, so you can let your baby fall asleep with these.

Point to Remember

For some of your baby's sleep times, remove the breast or bottle and let them finish falling asleep without something in their mouth. When you do this, your baby may resist, root, and fuss to regain the nipple. It's perfectly fine to return them to the breast, or bottle, and start over a few minutes later or at the next sleep session.

Repeat. Repeat. Repeat. If you do this at least a few times a day, your baby will eventually learn how to fall asleep without having something resting in their mouth.

If you are a breastfeeding mother, please go back and reread the previous paragraph. It contains possibly the most important idea I can share with you at this time to prevent you from facing a common and difficult sleep problem a few months from now.

What About Pacifiers?

Pacifiers are one tool to help a baby who has a strong and constant need to suck, and if used properly can be helpful. Babies who are sick or have special needs might also find a pacifier helps with pain relief.

Once breastfeeding is firmly established and going well for both of you (three to eight weeks), or if your baby is exclusively bottle-fed, it is fine to offer your baby a pacifier to help them fall asleep, if you'd like, as it is a soothing non-food sleep aid and might possibly help reduce the risk of SIDS (see page 344). Use pacifiers judiciously, though, which often means keeping them linked specifically to sleep times, car rides, or colicky periods only. Don't replace the pacifier once it falls out after your baby is sleeping; and avoid having it become an all-day attachment or the first line of defense against fussiness.

What About Thumb and Finger Sucking?

If your baby falls asleep sucking their fingers, this is an entirely different situation from using a bottle, pacifier, or the breast. If your baby finds comfort in sucking their fingers, they are learning to control their own hands and will not always depend on someone else to help them. Current philosophies disagree as to whether letting a baby get into this habit is a good idea, but most experts agree that letting a young baby suck their own fingers poses no harm. The biggest problem, as you may expect, is that some babies don't give up the habit at any age, and you eventually have to step in, but for many parents this is an acceptable risk in trade for having a calm, happy baby now.

Those Newborn Sucking Marathons

There will be many days when all your newborn wants to do is suck. It's normal, it's natural, and it is utterly bone-deep exhausting for a parent to deal with. Here are some tips to make this short but challenging phase a bit easier.

Fill Baby's Tummy Before Sleep

Try to make the last feeding before bedtime a complete one. If your baby nods off after feeding from one breast or after taking half a bottle, shift them around, untuck the blanket, tickle those toes, and encourage them to finish the feeding; otherwise, they may wake up very soon to "finish" the feeding.

Create Restful Feeding Sessions

One piece of advice you will hear over and over is "sleep while baby sleeps during the day." Nice idea, but as a busy parent, often the last thing we can do is sleep when baby sleeps! Therefore, long, blissful naps are usually out of the question. But, during the day, you can rest while you feed your baby. Your baby will feed frequently during these first few months. It is your job to relax and feed your baby. Don't sit there and fret about all those things that you "should be doing." This *is* what you should be doing during these first few months of your baby's life.

Follow these steps each time you sit to feed your new baby:

- Relax. Breathe slowly.
- Push your shoulders down, and relax them. (Parents tend to tense up and raise their shoulders during feeding, especially during the first few months. When your shoulders are up around your ears somewhere, this creates muscle tension in your arms, shoulders, and neck.)
- Circle your head, stretch out your arms and legs, and arch your back to work out the stress.
- Enjoy a few minutes of peaceful baby time; take advantage of this opportunity to gaze at your precious little one. Start making memories.
- Read, if you enjoy it. (Or read to your baby.)
- Watch television or a movie, scan your social media, or listen to music, if any of those things relax you.

Simplify Your Life

Simplify your life as much as you can during these early months of your baby's life. Relax your housekeeping standards. Graciously accept any help that anyone offers to you. (Repeat after me: "Yes, thank you, that would be nice.") Your first priority right now is to take care of your new baby.

Have Realistic Expectations

Your newborn baby will not sleep through the night. There are no magic answers and no shortcuts to sleep maturity. If you focus on your wish for a full night's sleep, you'll just push yourself to the point of weeping over what you cannot have right now. The best advice I can give you is to remind yourself that these early months with your baby will pass quickly. And then you'll be looking back fondly on those memories of holding your newborn in your arms.

Key 10: Help Your Baby Make Friends with the Bassinet

Where does your baby feel the most comfortable and secure? In your arms. Where is your baby most at peace? In your arms. If given the choice, where would your new baby want to sleep? In your arms, of course!

There is nothing—absolutely nothing—as endearing and wonderful as a newborn baby falling asleep in your arms. I know that I found it nearly impossible to put my sleeping babies down.

I can tell you that I became an expert at typing with one hand. I can do—and have done—anything with a sleeping baby in my arms—including coaching my daughter's softball team (dugout baby in team-colored sling), chairing a PTA meeting, and even using the toilet. (Oh, you thought you were the only one to do that?)

But—Danger! Alert! Warning! A baby who always sleeps in your arms will—you guessed it—always want to sleep in your arms. Smart baby! A baby who cries for the comfort of mother's or father's arms, and the parent who responds, is working within the natural framework of instinct that has helped ensure infants' survival from the beginning of time.

Asa, two-months-old, and Daddy

This very natural and all-consuming connection would work perfectly in a perfect world—where parents did nothing but care for their babies that entire first year or two of life. A world in which someone else tends the home, makes the meals, provides the means to pay the bills—while parent and baby spend their days enjoying each other and doing those nourishing, bonding things nature intended. Alas, such a world doesn't exist. Contemporary life, with its demands, does not provide such privilege. We have much to do, and we must strike a balance between instinct and practicality.

Choosing to Honor the Instinct

Many parents of newborns give in to their basic instinct to hold their sleeping babies for naps and to bed-share at night. This is a perfectly natural and normal situation the world over and is much too lovely of an experience to pass up. There are plenty of times when you should relish this lovely experience, and I encourage you to do so whenever it's possible and practical. And when you do, breathe in every moment of the sweetness of your precious baby.

Mother-Speak

"You know, when Zach fell asleep nursing in my arms, I did just this. I traced the outline of his nose, I smelled his hair. I played with his fingers. I wanted to suck up every little thing I could about him when he was a baby, because he is my fourth child, and I'd learned how very quickly it all goes."

Vanessa, mother of two-year-old Zachary

Newborns aren't newborns very long. In a blink they will be toddling off on wobbly legs, and another blink after that they will be on the school bus, and next thing you know they'll be driving off in their own car. As a mom of four grown children, trust me when I say the days are long but the years are short. So, some of you will choose to honor the instinct to keep your baby in your arms or at your side throughout the newborn months, and if it suits you, carry on! (Please do read the safety list on pages 369–373 if you choose to bed-share.)

The Benefits of Bassinet Sleep

Even if you are one of these parents who loves to keep your baby at your side for sleep, I urge you to allow your baby to get used to sleeping alone at least *some of the time*. It's a rare mother or father who has the time or ability to cater to an in-arms-sleeping baby for every single nap, and all night long for the next one, two, or more years! Babies need much more sleep than adults do. I've worked with many parents whose babies are so accustomed to a parent's presence in bed that Mom or Dad has to go to bed at 7:00 P.M. and *stay there* because their baby has built-in radar that won't allow them to leave the room. A parent also has to take daytime naps, whether they want to or not, or hold a gangly toddler for a two-hour on-the-lap nap! A better idea is to enjoy the in-arms and bed-sharing times with your baby, when it works for you, but teach your little one that they can sleep alone, too.

> **Point to Remember**
> It may be a good idea to get your baby accustomed to sleeping in a bassinet some of the time, even if you don't think you will need or want this option. You might wish to take a shower, exercise, or use the toilet without a babe-in-arms once in a while!

So, as difficult as it may be, I recommend that when your baby is asleep, *at least once every day: put your sleeping baby down in a cradle, bassinet, or crib.* If you start this from the beginning, your baby will learn to enjoy independent sleep.

In addition to arranging at least one nap per day in the crib, it's very helpful to have at least one nighttime sleep cycle in the crib. (If you've looked at Part V on safety, page 343, you know that your baby's crib or cradle should always be located in your bedroom during the newborn months.)

An easy way to make a crib-sleep session happen is to select the first sleep time of the night as the crib sleep. Feed your baby in a chair or on a sofa that is *not* in your sleeping room—and then move your baby to a cradle, crib, or bassinet for the first sleep segment of the night. (The first segment of the "night" happens any time after 5:00 to 6:00 P.M. when your baby is showing you clear signs of being tired, or when they normally have their first long sleep of the night.) An advantage of doing this for your baby's first sleep of the night is that you are less likely to fall asleep with your baby feeding in a chair, recliner, or sofa, which can happen during night feedings and is a very risky situation.

Once your baby has fallen asleep in the crib, even if it turns out to be only for a short five-minute snooze, the experience will help to make it a familiar sleep place. After this, when your baby wakes during the night for feeding, you can either return your baby to the crib or bring them in to your safely arranged family bed.

See Key 12, "Give Your Baby Opportunities to Fall Asleep Unaided," for more tips on bassinet or crib sleep.

Good Advice, Briefly Modified

After I wrote the above section for the original edition of this book, I took a break to pick up my then-teenaged daughter from an early-release day at school. We spent the afternoon together—had manicures and then went out for lunch. As we sat and talked and giggled like girlfriends, I thought how terribly I would miss her when, in a few short years, she would leave the nest for college or wherever her nearly adult status took her. When Angela and I returned home from that outing, the two of us sat with Coleton, who was then such a tiny baby, while he entertained us by making faces and noises.

I recall thinking that every moment of our children's lives is incredibly precious and irreplaceable. How fleeting each phase, and how I wish I could bottle and save each of them to view and treasure. Today, my sweet daughter is a wife and mother herself, and those years are so far behind us. So my advice to put your baby down to sleep is so easily given from where I sit. I'll be totally honest with myself and with you, though. My grandson would frequently find himself exactly where his mother, aunt, and uncles did—sleeping in my arms—with his little head bopping to the tune of my computer keys.

So, allow me to amend my advice just a bit, please. Understand that those beautiful, bonding, peaceful habits are very hard to break, and choose carefully when you want to break them. If you can, and when you can, put your baby down so that they are able to sleep alone, as well as in your arms. And when you don't put your little one down, hold them with your heart, too, and relish every gurgle, flutter, and little sighing breath. Trust me when I say, "You will miss this." You will. Even the dark, exhausted nights will take on a certain romance in your memories, and those recollections will bubble to the surface when your "baby" drives off in their first car, graduates from school, gets married, and has their own baby.

There are no absolute rules when it comes to these Keys. If you are a 100 percent bed-sharing family, everyone is sleeping well enough, your baby is sleeping safely, and you are comfortable with having your baby in your arms or your safely arranged family bed, then just skip this key, and live life your own way.

Key 11: Swaddle Your Baby at the Right Times in the Right Way

After nine months of living in a snug body-hugging, pretzel-folded space, your newborn can find it very unsettling to be put on their back on a flat surface—yet this is the safest way for your newborn to sleep to protect against SIDS. To help make sleep more pleas-

Izadora and Antonella, one-month-old

ant, many babies are comforted and sleep better and longer when parents create a womb-like experience for sleep by wrapping them securely in a receiving blanket—swaddling. When done correctly, swaddling can be an effective technique to help calm infants and promote sleep. In addition, when new babies are wrapped snugly, this prevents their natural startle reflexes from waking them up.

Your pediatrician, nurse, midwife, doula, or a lactation consultant can teach you how to swaddle your newborn. You can also find step-by-step instructions for swaddling your baby in a baby care book or a YouTube video. Check reputable sources for safe and proper swaddling techniques, such as the International Hip Dysplasia Institute.

If you decide to swaddle your baby investigate all the do's, don'ts and safety rules. Here are some of the most important points:

- Swaddle only a full-term, healthy baby who sleeps in your bedroom (or if a doctor gives the okay for your special baby).
- *Always* put your swaddled baby down on their back for sleep.
- NEVER swaddle your baby when you bed-share.
- Make sure your baby's legs can bend up and out (froggie style) when swaddled to protect hip development.
- Don't allow your baby to overheat. Choose a lightweight, breathable fabric for a swaddle and appropriate-weight pajamas.
- Swaddle snugly enough so that baby can't become unwrapped, but not so tight that it affects breathing or circulation. There should be space for two or three of your fingers to slide easily between your baby's chest and the fabric.
- Get an OK from your health provider to be sure swaddling is a safe choice for your baby.
- Swaddle only for sleep. Unwrap your baby when awake.
- End swaddling when potential risks outweigh the benefits, such as when your baby begins to roll over or can wiggle free from the blanket.

Point to Remember

If your newborn baby enjoys swaddling, and if it helps them sleep better, you can swaddle every day for naps and at night-time, right from the day of birth, provided that you adhere to all the safety aspects of proper swaddling.

Key 12: Give Your Baby Opportunities to Fall Asleep Unaided

Having a newborn fall asleep in your arms, at your breast, or in a sling is one of life's greatest pleasures and should be enjoyed fully. It's easy to keep these precious little packages in your arms long after they have fallen asleep, and it is a joy you should treasure every time it happens. This key is about understanding how this lovely routine can affect your baby's sleep rituals over time and suggests ways to enjoy a balance between holding your sleeping baby as they fall asleep versus allowing them a chance to fall asleep on their own.

The reason that this concept is important is not about today. It's about next month and the month after that, and the year after that. Babies love being nurtured to sleep; however, if you always hold or nurse your baby to sleep, they will very easily

Amelia, two-weeks-old

become accustomed to being held as they fall asleep and as they move between sleep cycles. Eventually your little one will be *unable* to fall asleep or maintain sleep on their own, and this is when nighttime parenting often falls to pieces. Most parents cannot maintain the pace of being the sandman every hour or two all night long for the first year or two of their child's life, and it's wise to keep your eye on this factor as you move past the newborn phase.

This key is all about putting your baby into bed when they are sleepy instead of sleeping. A tired newborn, too young yet to have ingrained habits, will often accept being put into the crib or cradle while still awake, where they will then fall asleep on their own. When you first try implementing this idea, sometimes your baby will go to sleep, and sometimes they won't. When your baby does not settle and fusses instead, you can rock, pat, or even pick your infant up and help get them settled, and then start over either in a few minutes or for the next nap.

Mother-Speak

"I think one of the most helpful ideas was to put him down when he was tired but awake—he surprised me by allowing it so often!"

Judith, mother of three-month-old Harry

You can avoid creating the almost inevitable scenario of a totally sleep-dependent child by placing your baby in the crib, cradle, or cradle-swing (lying flat) when comfortable and drowsy, but not entirely asleep *at least some of the time*. Most newborns will accept this idea much more easily than an older baby who has come to learn that sleep only comes when mommy, daddy, Nana, or another loving adult is there to provide it. If you think you like the sound of this idea, there is no harm, no risk, and no tears involved in giving it a try.

Make Your Baby Comfortable

Babies are as different from each other as we adults are, and you'll learn to understand your own baby's preferences over time. Here are a few ideas for making your baby comfortable enough to fall asleep unaided. Experiment with them, and you'll soon discover which work best for your little one.

Cozy Cradle, Sleepy Place

It can help to set up a welcoming sleep place to aid with falling asleep. Make sure your baby's mattress is comfortable, as many that come included in a cradle or bassinet are hard and stiff. Use soft sheets, such as fleece or flannel (always use bedding made to fit your baby's exact mattress size), and keep the room dark and quiet except for your baby's white noise.

Smaller Space

Many newborns feel overwhelmed in a big crib. Your baby may be one of those who finds a smaller cradle or bassinet more to their liking. There are cradles made for use alongside an adult bed, which is very helpful for ease of night feeding and for reaching over to settle your baby. One of these bedside cradles can be a perfect choice since it keeps your baby at arm's reach but still nestled in their own little space.

Many babies even scoot up to the corner of the cradle to wedge their head into the crevice—much like they were wedged into your pelvis. Make sure that if your cradle can rock that you lock it into a stationary position when your baby is sleeping unattended, and that it cannot be tipped over if they do this creeping-into-the-corner routine.

Good Smells

A baby's sense of smell is more keen than that of an adult. Research shows that babies can recognize their own mother or father by smell. If you have a small stuffed animal or baby blanket, you can tuck it in your shirt for a few hours, and then place it beside the cradle while baby sleeps. Follow all safety precautions, which include not placing this object directly in bed with your newborn. (You might try putting your baby's fitted bedsheet in your shirt for a bit if you don't mind having to remake the bed.) Avoid using perfume, cologne, or scented deodorant if trying this idea, as your baby's sense of smell is sensitive.

A Warm Bed

When a sleepy baby is placed on cold sheets, they can be jarred awake. While you are feeding your baby, you can warm the sleeping spot with a wrapped hot water bottle or a heating pad set on low. Remove the warmer from the crib before you lay your baby down, and always run your arm slowly over the entire area to make sure it's not too hot. An alternative is to use flannel or fleece crib sheets rather than the colder linen or cotton blend types.

A Gently Rocking Bed

Many newborns fall asleep much more easily in a moving bed that is gently rocking or swaying rather than a still surface. Check out the ideas in Key 13 for adding motion for peaceful sleep.

Perfect Timing

Check out the sleep hours chart on page 204, paying close attention to the happily awake span. Watch the clock for approximate sleep time and observe your baby for signs of tiredness. Make sure your baby is well-fed and has a dry diaper, then place your baby into bed.

So you see, over the first few months of life, you can gradually and lovingly help your baby learn how to fall asleep without your help. And you can do this without tears (yours or theirs).

Key 13: Provide Motion for Peaceful Sleep

Prior to birth, 100 percent of a baby's sleep occurs in a cozy bed of fluid that sloshes and moves along with Mother's every step and motion. She walks, bounces up the stairs and maybe even jogs or bikes! Even during the typically disjointed sleep that pregnancy so kindly provides, Mama likely shifted and moved throughout the

Maja, fourteen-months-old, and Mommy

night. That's why babies are naturally attracted to motion for sleep and why lying on an unmoving, rigid crib surface can be unsettling to your new baby.

In the womb, the fluid sway of movement was a constant, soothing sleep-inducer, and that is now missing. At birth, your baby is still the same motion-loving person from just a minute before; they don't magically transform into a different life form! That's the reason that the first three months of life are often referred to as the "Fourth Trimester." It is a time of transition.

Babies often sleep better when we re-create some of the experiences from the womb. This explains why infants enjoy a sleeping place that is warm, closely held, filled with a rhythm of white noise and gently moving. Being held in a parent's arms creates the perfect combination of these things—but most busy parents cannot possibly hold a napping baby for the many hours that a newborn sleeps every day. The next best solution: a swing, glider, stroller, or rocking cradle. One of these will very often become a baby's favored location for napping over a stationary cradle, crib, or bed. (Don't use a baby hammock as these have not been deemed safe. As wonderful as they appear, a baby could sleep in the dangerous chin-to-chest position that can impede breathing. Though keep your eye on the news as I suspect someone will invent a safe baby hammock at some point in time!)

When used properly, these devices are not only safe and helpful—they can be sanity-savers. The biggest risks are the temptation to overuse them, and the possibility that your baby will become so accustomed to them that you'll be battling a set-in-concrete sleep association six months from now. Which, for some parents of colicky infants, or for those who are desperate to find a way to help their infant sleep better, can be risks they are willing to take.

When using a bed of any type for motion, make sure it's made especially for a newborn and that it allows your baby to lie flat, like on a bed, since newborns should not be left to sleep in a sitting position.

Professional-Speak
Busting This Myth About Baby Sleep

"Sleeping in your arms, a sling, a stroller, or a swinging cradle is "junk" sleep and it won't refresh your baby's brain. . . ."

Clearly these scaremongering fools have never been stuck at home all day so their baby can sleep while their own brains turn into scrambled eggs. Luckily you would only believe this bit of nonsense if it was your first kid and you didn't have to also do school runs or get to soccer practice with your other kids. Sleep is sleep. A baby who can snooze on the move is a lot easier than one who will only ever sleep in a darkened room at home, in his safety standards-approved crib, in his own interior-designed nursery.

We have been rocking babies to sleep for generations, so there just might be something in it (or in us) that's pretty innate, don't you think? If your baby sleeps in a stroller, a sling, or your arms, the rocking motion while he is sleeping is actually great for his tiny brain: movement helps develop his vestibular apparatus, a series of canals inside the inner ear that, as fluid moves over them (with movement), send out messages to the nervous system. This helps with the development of speech and language, balance, and sensory integration (making sense of all the sensations of sound, movement, taste, smell, and visual stimuli). So, ditch the guilt and worry, pop your baby in a carrier or the stroller, and get up and go!

Pinky McKay, author of *Sleeping Like a Baby* and *Parenting by Heart*

While motion sleep is helpful, having 100 percent of naps occur with motion can lead to dependence, so avoid excessive reliance on this. Other than that, every baby benefits from a unique balance of the two—motion sleep and stationary sleep. After the first few weeks of your baby's life, I recommend that you intentionally balance motion naps with some stationary crib naps. If your baby can fall asleep in several different ways, this can give you more flexibility and will likely make it easier if you wish to modify sleep locations down the road.

Key 14: *Develop a Hint of a Bedtime Routine*

Newborn babies don't require much of a bedtime routine since they sleep and wake all through the day and night. But there are many simple things you can do to help the sleep process flow

Penelope, two-weeks-old

more easily and to gradually build a good bedtime routine that will hold you in good stead as your baby becomes a toddler. In addition, introducing a routine can help you to identify and reinforce your baby's ideal point of "tired-but-not-overtired" by including factors that help your baby reach that sleepy point precisely at bedtime.

The following bedtime routine factors are helpful to almost all babies:

- Help your baby "wind down" for ten to twenty minutes before sleep time by keeping the people around him quieter and relaxed. Turn down the music or TV, and keep your voices hushed.
- Dim the lights in the fifteen to thirty minutes before a nap or bedtime. Bright lights are an alerting factor in the biological clock process, whereas darkness brings relaxation and sleepiness.
- Use white noise to mask harsh sounds and create a soothing pre-bed mood. This also creates a powerful sleep cue.
- Hold and rock your baby, feed them, or give them a massage. Warm touches are relaxing and can help your baby fall asleep.
- Talk, sing, or hum to your little one. Your voice is your baby's favorite sound—so read a book (even a novel will do at this age!) or sing a lullaby or your favorite song.
- Create a short but peaceful pre-sleep routine, possibly including a change into pajamas, a quiet diaper change, and taking the last feeding in a specific and relaxing location.

Key 15: Live by the No-Cry Philosophy and Enjoy Your Happy Family

To be a kind, compassionate parent, view your actions through the eyes and the experiences of your child. Be a knowledgeable parent.

Read, listen, and learn. Make thoughtful, purposeful decisions. Build a friendship with your child right from the start. Enjoy the moments and rise to the challenges. Don't be so focused on sleep issues or any other distraction that you miss the glorious loveliness of your new baby—this time passes in a blink of an eye. When your baby is (finally) asleep, take a few minutes to bask in the breathtaking beauty of their soft hair, tiny ears, smooth-as-silk skin, the gentle rise and fall of their breath, or those adorable baby snores. These are the moments when memories are built.

Zoey, six-years-old, and Willow, three-weeks-old

Tune out the outside advice or criticism that doesn't fit with your parenting style. There are no absolute rules about raising children and no guarantees for any parenting techniques. Raise your children how you choose to raise them and in ways that are right for you, and politely ignore those who feel they must provide their opinions. Don't create or imagine problems because someone else has a different lifestyle than you do. Be true to yourself.

Understand that sleep success and problems are an ever-changing state of affairs. Throughout childhood, there will undoubtedly be many disruptions to your child's sleep: colic, teething, growth spurts, illness, vacations, separation anxiety, or starting daycare. When real problems arise, or issues need to be addressed, take a deep breath, do your research and make a plan. As sleep needs evolve and change over time, keep in mind that there are always gentle No-Cry sleep solutions to address them.

Understand that raising a child is a complicated lifelong undertaking, and that you are, and always should be, the best expert on your own child.

Raising your child only starts with the blur that is babyhood. This time now is only the beginning; it is the setting in motion of a relationship that will blossom from what you plant today.

Part Two: Solutions for Older Babies— Four Months to Two Years

The following section presents an assortment of ideas geared to babies who are past the newborn stage, up to two-years-old and sometimes a little older. If your baby is on the young side of this range, you may want to also read the section particularly for newborn babies that begins on page 121.

You won't use every idea here. You'll want to review and use those solutions that suit your family and match up to your individual baby's needs. Even if a certain idea resonates with you, it might still be that modifying the suggestion a bit will result in the best solution.

> **Point to Remember**
> There is no one-size-fits-all sleep solution. Every baby is unique, so sleep plans must be unique. You know your baby better than anyone else in the world, so only you can create a customized sleep plan that works best for your child.

⭐ Get Yourself Ready

In the course of my research and through my own experience, I have discovered that our own emotions often hold us back from making changes in our babies' sleeping habits. You yourself may be the very obstacle preventing you from changing a routine that disrupts your life—in this case, your baby's sleep habits. After all, you probably wouldn't be reading this book unless you find your baby's sleep routine difficult to mesh with your own life. So let's figure out if anything is standing in your way.

Examine Your Own Needs and Goals

Before you read another page of this book, you must ask yourself a few questions, and make a decision. In your heart of hearts, are your baby's wakeful ways and your coping strategies truly upsetting to *you*? Or does the problem lie more in the perceptions of those around you? Let me put it another way. Your baby's sleep habits are only problematic if *you* feel they are. Today's society leads us to believe that "normal babies" sleep through the night from about two months on; my research indicates that this is more the exception than the rule. I've discovered that until about age three, a

Ailee, seven-months-old, and Maman

great percentage of children wake up during the night needing a parent's attention. The number of families in your boat could fill a fleet of cruise ships, so don't feel that you must pressure yourself or your baby to fit into some imagined sleeping requirement.

You must figure out where your problem lies. Is it in your baby's routine, in your management of it, or simply in the minds of others? If you can honestly say you want to change your baby's sleep habits because they are truly and personally disruptive to you and your family, then you're ready to read on. But if you feel coerced into changing your baby's patterns because Aunt Martha, Great-Grandma Beulah, your friend from playgroup, or even your pediatrician says that's the way it should be, it's time for a long, hard think.

Every baby is unique, every parent is unique, and every family is unique. Only you can determine the right answers for your situation.

Once you decide how you truly feel about your baby's sleep habits, you can read this book with a better understanding of what you expect from the things that you learn.

This is a good time to take stock. Compare your baby's sleep pattern to the information in Chapter 2, which explains a baby's average sleep requirement. It also covers how often *typical* babies wake up at night. Use that information to help you determine realistic goals for your baby's sleep.

Certainly, if your little one is waking you up every hour or two (as my Coleton did), you don't have to think long on the question, "Is this disruptive to me?" It obviously is. However, if your baby is waking up only once or twice a night, it's important that you determine exactly how much this pattern is disturbing to you, and decide on a realistic goal. If you are wishing for twelve hours of solid sleep—from 7:00 P.M. to 7:00 A.M.—your goal may not be reasonable. After all, waking up once or twice a night is really normal during the first few years of life, even though many books and articles paint a different picture. I have found it odd that when more than 50 percent of babies younger than two years of age wake up during the night this is labeled a "disorder." With that high of a percentage I'd label it "normal." Just because it's normal, though, doesn't mean you can, or should, live with it. You can do many things to encourage your baby to sleep better.

So, be realistic in determining your goals and honest in assessing the situation's effect on your life. Some people can handle two night wakings easily, while others find that the effect of even one night waking is just too much to handle. The key is to evaluate whether your baby's sleep schedule is a problem in your eyes or just in those of the people around you who are not as informed as you are now about normal sleep patterns.

If your baby's sleep pattern is a problem for you, this book will help you solve it. And even if you've decided that one or two night wakings really aren't so bad after all, you can still use these concepts to gradually help your baby eliminate them sooner than would happen if you didn't change anything at all.

Begin today by contemplating these questions:

- Am I content with the way things are, or am I becoming resentful, angry, or frustrated?
- Is my baby's nighttime routine negatively affecting my marriage, job, or relationships with my partner, friends, or my other children?
- Is my baby happy, healthy, and seemingly well-rested enough to get through the day?
- Am I happy, healthy, and well-rested?
- Based on the facts in this book (see Chapter 2), what is a reasonable expectation for my baby at this age?
- What naptime and bedtime situation would I consider "acceptable"?
- What naptime and bedtime situation would I consider "pure bliss"?

Once you answer these questions, you will have a better understanding of not only what is happening with regard to your baby's sleep, but also how motivated you are to make a change.

Your motivation is a key component to finding success using this plan.

Reluctance to Let Go of Those Nighttime Moments

A good, long, honest look into your heart may truly surprise you. You may find you actually *relish* those quiet night wakings when no one else is around. I remember in the middle of one night, I lay nursing Coleton by the light of the moon. My husband, the other three kids, and Grandma were all asleep. The house was perfectly, peacefully quiet. As I gently stroked his downy hair and soft baby skin, I marveled at this tiny being beside me—and the thought hit me, "I love this! I love these silent moments that we share in the night. And I love being needed by this precious baby." It was then that I

Chantelle, twelve-days-old

Mother-Speak

"Well, if I'm honest with myself, I must say that I—in no uncertain terms—fit into this category very nicely. I always loved waking with my babies to nurse at night. Snuggling and nursing a soft warm bundle in the semidarkness when the rest of the household is quiet is one of the most wonderful things about being a mommy. We mommies are paid not with a check, but in hugs, cuddles, and kisses. These nighttimes together are the equivalent of making overtime money or maybe a holiday bonus. Is it any wonder I've been reluctant to give that up?"

Donna, mother of nine-month-old Zachary

realized I needed to *want* to make a change in our night-waking habits before I would see any sleep success.

You may need to take a look at your own feelings. And if you find you're truly ready to make a change, you'll need to give yourself permission to let go of this stage of your baby's life and move on to a different phase in your relationship. There will be lots of time to hug, cuddle, and love your little one, but if this plan is to work, you must truly feel ready to move those moments out of your sleeping time and into the light of day.

Worry About Your Baby's Safety

We parents worry about our babies, and we should! With every night waking, as we have been tending to our child's nightly needs, we have also been reassured that our baby is doing fine— every hour or two all night long. We get used to these checks; they provide continual reassurance of our baby's safety.

As soon as you decide to help your baby sleep for longer time periods, you will probably move into an overprotective "mother or father bear" response. When three, four, or more hours have passed, you may worry. Is your baby breathing? Hot? Cold? Wet? Tangled in the sheet? Lying on their tummy?

Mother-Speak

"The first time my baby slept five straight hours, I woke up in a cold sweat. I nearly fell out of bed and ran down the hall. I was so sure that something was horribly wrong. I nearly wept when I found her sleeping peacefully."

Azza, mother of seven-month-old Laila

These are very normal worries, rooted in your natural instincts to protect your baby. Therefore, for you to allow your baby to sleep for longer stretches, you'll need to find ways to feel confident that your baby is safe—all night long.

The best way to do this is to review the safety checklist in Part V and take all necessary safety precautions. If your baby sleeps in a separate room, you may want to keep your bedroom doors open or your baby monitor turned up so that you know you'll hear your baby during the night if your little one calls for you.

Parents who bed-share are not exempt from these fears. Even if you are sleeping right next to your baby, you'll find that you have become used to checking on them frequently through the night. Even when they are sleeping longer stretches, *you* aren't sleeping, because you're still on security duty.

Once you reassure yourself that your baby is safe while you sleep, you can calmly take the steps toward all-night sleep.

Belief That Things Will Change on Their Own

You may hope, pray, and wish that one fine night, your baby will magically begin to sleep through the night. Maybe you're crossing your fingers that they'll just "outgrow" this stage, and you won't have to do anything different at all. I have to tell you that it's a very rare night-waking baby who suddenly decides to sleep through the night all on their own. Granted, this may happen to you—but your baby may be two-, three-, or four-years-old when it does! Decide now whether you have the patience to wait that long, or if you are ready to move the process along.

Too Fatigued to Work Toward Change

Change requires effort, and effort requires energy. In an exhausted state, we may find it easier just to keep things as they are rather than try something different. In other words, when your baby wakes for the fifth time that night, and you're desperate for sleep, it's so much easier just to resort to the easiest way to get your baby back to sleep (rock, nurse, or replace the pacifier) than it is to try something different.

Only a parent who is truly sleep deprived can understand what I'm saying here. Others may be able to calmly advise, "Well if things aren't working for you, just change what you're doing." However, every night waking puts you in that foggy state where the only thing you crave is going back to sleep—plans and ideas seem like too much effort.

If you are to help your baby sleep all night, you *will* have to force yourself to follow your plan, even in the middle of the night, even if it's the tenth time your baby has called out for you. The best defense here is to tell yourself, "In a month or two my baby will be sleeping all night long. I can do this for a few short weeks." And you can. (Especially when you consider the alternative: dealing with night wakings for another year or more!)

So, if after reading this section you're sure you and your baby are ready, it's time for you to make a commitment to change. Now. *Tonight.* This is the time.

Get Your Baby Ready

Before you attempt to make any changes in your baby's sleep routine, make certain that your baby is comfortable, healthy, and well fed. A baby who is hungry, cold, or has an ear infection, allergies, or any other health problem may wake at night because of pain or discomfort. Rule out these issues before you embark on your plan for better sleep. (For more information on medical and health reasons that keep your baby up at night, see Part III.)

Fill That Daytime Tummy

Make sure your baby is getting enough to eat during the day. Some babies get in the habit of nursing or drinking bottles all through the night, taking in an inordinate percentage of their daily calories then. To sleep longer at night, these babies need to tip the feeding scales back toward daytime.

For those little ones eating solids, make sure that *most* food choices are healthful ones. Sure, your toddler loves cheese and that's the only thing they want to eat, but the rules of good nutri-

---

Mother-Speak

"My fourteen-month-old baby was waking up crying and taking forever to fall back to sleep. I was so frustrated and wide awake at one point that I brought him downstairs and turned on the TV. He let out a big yell, and by the light of the screen I could see inside his mouth—he had three huge purple and white bumps on his gums where his molars were coming through. The poor thing was likely in too much pain to sleep. I let him chew on a cold, wet towel for a while, and he calmed down and fell right back to sleep."

Jessie, mother of fourteen-month-old Blaine

tion say they should be eating more variety. Good nutrition is important for overall health, including good sleep.

Take a look at what your toddler eats in the hours before bedtime and make sure they munch on foods that are conducive to good sleep. Some foods are more easily digested than others and are less apt to disrupt sleep cycles. Think "comfort food"—complex, healthful carbohydrates and nourishing proteins. The choices are endless: whole-grain cereals (easy on the sugar!), oatmeal, brown rice, yogurt, cheese, leftover meats. Fruits can satisfy sweet cravings.

In contrast, many foods tend to "rev" the body a bit. Look for hidden caffeine and other stimulating substances. While current scientific thought says sugar does not cause hyperactive behavior in children, I still suspect some effect on the ability and willing-

Cairo-Jaxx, two-years-old, and Daddy

ness to calm down and fall asleep. Sugar cookies and chocolate cake simply aren't good choices for late in the day.

If your toddler, like most, goes on food jags, take heart. Remember that nutritionists look at a child's diet from the standpoint of a week, rather than a day. In other words, when evaluating the healthfulness of your child's diet, think about proportions of major food groups consumed over the course of an entire week.

Breastfeed More During the Day

If your baby is used to frequent night feedings, they are taking in a good portion of their nourishment during those long, relaxed feeding sessions. You may have to nurse more often during the day for a while to make up for the nighttime feedings your baby will be giving up.

Your baby may be hanging on to night wakings as much for the comfort and emotional connection as for the milk—particularly if you're busy working or tending to other children during the day. If you are sensitive to this, you can give your little one extra cuddles and extra nursings during the day to help them adjust to giving up those nighttime nursing sessions.

Pay attention to the types of foods that *you* eat, because they can affect your breast milk. Watch for your baby's reaction when

---

Mother-Speak

"Austen hardly eats at all during the day and then nurses all night long. I try to offer her food several times a day, but most times she's too busy or distracted to eat. She really likes the time we spend before bed. It seems to always take more than an hour to get her to sleep, and her middle-of-the-night-feeding sessions are long ones."

Annette, mother of twelve-month-old Austen

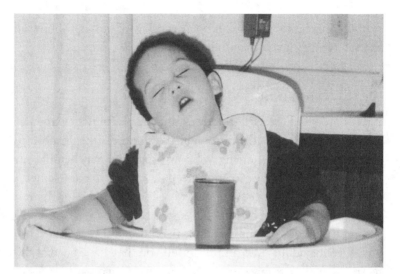

Jarell, twelve-months-old

you drink coffee, tea, or cola, or when you have dairy, nuts, or gassy foods such as broccoli, beans, and cauliflower.

Your curious, busy toddler may be too active to stop during the day to eat or even to nurse. In this case, try providing your energetic baby with "food on the run"—finger foods. Another option is to offer bites of food during playtime. (Fill a muffin tin with healthy nibbles and keep it within reach.) The key is to help your child get their full day's calories into the daytime and out of the nighttime.

Check Baby's Nighttime Comfort

Make sure Baby's bed is very comfortable. Dress them according to the temperature of the room, taking care that they are neither too cold nor too hot. If your home is cool at night, buy thick blanket sleeper pajamas (the full-body kind that snap at the crotch) or baby-bag sleepers, and put them on over a T-shirt. If the season is hot, cool the room with an open window or fan, but follow all the safety rules if you do either of these.

Get to Know Your Baby

Babies are similar in their actions and needs, but they are also beautifully unique with individual likes and dislikes, emotions and character traits. Getting to know your child may be not only the most important key to good sleep, it may be the most important key to every single parenting decision you make for the rest of your life.

I am the mom of four children, two boys and two girls. They are all young adults now, and I can tell you they have been as different as apples, oranges, chewing gum and tango dancing, since the day they were born! Given identical situations I must respond differently to each child if I am to achieve the best outcome. Keep this in mind as you make decisions about your baby's sleep issues. Family units also are unique in how they function, and in their core beliefs. A solution that works wonders for your sister, your best friend or your neighbor, may be totally wrong for you. Even a plan that worked perfectly for your child's older sibling may fail miserably when applied to this individual child, so cueing in to your unique baby may be your first and most important task.

Learn to Read Your Baby's Sleepy Signs

By getting to know your baby you will master the important task of reading the unique and sometimes subtle signs of fatigue that appear, and will be able to put your child to bed at exactly the right moment.

Tired babies fall asleep easily, and they give signals that they are ready to sleep. If they aren't tired they will resist sleep with all their might, but if they are, and you miss the sleepy signals, your

Saunders, one-month-old

baby can easily become *overtired* and will then be unable to fall asleep when you finally do put them to bed. It's a balancing act, for sure, but an important aspect to helping your baby sleep well.

Figuring out the best sleep times for your baby is a process. When they are infants you should put them to bed every time the sleep indicators show themselves. For older babies and toddlers, if you watch your child's signs over a week or two you should be able

Point to Remember

Babies sleep better when you properly read their unique signs of fatigue. (And by babies, I mean *all* babies.)

to create a good nap and bedtime schedule based on their personal daily biological rhythm. Use the time you pick as a guideline, and then use your child's tired signals as the main cue for sleep time. If you spot the signals, don't begin a lengthy routine—just get your tired little one off to bed!

Typical Signs of Tiredness

While babies are unique, they are also similar in their signs of fatigue. Your child may demonstrate one or more of these signs that tell you they are tired and ready to sleep—*now*:

- Reducing their level of activity; making slower motions
- Quieting down, making fewer or simpler sounds
- Losing interest in people or toys; looking away
- Rubbing their eyes or ears
- Looking glazed or unfocused; staring off in the distance
- Having a more relaxed jaw, chin, and mouth (droopy looking)
- Head nodding or clumsy movements
- Eyes wide open and unblinking; or making long slow blinks
- Becoming whiny and cranky
- Fussing or crying
- Losing patience with toys or activities
- Having tantrums
- Yawning
- Lying down or slumping in their seat
- Watching TV or a video with a blank expression
- Caressing a lovey or blanket
- Asking for a pacifier, for a bottle, or to nurse

In addition to those signs of normal tiredness, babies will also accelerate their signals when they become overtired. There is often a fine line between tired and overtired, but when you pass that line your baby becomes more difficult to soothe. They get a second wind and become too wired up to relax. At this point they will become very irritable and will often fight sleep—the very thing they need most.

Typical Signs of Overtiredness

Your baby has passed from tired into overtired when they show some of these signs:

- Fretful, intense crying often without apparent reason
- Arching backward or stiffening their body out
- Flailing, jerky, uncoordinated movements
- Drooping or fluttering eyelids
- Dark circles appearing under the eyes
- Difficult time latching when feeding
- Won't settle when you use techniques that usually work

(Note that some of these signs can also signal illness or pain.)

Once you learn to identify your child's early signs of tiredness you can get your little one to bed at exactly the right moment—making bedtime or naptime much more pleasant.

Identify and Respect Your Baby's Happily Awake Span

One important factor to consider as you learn to read your child's signs of tiredness is how long they have been awake. Pay attention, be certain that they have their much-needed naptime each day, and that they have a bedtime that aligns with their sleep needs. As a guide for this span see the column for "Endurable Awake Hours" shown on the sleep hours chart on page 204.

Babies need a consistent daily routine of naptime to refresh and take a break from their busy world. Even those who are great nighttime sleepers require daytime naps to rejuvenate in between

Mother-Speak

"This baby in general is easier than my now-three-year-old was. She is a lot less fussy, has more quiet alert times, and naps more often. I think it's because I didn't understand the "happily awake concept" with my first. I had no idea that her long periods of being awake were the cause of her crabbiness. Paying attention to how long this baby has been awake has been super helpful, so I've referenced the chart often. She is generally content, since if I'm aware that she's been awake for about an hour I can start watching for sleepy signs more carefully, and start preparing to help her get back to sleep *before* she starts to get fussy. It has made an amazing difference."

Megan, mother of three-year-old Anna and two-month-old Felicity

lifetime learning segments of time. Each and every time that your baby sleeps, they are gifted with an amazing array of benefits to their physical and mental health. Naps also improve your child's overall temperament; they can dramatically reduce the amount of fussiness and tears throughout the day.

Every time your baby sleeps, it enables their body to release cortisol and other hormones that combat stress and tension. Without the release of these hormones, they build to uncontrollable levels, which create inner pressure that erupts as fussiness and crying. Babies and toddlers who stay awake for too long can dissolve into tears much more easily than those who get sufficient rest breaks. (This concept is at the heart of the "terrible twos" we hear so much about—toddlers who give up naps before their biology has eliminated the need for them.)

The Happily Awake Span

As shown on the sleep hours chart on page 204, the length of time that children can stay happily awake increases as they age. In the first few weeks, most newborns can only handle 45 *minutes to two hours of wakefulness*—and at times even less than that. By three months of age, many babies can stay happily awake one to three hours, but it isn't until about seven to nine months that some babies begin to stay awake for four hours without a meltdown. Some don't reach that happy four-hour mark until eighteen months of age.

When babies are pushed beyond their biological waking span without a break, they become fatigued and unhappy. As the minutes pass and the sleep pressure builds, a baby becomes fussier, whinier, and less flexible, and will have more crying spells. You may notice a loss of concentration and a drop in the ability to take in new information. As always when dealing with children, these guidelines don't apply precisely to every individual, and a few

Point to Remember

Do not let your baby stay awake for too long at a stretch. Newborns can only stay happily awake for forty-five minutes to an hour or two at a time. By three months of age many babies routinely enjoy a two- to three-hour awake span, although some still can barely make it an hour without getting tired.

If your baby has been awake for too long, you have likely missed their sleepy signals, and they are overtired. An overtired baby will find it hard to sleep yet hard to stay happily awake. This becomes a pattern that can disrupt both sleep and temperament. So, keep one eye on your baby (watch for tired signs) and one eye on the clock. (Set your phone to buzz for when time is up and you should watch for those sleepy signals.)

babies make up their own rules about their best "happily awake span"—but trust me, they all have one! Don't try to push your baby into a strict schedule if their cues just do not match. Always go back to reading your unique baby's telltale signs and respond by providing adequate rest breaks and naps.

Develop a Bedtime Routine

Creating and following a bedtime routine can make your evenings run more smoothly and peacefully. A bedtime routine can help guide you at the time of day when you are most tired, and can send a signal to your baby that bedtime is here. It invokes a conditioned response from baby: "Oh! It's bedtime! I should be sleepy!"

But What If I Hate Routines?

Some parents avidly reject the idea of any kind of routine for babies. This is usually because when they hear the word *routine* they think of a rigid English nanny demanding a clock-driven schedule with feeding and sleep charts. This isn't at all what I mean here! This is a "soft routine," if you will: a guideline that helps you to gently create patterns that help your baby nap effortlessly and ease into bedtime each night. It's important to have a flexible routine that is adapted each day to your baby's life and needs. Use your intuition and your baby interpretation skills to customize the routine each night to best suit your baby.

I do want to add that if you truly, totally hate the idea of any kind of routine, then skip this section entirely. Instead, watch your baby from dinner time onward—very closely—and head for bed whenever the signs are there. You can keep up this same approach throughout childhood, if you remain diligent about your child's individual sleep needs. Children change their own sleep needs from time to time, and you can help yours be happier and healthier by making certain they get all the sleep they need.

Anzel, eight-months-old, and Daddy

A Sample Bedtime Routine

A routine for the hour before bedtime is helpful in cueing and preparing your baby for sleep. Include any of the following that you enjoy and that help soothe and quiet your baby. Keep in mind that each baby is unique and what may relax one might rev up another. As an example, many babies find a warm bath soothing, but others think they are at a water park and find a dip in the tub invigorating, so take this list as suggestions and create your own child's best pre-bed steps, including some of these things:

- Give your baby a warm, calm bath
- Massage
- Read books
- Sing songs
- Play soft music
- Take a walk
- Talk about your day
- Rock in arms or in a rocking chair
- Breastfeed
- Bottle-feed

The hour before bed should be peaceful. Your routine should take place in a quiet room with dim lights. Your last step should end in the quiet, dark bedroom with your usual go-to-sleep technique. Write down your routine, and make it very specific.

A sample bedtime routine might look like this:

1. 7:00 P.M.—Bath
2. Massage with baby lotion
3. Put on pajamas
4. Read three books
5. Lights out
6. Sing lullaby
7. Breastfeed or bottle-feed
8. Rub back
9. Sleep

Use the form on page 70 to write down your own bedtime routine.

Follow your *exact* routine every night. (Once you and your baby are both comfortable with the routine, and your baby's sleep is consistent, you won't need your written list, though some parents continue to use a written bedtime routine up through elementary school.) Try to avoid going out around your baby's bedtime during this adjustment period. If you absolutely have to go out and come home later than your usual bedtime routine starting time, make sure you still go through the entire routine, even if you have to shorten the steps—for example, reading just one book instead of three.

A Routine Helps Set Baby's Biological Clock

In addition to the routine itself, if you can put your baby down for naps and bed at about the same time every day, you will achieve sleep success much sooner, because the consistency will help set your baby's internal clock. Your child's biological clock has a strong influence on wakefulness and sleepiness. When your child's biological clock is ticking in time with their daily activities they will be tired at naptime and bedtime, fall asleep easily, and wake up refreshed. The human clock must be reset daily to work effectively. The first key to this process is to establish a set time for bedtime and stick to it seven days a week. A few babies do well with a varied bedtime, but if you are struggling with any sleep-related issues this is an important solution to try.

An added bonus of implementing this idea is that adhering to a specific routine organizes your life, reducing your stress and tension.

A Flexible Routine Is Best

When I talk about "routine" I certainly don't mean a rigid routine that is set in stone! Remember that I'm a mother and grandmother, too, and I know that flexibility is very important when it comes to— Oops! I'll be right back. Hunter just woke from a nap and I need to go get him, make a snack, and create some Play-Doh snakes—I'm back, and as I was saying . . . what was I saying? Oh yes.

Flexibility is important when you have a little one in your life! Try to maintain your bedtime routine as often as possible, but watch your child too. If they are fussing and yawning it's not the time to have a bath and read a bedtime story! It's the time to skip some steps and get them to bed ASAP! You may also have to forfeit your entire routine some nights; if Great-Grandma is having her 100th birthday party don't feel that you have to leave at 6:00 p.m. sharp to get your bedtime routine going. There are times when you'll have to go with the flow and get back to routine the next night.

Mother-Speak
"I have found the bedtime routine idea is essential. Since you mentioned this I have realized that on the nights I skip parts I always have more trouble getting him to sleep."

Diane, mother of seven-month-old Jamar

Bedtime Routine Is Important Throughout Childhood

Don't consider your bedtime routine burdensome, unimportant, or unnecessary. A loving bedtime routine is *always* important for children. Until about age ten or so, a child thrives on spending special quiet time with a parent before bed. Reading books, talking, giving back rubs, and simply being together quietly are all important prebed rituals. Actually, I find that most parents who do *not* have a formal bedtime routine typically spend that last hour before bed fighting with their children about going to bed—now *that* is unpleasant and unnecessary.

At some point, a child no longer needs the ritual, and most parents mourn the loss of that special, quiet time in the day. Life changes, and so do those bedtime routines, so enjoy that special bonding time.

Establish an Early Bedtime

Many people put their babies to bed much too late, often hoping that if they are "really tired" they will will sleep better. This often backfires because baby becomes overtired and chronically sleep-deprived. In *The Promise of Sleep* (Dell), Dr. William C. Dement (a leading authority on sleep) states, "The effects of delaying bedtime by even half an hour can be subtle and pernicious [very destructive]" when it comes to babies and young children.

A baby's biological clock is preset for an early bedtime. When parents work with that time, a baby falls asleep more easily and stays asleep more peacefully. Most babies are primed to go to sleep

Mother-Speak

"One evening we were visiting friends and in all of the excitement we missed the 'window of opportunity' for getting Alicia to sleep. She passed into the 'downright weird window.' She was motoring through the house like a race car with no driver. When I finally convinced her to lie on my lap to nurse, it was like nursing a baby monkey! It took forever for her to settle down and fall asleep."

Robin, mother of thirteen-month-old Alicia

for the night as early as 6:00 or 7:00 P.M. It is helpful if you establish your baby's bedtime and plan for it by beginning your prebed routine an hour before, if at all possible.

I often hear about how babies and young children have a "meltdown" period at the end of the day, when they get fussy, whiny, and out of sorts. I suspect that it's simply a sign of overtired children longing for sleep.

Early to Bed, Early to Rise?

For babies, early to bed does *not* mean early to rise! Most babies sleep better and *longer* with an earlier bedtime. Many parents are afraid to put their baby to bed so early, thinking that they will then face a 5:00 A.M. wake-up call. Or they may come home from work and *want* to keep Baby up late to play. But keeping your little one up too late backfires, and they become overtired, distressed, and too wound up to settle down, and more often, a late night is the one followed by that early morning awakening.

Prior to my sleep research, my little Coleton used to go to bed at 9:00 or 9:30 P.M., the time when my older children went to bed, because it was convenient for me. At that time in the evening, it would take him a long time to get settled. I never connected his inability to settle with his late bedtime. When I started putting him to bed between 7:00 and 8:00 P.M., he fell asleep much more quickly and slept more soundly. And as an added bonus, I recovered some quality "me" time in the evening that I had long forgotten about. This has been a common experience among my test parents. Many were truly surprised to find that an earlier bedtime really did help their baby fall asleep easier and faster and often encouraged better sleep and a later waking time. Of course, when we are talking about children there are always those that break all the rules and insist on doing things there own way! So, a few babies are more than happy to stay up until midnight and then sleep until

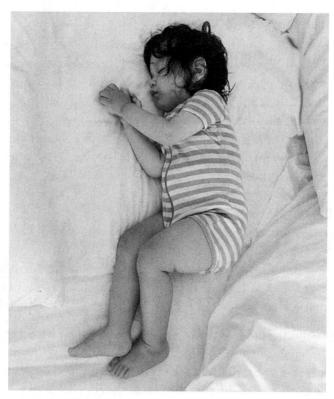

Leo, sixteen-months-old

noon! As long as your baby is happy and healthy, and it works for your family, you can relax about their unique schedule.

What About Conflicting Work Schedules?

If you are a working parent, and your evening with your little one *begins* at 6:00 or 7:00 P.M., you may find yourself torn between keeping your baby up for some playtime and sticking to an early bedtime. Because you are reading this book, I know that you would like your baby to sleep better. Early bedtime is a key idea, so it may be worth trying it out to see what the results are for you.

Some working parents find that when their babies go to sleep earlier, they sleep better and awaken in a pleasant mood, eager to play. Because you, the parent, have gotten a better night's sleep too, you can consider getting up earlier in the morning and saving some time before work to play with your baby, as an alternative to that late-evening play session. You'll both enjoy that special morning time. Later, when your baby is consistently sleeping all night, every night, you can then move bedtime a little later and judge whether the difference affects your baby's sleep.

Finding Your Baby's Best Bedtime

It can take some experimentation to find your baby's best bedtime. If you have been putting your little one to bed too late in the evening and you are seeing negative repercussions from this, you can approach this adjustment to an earlier bedtime in one of two different ways:

- Adjust your baby's bedtime to be earlier by fifteen to thirty minutes every two or three nights. Pay attention to how easily your baby falls asleep as well as their awakening time and mood to gauge the effectiveness of the changes until you settle on the best bedtime.

Mother-Speak

"I had been waiting until 10:00 P.M. to put Brooklyn to bed because that's when I go to sleep and it seemed easiest. But your suggestion made so much sense that last night I put her down at 8:00 P.M. I loved having the rest of the evening to spend with my husband. We haven't spent that much time alone together in months! And the baby actually had a better night's sleep. I'm happy that all our needs can be met in such a pleasant way."

Tammy, mother of seven-month-old Brooklyn

- Beginning at around 6:00 P.M., watch your baby closely. As soon as they exhibit any signs of tiredness put them right to bed, even if their previous bedtime has been 11:00 P.M. (For a list of the signs, see page 136.) When you do this, keep your home quiet and the baby's room dark so that it resembles the usual environment in the middle of the night. If this bedtime is substantially earlier than usual, your baby may think they're going down for a nap and awaken after a short snooze. If they do this, respond very quickly so that they don't fully awaken. Follow your usual method for helping your baby fall right back to sleep, such as rocking or nursing; keep the room dark and quiet as you do during the middle of the night. It may take a week or more of adjustment to settle into a new bedtime.

Follow a Flexible Yet Predictable Daytime Routine

During the first year of life, a baby's biological clock slowly matures. According to Dr. Dement, "As the weeks go by, the baby starts sleeping longer and being awake longer. This is caused by the consolidation of sleep periods. Then, around the fortieth week, the baby has started waking and going to sleep about the same time each day. Their biological clock becomes in tune with the twenty-four-hour day."

Yes, you read that correctly. He wrote *the fortieth week*! That's over nine months! In other words, we cannot force a baby to conform to a parent's desire for a pleasant day, a lengthy nap, and a long, uninterrupted night's sleep. We need to make baby's world conducive to sleep in every way we can. We must remove any obstacles to peaceful nighttime sleep, and wait patiently for nature to do what's best. Yes, some babies do consolidate their sleep earlier than forty weeks (lucky you if you had one of those!) and some require longer. (OK, I'll say it—some, much longer.)

Why Wake-up Time Is Important, Too

Even given the constraints of your baby's natural sleep consolidation schedule, you can help this process along by making sure that when your baby wakes in the morning, they are exposed to bright light (preferably natural daylight) and that the hour before sleep at night is dimly lit, relaxed, and quiet. Waking up at about the same time every morning can help set your baby's biological clock, too. A hefty portion of setting your child's biological clock is connected to the time they wake up every morning. A bit of difference is fine, but if weekday mornings start at 7:00 A.M. while on weekends and holidays everyone sleeps in until 9:00 A.M., your child's clock can be knocked totally out of sync. A regular wake-up time can help set the day's nap schedule and bedtime as well. Yes, that means that *you* have to get up at the same time every morning, but this will help set *your* biological clock as well as your baby's.

Routine Days, Routine Nights

Keeping a regular feeding, napping, and activity schedule helps set your baby's internal clock. As an example, while you may enjoy veering off from your weekday meal and sleep routines on the weekends, this can disrupt your baby's regular schedule; they neither know nor care what day it is. Any changes to their normal sleeping and eating pattern prevent their biological clock from working properly. (By the way, this is true for adults, too. One of the best ways to treat adult insomnia is to set a wake-up time and adhere to it seven days a week. You can read more about that in Part IV.)

As I have said before, I am not suggesting a clock-watching program. Such regimens only put unnecessary stress on you and your baby. If your baby is breastfed, you shouldn't be on a schedule anyhow; your little one should be fed when you're cued by signs of hunger, not fed by the clock. Instead of a rigid schedule, set up a typical daytime routine and adjust it daily based on your baby's cues and any situations that arise. What you want to avoid is a haphaz-

Mother-Speak

"I am not big on 'routines,' but with the twins I have had to discipline myself to have somewhat of a routine. I try not to be an avid clock-watcher; instead, I pay attention to the babies' cues. For example, I try to put the babies down for a nap around 9:30 A.M. This morning Rebecca was obviously tired at 9:30 A.M. Thomas, on the other hand, was in great form, laughing, playing, and enjoying life—not in the least tired. So I put Rebecca down for a nap and kept Thomas up for another thirty minutes. If I had tried to put him down when he wasn't tired, I would have eventually gotten him to sleep, but it would have been a struggle. By waiting thirty minutes, until he showed signs of tiredness, I got him to sleep easily. In other words, I have a vague structure to my day, with some flexibility depending on my babies."

Alice, mother of six-month-old twins Rebecca and Thomas

ard week of events—awaking Monday morning at seven, Tuesday morning at nine; lunch on Wednesday at eleven, on Thursday not until one; naptime on Monday at eleven, on Tuesday at one. When your schedule (or shall I say, lack of schedule) looks like this, your baby's biological clock isn't able to work properly. It's much better to have a predictable pattern, allowing for flexibility.

A daily routine for a two-year-old might look like this:

7:00 A.M.—Up for the day
Get dressed
Have breakfast
Playtime
11:30 A.M.–12:00 P.M.—Lunch
12:00–12:30 P.M.—Down for a nap
After nap, midday snack
Playtime

5:00 P.M.—Dinner
6:30–7:00 P.M.—Bath and start bedtime routine
7:30 P.M.—Light pre-bed snack
8:00 P.M.—Bedtime

(This is just a rough example; yours may be very different.)

When you have a daily eat, sleep, and play routine, you will find that your baby is more willing to nap, eat, and sleep when the regular time comes, because your child's internal clock ticks along with your predictable schedule. Of course, if your baby is strictly breast- or formula-fed, they should be "demand-fed" (or a softer-description that I prefer: "cue-fed") whenever they are hungry. However, you can build a predictable routine around the other parts of your day. If you are lucky enough to have one of those rare super-flexible babies who easily goes with the flow, then you can be super-flexible, too!

Have Your Baby Take Regular Naps

Naps take only a few hours of time each day, but naps—or lack of naps—can shape all twenty-four hours of your baby's day. The quality and quantity of naps influence mood, behavior, health, and even brain development. Naps can affect how happy your child is when they wake up in the morning and how easily they'll go to bed at night. An appropriate nap schedule is a vital component for your child's healthy, happy life. When you consider all of this, you'll also understand that your child's naps—or lack of naps—can affect all 24 hours of your day, as well as your child's!

Point to Remember
Science proves what parents instinctually know: Naps are absolutely, positively necessary.

What About Catnaps?

A nap less than an hour in length does not really count. I'm not dictating a random number here—it's science! Catnaps can take the edge off, but because the sleep cycle is not complete, your baby doesn't gain the benefits of a full sleep-cycle nap, since many of the benefits show up after that one-hour mark. These short naps can just make your baby fussier in the long run, and don't improve health and brain function in the same way as a longer nap. A few babies seem to rewrite this rule and function beautifully on a forty-minute nap, but don't assume this to be the case for your baby

Ella, two-months-old, and Thea, two-years-old

Mother-Speak

"Now that I am more aware of the importance of naps I try very hard to make sure she has a good nap every day. She really does then sleep better at night. It's amazing what a difference naps make!"

Tina, mother of twelve-month-old Anjali

unless both their nap and nighttime sleep are consistent, and they seem happy and well-rested throughout the day.

How Much Naptime Does Your Child Need?

Babies differ in their needs for nap length and number of naps. They also differ in the length of time they can stay happily awake between sleep sessions (see Newborn Key 4, page 136, regarding this concept). The following table is a general guide that applies to most babies and will give you the information you need to calculate the best number of hours to aim for with your child.

Average Number and Length of Naps for Children

Age	Number of naps	Total naptime hours	Endurable awake hours
1 month	3–5	6–7	1–3
3 months	3–4	5–6	1–3
4 months	3–4	4–6	1–3
6 months	2–3	3–4	2–3
9 months	2	2½–4	2–4
12 months	1–2	2–3	3–5
18 months	1–2	2–3	4–6
2 years	1	1½–3	4–6½
5 years	0–1	0–2	6–12

Frankie, one-month-old, and Daddy

When Should Your Baby Nap?

Timing of naps is important, too. A nap too late in the day will negatively affect nighttime sleep. Your child may not be tired when bedtime arrives, pushing sleep time later, possibly creating more night waking, as well as a disrupted waking time the following morning. Certain times of the day are better for napping because they suit your baby's developing biological clock; these optimum periods help to balance sleep and wake time to affect night sleep in the most positive way. Again, all babies are different, but generally, best times for naps are as follows:

- If your baby takes three naps: midmorning, early afternoon, and early evening
- If your baby takes two naps: midmorning and early afternoon
- If your baby takes one nap only: early to mid-afternoon

If you want your baby to welcome naptime, use the general guidelines already described and watch for sleepy signals. Naps should happen *immediately* when your child shows signs of tiredness. If you wait too long, they become *overtired*, "wired," and unable to sleep. Once you are familiar with your baby's nap needs, you can plan for your nap routine to start the wind-down process. If consistent naps are new to you, look more for your baby's signs of tiredness and scrimp on the routine until you settle into a predictable pattern. In other words, don't begin a lengthy prenap routine if your baby is clearly ready to sleep.

Watch for these signs of fatigue; your baby may demonstrate one or more of these:

- Decreasing activity or slower movements
- Quieting down, talking less or making fewer or simpler sounds
- Losing interest in people, toys, or activities
- Rubbing eyes, ears, or face
- Looking "glazed" or staring off into the distance
- Limp, relaxed face and jaw
- Dark circles appearing under eyes
- Drooping eyelids or slow blinking
- Fussing or whining
- Yawning
- Lying down on the floor or on a chair
- Caressing a lovey or asking for a pacifier, a bottle, or to nurse
- Being awake longer than the "Endurable Awake Hours" span shown on the chart on page 204

This timing of naps is very, very important! You have probably experienced this scenario: Your baby looks tired and you think, "Time for a nap." So you change their diaper, answer a phone call, put out the dog, and head for your baby's crib, only to find that they're suddenly wide awake and eager to play! What happened?

Your baby has moved through the window of tiredness and gotten a "second wind" that buys another hour of two of alert time before reentering a tired state. This can then happen later in the day. Suddenly your baby is (finally!) ready for a nap at dinnertime, and the plot thickens—do you put them down for a late nap and thus extend bedtime, or keep them awake and deal with a tired, fussy baby? Rather than face this ordeal, respond earlier to signs of fatigue and get your baby in for a nap immediately when tired signs appear.

Once you have watched your baby carefully for a week or so, you should be able to create a nap schedule that works with their daily periods of alertness and tiredness, thus making your nap schedule easy to adhere to. (Keep watch though, as children's sleep needs change over time, so the nap schedule will change, too.)

The Nap Routine

Once you've established a nap schedule for your baby, create a simple but specific nap routine that is different from your night-time routine. It can have similarities that signal sleep, for example, the presence of a lovey or special sleep-inducing white noise. Follow your nap routine the same way every day. (Except, as I mentioned before, if your baby is showing clear signs of being tired and ready to sleep. Then abbreviate or even eliminate your routine for that day.)

For a reluctant napper, your routine may include some relaxing motion (rocking, relaxing in a swing, or walking in a sling or stroller).

A nap routine doesn't have to be long and involved to be effective. If your baby's nap occurs about the same time every day, many subtle cues—such as the timing of lunch—will tell your baby that naptime is nearing.

Point to Remember

If you are working on solving a frequent night-waking problem, do anything and everything that works to get your baby to nap during the day; a well-rested baby will respond better to the nighttime sleep ideas.

When it comes to babies, more sleep brings better sleep. Lack of naptime during the day can actually make it more difficult for your baby to fall asleep at bedtime—and stay asleep all night—due to overtiredness and sleep deprivation.

Once your baby is sleeping well at night you can then work out the particulars for nap sleep, including modifying associations and routines.

⭐ Getting the Short Napper to Sleep Longer

Some babies will show you their tired signs and go down for a nap rather easily, but then, twenty minutes or so later, they're up again. Most parents resign themselves to this short nap routine. But it is very important to your child's health and well-being to work towards lengthening these short naps. Sleep research shows that a nap should last at least an hour (but preferably an hour and a half) for maximum sleep benefits. Shorter catnaps don't suffice since many of these benefits occur in the later stages of sleep. These include:

- Strengthening memory
- Boosting the immune system
- Repairing bone, tissue, and muscles
- Regulating appetite
- Sharpening perceptual skills
- Reducing stress
- Releasing growth hormones

Catnaps appear to happen when your baby moves through a sleep cycle and then awakens fully when they hit their first brief awakening mid-cycle. (Remember this from the Basic Sleep Facts in Part I?) The key to getting your short napper to lengthen naps is to help them go right back to sleep when these brief awakenings occur. Here's how to make that happen:

Put your baby down for a nap. Set a timer or keep your eye on the time. About five or ten minutes before the usual awakening time, sit outside the bedroom door and listen carefully. (Use this time to read a book, catch up on social media, or do some other peaceful, pleasant activity. Or be practical and fold laundry or pay your bills. Or maybe even take care of your own sleep deficit and snooze next to your little one.) The minute your baby makes a sound, go in quickly. You'll find your baby in a sleepy, just-about-to-wake-up state. Use whatever technique helps them fall back to sleep—breastfeeding, rocking, or offering a bottle or pacifier. If you've caught them quickly enough, they will fall right back to sleep. After a week or so of this intervention, your short napper should start taking a much longer snooze without any help from you.

Help Your Baby Learn How to Fall Asleep Without Help

As we've discussed, every human being has night wakings. If your baby is waking you up frequently at night for help, the problem is not the awakenings, but that they don't know how to go back to sleep on their own. There are gentle ways to help babies feel comfortable and secure when they wake up so that they can go back to sleep without your help.

Corra, sixteen-months-old

"My Bed Is a Nice Place!"

This first idea helps your baby learn that their bed is a safe, comfortable place.

Spend some quiet, happy time during the day in the place you want your baby to sleep at night. Read, talk, sing, or play. Have two or three of these very pleasant interludes during the day with your baby in this sleeping place. If your baby responds positively, try to get them interested in watching a mobile or playing with a toy as you fade back and sit quietly in a chair nearby and watch.

By following these steps your baby will come to know their crib as a welcoming, safe, and comfortable haven. It will become familiar. Your little one will find comfort in waking there during the night

Mother-Speak

"As you suggested, we played with Dylan in his crib so he could get used to it. He has this really cool mobile that he loves and we let him 'play' with it two or three times a day. This has really helped him get used to his crib. I think that's one of the reasons he is starting to put himself to sleep when he wakes up during the night."

Alison, mother of five-month-old Dylan

and find it easier to go back to sleep. (This is an especially important idea if you've attempted to let your baby cry it out in the past. It can help banish any negative memories and replace them with a sense of peacefulness about being in the crib.)

Falling Asleep in Different Ways

Right now, your baby may fall asleep in only one way, such as nursing, rocking, or having a bottle. This activity is a very powerful signal that your baby associates with falling asleep. It is so powerful that they may believe that the only way they *can* fall asleep is when this signal is present.

Mother-Speak

"Emma has always fallen asleep breastfeeding. Once in a while my sister baby-sits her while my husband and I go out. It never fails that she'll be wide awake when we get home, no matter how late. My sister says she tries everything, but the little stinker waits until I walk in the door. Two minutes of nursing and she's sound asleep."

Lorelie, mother of six-month-old Emma

If your baby relies on one specific signal to fall asleep, you can help change this association so that your baby can learn to fall asleep in different ways.

If you choose to follow this suggestion, creating and following nap- and bedtime routines prior to sleep, as discussed earlier in this chapter, will help. But the final step occurs in several different places.

Usually, it's easier to begin this plan with naps before tackling nighttime. Does your baby fall asleep in the swing? While rocking, using a pacifier, or walking in the stroller? Find and use alternative ways to help your baby to fall asleep for naps. Try to get your baby comfortable with a variety of ways to fall asleep—but do this every day at the same time. One day, go for a walk in the stroller. The next day, put Baby in a swinging cradle. The third day, walk your

Henry, two-years-old, and Alice, thirteen-days-old

baby around the house in a sling or carrier, or spend time in a rocking chair. After you have done this for a week or more, you can begin to use your alternate "signals" to bring your baby to a very sleepy state, and then transition them quietly to bed.

At this point, stay with your baby, and pat or touch them in the way that is soothing. If you have been using a nap routine and watching for sleepy signals, your baby should then be able to fall asleep on their own. If they don't, you can go ahead and use the method that works best. Your goal, after all, is for your baby to take a nap.

You may then gradually shorten your routine until it is comfortable for both of you. Once your nap schedule is in place, and your nighttime sleep is settling down, you can eliminate all those alternate methods for falling asleep and use the one that is most convenient for you.

Introduce a Lovey

Some babies attach themselves to a blanket or toy that becomes a "lovey." This is a transitional object that comforts your baby in your absence. In some cases, you may be able to help your baby become attached to a lovey or comfort object so that they have something to cuddle and help them fall asleep without your help.

A lovey does *not* take your place. Instead, it is something that your baby can use to feel safe when you are not there. Interestingly, only one of my children discovered her own lovey: my award-winning-sleeper baby, Vanessa. Appropriately enough, her lovey was a red pillowcase named Pilly. Angela and David had favorite cuddly toys, but none that would qualify as a lovey. With Coleton, I was able to encourage his attachment to a lovey. It wasn't nearly as intense as with Vanessa, but it became a sleep cue and was a helpful piece of the whole sleep plan that I created for him.

Keagan, one-year-old

Some children adopt a lovey in babyhood and continue to use it all through childhood. Others switch to a new lovey from time to time, other children find solace in any soft, fuzzy toy, and some never do take to the idea of a lovey. You'll be able to tell which category your child fits in by watching their actions.

Choose a Safe Lovey

Choose a soft toy that your baby is already attracted to, or pick a safe stuffed animal that meets these criteria:

- No button eyes or nose, nor any small, potentially removable pieces
- No clothes, hats, or other removable pieces of fabric
- Firm, not floppy
- Small and easy for baby to hold and manipulate, but not so small that it poses a choking hazard
- Made of a safe, organic material, since your baby might chew on this

The ideal lovey is a stuffed animal created for babies. For example, I purchased a little flannel doll for Coleton. After he became accustomed to having it in bed, he let us know that he was tired by asking for his lovey. (Or we would encourage him to *get* tired by cuddling him with his soft toy.)

When you have carefully chosen the lovey, place it between the two of you whenever you nurse your baby, give them a bottle, or rock them. At other times of the day, you might even want to

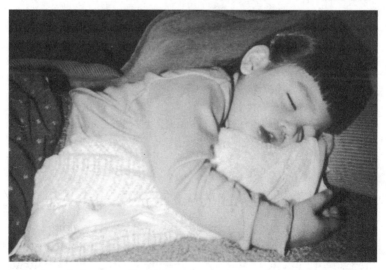

Emily, twenty-four-months-old

"wear" this lovey inside your shirt for a few hours to give it that lovely Mommy or Daddy smell, because babies can recognize their parents' scents. At first, it is best to use this lovey only at sleep times so it becomes one of the sleep-time cues.

You can introduce a lovey at any age. If your baby is young, you can choose something yourself, and gauge your baby's response to the toy. As your baby gets older, they will have a definite say in determining which toy attracts and soothes them; this is evident anytime you see a child wandering around with a well-worn blanket, a hairless teddy bear, or a scrap of Mommy's old nightie. When your baby becomes a toddler, you may find that they will expand the usefulness of this lovey by holding onto it whenever they need a little extra security. So if you have any say in the matter, do direct your child toward something that you'll enjoy having in the family for years to come.

If your baby does indeed get attached to this lovey, be sure to buy at least two to prevent any lost-lovey disasters—or at least choose one that's easily replaceable or commercially available.

Mother-Speak

"I finally found a lovey that I like for Carrson, and he likes it also. When we hold it between us when we nurse, he plays with it and talks to it. It's becoming a 'friend.'"

Pia, mother of eight-month-old Carrson

⭐ Make Night Sleeping Different from Daytime Naps

When your baby wakes up, he doesn't know if he's waking from a nap or from nighttime sleep, so you might want to differentiate the two for him. You can help your baby stay in a sleepy state all night by keeping nighttime quiet and dark. These are some ways to make night sleeping unique:

- When your baby wakes in the night, do not talk. Say "shhhh" or "night-night," but refrain from conversation.
- Do not turn on any lights. Even a twenty-five-watt bulb can trigger your baby's biological clock to signal "wake-up time." (Use a low-wattage night-light for diaper changes.)
- Keep your activity slow and quiet.
- Put your baby in absorbent nighttime diapers with lots of ointment. Change only a soiled or very wet diaper or if baby desires a change. Every diaper change could wake up your baby and reinforce night waking. (Think of it this way: when your baby is sleeping through the night, you won't be getting up to change your sleeping baby's diaper, will you? Also, as your baby is waking up less to nurse or have a bottle, their diaper won't get as wet.) When you do change a diaper, have all your supplies organized and close by so that you can do it quickly. And make certain you use a warm wipe on that sleepy bottom, since a cold, wet washcloth is a sure way to wake your baby up.

Mother-Speak

"I have always had this approach, simply because I am way too tired to change diapers, talk to the baby, or play with the baby at night. It works really well. In the last five years with my four children, I have only rarely been awake for long periods deep in the night with a baby. Many of my friends have this problem on a daily basis. But for me, even with night-waking twins, I am far better rested than they because my babies go back to sleep so quickly."

Alice, mother of six-month-old twins Rebecca and Thomas

- If you have windows that let evening or early morning light in, cover them up with something dark or opaque, like light-blocking blinds, thick curtains, or even a temporary shield of cardboard. (Leave the covers off during daytime naps.)
- Keep activity toys out of the sleeping area. One stuffed animal or your baby's lovey should be the only toy in their bed. When baby wakes during the night, you don't want the notion of playtime entering that little mind. Like loveys and routines, the presence of toys is a cue—but of the wrong kind for this hour.

⭐ Develop Key Words as a Sleep Cue

You can condition your baby to know it is sleep time when you say certain words in a certain way. Begin now by deciding what your sleep-association words will be. The standard quiet sound of "shhh" is often helpful because it resembles the sound that your baby heard in the womb. Your key words can be something like a whispered "shhh, shhh, it's OK, sleepy time." Or "night-night, shhh, shhh, night-night." Or, "Enough, already, just go to sleep!" (I'm obviously kidding on that one, although I remember distinctly saying that to Coleton one night.) An alternative to establishing key words is to quietly hum a special relaxing melody.

Once you decide on your key words, get your baby accustomed to them by saying them each time your baby is quiet, peaceful, and falling asleep. Once your baby is familiar with the words, use them to settle them at bedtime or if they wake up during the night.

How to Introduce Your Key Words

For the first few weeks, use your key words only when your baby is actually falling asleep. You want your key words to be associated

Winter, ten-days-old, and Daddy

with this sleepy state. *Do not* use the key words when your baby is crying or unhappy, as *that* is what they will associate the words with. Funny enough, I learned this from my dog trainer! Yes, *dog trainer*. She says most people say, "No barking" when their dog is barking, so the dog thinks that "No barking" is an order to bark! She suggests saying it when the dog is in a quiet state so he associates the command with quiet. I heard something similar in a lecture on word association. The speaker suggested repeating words such as "relax" when you are feeling relaxed, so that you can replicate your relaxed stage when you are in stressful situations. So, at first, use your key words when your baby is in a quiet, nearly asleep state. Later, when the association is made, you can use your key words to help them calm down and fall asleep.

Use Music or Sound as Sleep Cues

Many people tiptoe around sleeping babies thinking that any noise will wake them up. This isn't exactly the case. True, there are many noises that wake a sleeping baby, but many sounds that actually soothe them to sleep.

> **Point to Remember**
> "White noise" sounds can help many babies to relax and fall asleep—and stay asleep—much more easily than a totally quiet room. This is partly because these sounds originate in the womb where your baby was always surrounded with sounds of your heartbeat, digestive noises, the soft whoosh of blood through your arteries, supplemented with the muffled outside sounds of your voice and the world.

White noise is sound that contains many frequencies of equal intensities so that the individual sounds are not heard, but rather a blended hum of sound results, serving as indistinct background noise. Examples are the drone of a fan, the rumble of an airplane engine, or the muffled hum of voices at a large gathering of people.

Even adults can find white noise sounds comforting and helpful in aiding sleep. For many people, it's relaxing to nod off to the hum of a fan or the steady tranquil lapping of ocean waves. This is because white noise reduces the audio clutter surrounding you, distracting you with an almost hypnotic beat and helping you tune out other sounds and thoughts that can keep you awake.

Four Ways That White Noise Works

The right kind of background noise is a perfect sleep aid for most babies. Whether your baby is an easy sleeper or a more challenging

Devi, three-weeks-old, and Mummy

sleeper, white noise can be helpful to your little one in four different ways:

1. **The gentle, consistent sound can be very effective at soothing your baby to sleep.**

    From the beginning of time, adults have used the sounds of "shhh shhh" or similar utterances to help calm a baby. It's an instinctual sound that mimics mother's heartbeat, and it works. When a baby hears these types of sounds, it brings the focus on them, and your baby can relax or fall asleep.

2. **The sound can mask other noises that can jar them awake.**

A steady hum of background noise can help block out sharp sudden sounds. Typically, it's not the noise itself that wakes your baby, but the sudden change in noise that jars your baby from sleep. White noise, played just loud enough, conceals these sharp sounds. You don't have to tiptoe around a sleeping baby, and the sounds of the house, like talking or soft footsteps, are soothing, as babies love to hear the sounds of the village as they sleep. However, sharp sounds like dishes clinking, dogs barking, or older siblings shouting can be sharp intrusive sounds that wake your sleeping child. Having white noise or soothing music playing can mask any of these baby-waking noises.

3. **White noise sounds can act as a bridge between sleep cycles.**

Daytime in your house is typically noisier than nighttime, both inside your home and outside, containing many abrupt baby-waking noises. And nighttime can also contain sounds, such as car horns, dogs barking or a television playing in another room. White noise can cover many of those disruptive sounds that happen during naps or in the middle of the night. When your baby is having a brief awakening between sleep cycles and hears these noises they can bring them fully awake. White noise can help your baby move seamlessly through sleep cycles (when hunger doesn't interfere) so that your baby has a longer nap or has fewer night wakings.

4. **A chosen sound used frequently for sleep times creates a consistent cue.**

When your baby hears the familiar sound it's a cue that it's time to sleep. When you routinely use the same sounds as soon as you notice signs of tiredness your baby comes to recognize it. Add some warm milk and a cuddle to easily lull your baby to sleep.

Your baby will become accustomed to these sounds for falling asleep, so it becomes an easy-to-use sleep cue, at home or away. If you purchase a small white noise machine it is easy to travel with or you can buy a white noise app on your phone or other device, or play a white noise video on YouTube—just keep in mind that you'll need to leave this running throughout your baby's nap.

White noise can be a magic answer for improved sleep for babies, children (and even adults!) You can leave it on for an entire nap and even all night long. These peaceful sounds are just one more piece in the puzzle that helps you to help your baby sleep better—gently, without any stress or crying at all.

What Kind of White Noise Is Best?

The sounds that help a baby to fall asleep and stay asleep are those that are steady and repetitive, without any major changes in volume or pitch, and don't contain any sudden sharp sounds. Typical white noise options mimic the sounds of ocean waves, rainfall, or other nature sounds. (Read about pink-hued white noise on pages 141 and 225.)

Negative Aspects of Using White Noise

As long as you use white noise properly, I've not discovered any dangers or side effects. The only negative mentioned is when the volume is too loud. To be certain you're using the correct volume I suggest that you put your own head down to where your baby's head will be resting to test that it's not too loud, so that you can protect your baby's delicate hearing. Always turn the sounds off when your baby is awake.

Likely the only real negative to using these sounds would be that your baby can become accustomed to the sound for sleep and you'll need to be sure you can accommodate this. That means finding a portable sound that can travel with you on vacation or when you're away from home. You'll also need to find out if your daycare supports the use of white noise for napping.

Finding the Right White Noise

As white noise has become more popular as a sleep aid, choices abound. There are machines, stuffed animals, CDs, MP3 tracks, digital music, YouTube videos, and apps. The best option may be the white noise machines that play various white noise options such as rainfall, a babbling brook, forest sounds, or ocean waves. Look for a white noise machine that can operate all night long. Some have automatic turn-offs, and they shut off just as baby is falling asleep and can wake them up with a click or sudden silence.

Choose white noise sounds that soothe your baby but also ones that you'll be happy to listen to. Once your baby is familiar with these sounds as a sleep cue, they can be used effectively for years to come.

Music Instead of White Noise

A few babies don't take to white noise and prefer actual music. If you opt for music for your baby, choose carefully. You'll want to find relaxing music, such as classical or soft jazz music, without any harsh or jarring sounds or sudden tempo changes. There are a wide variety of recordings available that have been created specifically for relaxation, yoga, meditation, or sleep that make great options for your baby.

Keep in mind, though, like in all things, babies are unique in their preferences. I have heard of several babies who fall asleep best to rock or rap music. (Of course, the rule for low volume still applies to protect your baby's hearing.)

The level and type of noise that disrupts sleep is different for each baby. Some children can sleep through a fire alarm siren, but some are awakened if you so much as drop a marshmallow, so you may have to try a few options to find your best match.

Make Your White Noise the Pink-Hued Variety

When it comes to the soothing nature of white noise, various studies show that *pink noise* is an even better choice for sleeping.

Pink noise is a variant of white noise that is filtered to reduce the intensity as the frequency increases. It sounds fuller, deeper, or richer than white noise. This further refined type of white noise seems to do an even better job of improving sleep because of its subdued quality. Interestingly, a heartbeat falls in the category of pink noise.

Most white noise machines and apps actually contain pink noise options, though they often aren't labeled as such, since "white noise" is the more commonly used term. To stay in the pink spectrum, choose sounds that are repetitive and use a lower, deeper sound and a slower pace. Perfect examples of pink noise are the sounds of a heartbeat, breathing, the hum of many quietly talking voices, a fan or humidifier, ocean waves, the pitter-patter of rainfall, the whoosh of a waterfall, the sound of rain falling on pavement, a car engine when driving on a freeway, or the rustling of leaves on a tree. In contrast, examples of white noise include things like a vacuum cleaner, the static between stations on a radio, and the squeal of a hair dryer, which are all a higher pitch and intensity, with a slightly harsh or tinny edge. As you can see, there are subtle differences that make pink noise gentler on the ear and a better match for aiding sleep.

While most white noise serves the purpose of masking sharp background sounds, pink noise adds a layer of relaxation and peacefulness. Pink noise might help you sleep better too. A study conducted at China's Peking University found that 75 percent of adults reported that they slept better, deeper, and longer when listening to pink noise as compared to having no sound in the bedroom. Another study in Germany found that pink noise improves brain wave activity during prolonged deep sleep, which represents enhanced memory retention.

It Doesn't Work for Every Baby . . . of Course

Babies are individuals, and just as with nearly every other piece of parenting advice, every idea doesn't work for every baby. The only way you can tell if the use of white noise works for your baby is to test it out. Does your baby fall asleep faster or stay asleep longer when you play the white noise? Experiment a bit so you can find the right answer for you. It may be that your baby prefers the quiet, or it could be that you need to make a different selection of the type of sound that you're using. Watch your baby for cues.

Mother-Speak

"I went out today and bought a small aquarium and the humming noise does seem to relax Chloe and help her to sleep. I didn't buy any fish though. Who has time to take care of fish when you're half asleep all day?"

Tanya, mother of thirteen-month-old Chloe

Eventually your baby will rely on white noise sounds less and less to fall and stay asleep. If you wish, you can help this process along by lowering the volume a small amount every night until you finally don't turn the music or sounds on at all. However, since there are no known negatives to using this solution, there's no need to eliminate this if it's working well for your child.

⭐ Change Your Baby's Sucking-to-Sleep Association

If your baby has learned to associate sucking (having your nipple or a bottle or pacifier in their mouth) with sleep, you can rest assured that your baby is perfectly normal. Babies are born this way, and nothing you've done has created your little one's attraction to this most popular baby sleep aid. I have heard a number of sleep experts refer to this as a "negative sleep association."

I certainly disagree, and so would your baby. It is probably the most positive, natural, pleasant sleep association a baby can have. The problem, of course, is that your baby may not be able to fall asleep any other way.

All-Day, All-Night Breastfeeders

The problem with our babies associating breastfeeding with sleep is not the association itself but our busy lives. If you had nothing whatsoever to do besides take care of your baby, this would be a very pleasant way to pass your days until your baby naturally outgrew the need. However, in our world, few parents have the luxury of putting everything else in their lives on hold until their baby gets older. With this in mind, I will give you a number of ideas so that you can gradually, and *lovingly*, help your baby learn to fall asleep without this very wonderful and powerful sleep aid.

Frequent Bottle-Feeding Babies

Your baby should be weaned from the need to have a bottle for sleep for a number of reasons. First, when your baby falls asleep with a bottle, the formula or juice might puddle in their mouth as they fall asleep and cause nursing bottle caries (cavities) syndrome. (Although much less of a risk, this can also happen with a breastfed baby who always sleeps while nursing if milk pools in their mouth.)

The second concern with using a bottle as a sleep aid is that your baby may not be hungry, but craves the sucking sensation to fall asleep. Therefore, they will be drinking more than they need.

The third issue is that it's simply no fun to be preparing and serving bottles all night when you'd much rather be sleeping!

Should You Use a Pacifier?

Once breastfeeding is firmly established (typically three to eight weeks), or if your baby is exclusively bottle-fed, it is fine to offer your baby a pacifier for falling asleep. There is no evidence that using a pacifier creates any health or developmental problems for young babies. Some studies show that pacifier use might possibly reduce the risk of SIDS, although it is unclear why the connection exists. Currently, medical organizations no longer discourage the use of pacifiers for naps and nighttime sleep for babies up to one year of age. They do not make a recommendation of pacifier use for all babies, but if your baby benefits from having a pacifier for falling asleep, you can now rest assured that it is fine to use one, as long as it doesn't interfere with your breastfeeding relationship.

Professional-Speak

"If used sensibly and for a baby who has intense sucking needs—in addition to, not as a substitute for, human nurturing—pacifiers are an acceptable aid."

—Dr. William Sears, author of *The Baby Book*

Scientists and breastfeeding groups feel that more research needs to be done before any specific recommendation of pacifier use should be made, since this might interfere with the quantity or length of breastfeeding for some babies. There are a few professionals who believe that a breastfeeding baby who sleeps close to the mother and wakes frequently to nurse has this same protection against SIDS, but it is all conjecture at this point. So watch the news and talk this over with your health-care professional as you make decisions about pacifier use.

Using a Pacifier Safely

Professionals encourage parents who use pacifiers for their babies to use them judiciously, which means keeping the pacifier linked specifically to sleep times, car rides, and colicky periods only, avoiding having it become an all-day attachment. Keep these important tips in mind when it comes to using a pacifier:

- Never use a pacifier to replace a feeding when your baby is hungry. (Remember that newborn babies can breastfeed every hour, and that is a need.) With any baby, but most specifically with a newborn, a pacifier should never postpone breastfeeding or bottle-feeding for a significant amount of time.
- Don't use the pacifier as a first choice when calming your crying baby—try holding, slinging, rocking, or singing to your baby first.
- Never use a string, ribbon, or other device to tie a pacifier to your baby or the crib.
- Use only a clean pacifier. (Keep them clean by popping them in the dishwasher.)

Mother-Speak

"He does sleep with six binkies, but that doesn't bother me because he sleeps all night long. We'll wean him eventually, but for now I enjoy getting a full night's sleep."

Jennifer, mother of six-month-old Coby

- Offer your baby a pacifier for falling sleep, but don't replace it once your baby is sleeping and has pushed the pacifier out of their mouth.

What About Thumb and Finger Sucking?

If your baby falls asleep with the comfort of sucking their own fingers, this is an entirely different situation from using a bottle, pacifier, or your breast. Your baby is in control of their own hands and able to use them whenever they wish. They are also not depending on someone else to help them every few hours all night long.

Current philosophies disagree as to whether letting a baby get into this habit is a good idea or not, but most experts agree that letting a young baby suck their own fingers poses no harm in the early months. The biggest issue, as you may expect, is that some children don't give up this habit on their own at any age, and you eventually have to step in when sucking could affect tooth, mouth, and speech development.

If you decide that you'd rather eliminate your baby's reliance on a pacifier or finger sucking now, read on for gentle weaning ideas.

How to Diminish the Sucking-to-Sleep Association

When your baby wakes looking for a bottle or to breastfeed, you most likely respond to these cues by providing the sucking that your baby is desiring. For some babies this sucking is the *only way* that they can fall asleep—or get back to sleep. The problem here is that this kind of baby's strong suck-to-sleep association most likely won't change until the second—or even third birthday, unless you take action to change things.

To take the steps to change your baby's suck-to-sleep association, you must complicate night wakings for a few weeks or even a month, but in the long run you can wean your baby from using your breast or a bottle as their only sleep association. In other words, be prepared to disrupt your own nights for a while to make some important, worthwhile changes, so that you aren't still dealing with this common sleep-disrupting process one or two years from now.

Yes, it's true that some babies *can* fall asleep for every nap and night sleep while sucking at the breast or bottle, and then nap well and sleep through the night. Count yourself very lucky if your baby is among this small group! However, if you have the much more common situation of a baby who absolutely requires sucking to fall asleep and then to fall back to sleep between every sleep cycle—all night long—and even mid-nap—this idea may be an important key to your sleep success.

This is a solution that you can also use for a baby over four-months-old to prevent them from developing such a strong suck-to-sleep association that it becomes an absolute necessity for sleep, and a firmly ingrained routine that becomes very hard to change.

Point to Remember

The beauty of this gentle plan is that it respects your baby's natural need to suckle to sleep by making changes gradually, peacefully, and respectfully.

Introducing *Pantley's Gentle Removal Plan*

Pantley's Gentle Removal Plan is simple in concept: After the first few months of life, and after breastfeeding is firmly established and without challenges, remove your baby from your breast or the bottle when they are done feeding, but before they begin the fluttery, on-and-off pacifying sucking that is nonnutritive but sleep inducing. Before your baby is totally limp-limbed and snoring, you remove them from the breast or bottle. You can then replace this with a pacifier, if your baby uses one for sleep (since the majority of babies will spit out the pacifier as soon as they are asleep).

If you are bed-sharing but aiming for independent sleep, you can then transfer your baby to the crib to finish falling asleep there. You will likely need to pat, rub, jiggle, or shush to help your little one fall asleep, at least at first. The value of this idea is clearest among breastfeeding mothers who must nurse their *toddlers* fully to sleep for every single nap and bedtime, or among parents who must wander the halls every few hours to refresh a bottle for a two-year-old—so to avoid that scenario, start with this idea early if you can.

Forest, seven-months-old, and Mama

Point to Remember

Enjoy and respect your baby's desire to nurse to sleep, but make sure it's not the one and only way your baby sleeps because it can become extremely difficult to change later.

To prevent a complete dependence on sucking to sleep, at least several times a day, and several times during the night, remove the breast or bottle from your baby's mouth and let them finish falling asleep without something resting in their mouth. If your baby enjoys it, you can replace the milk source with a pacifier. (Just don't put it back once your baby falls asleep and it falls out of their mouth.)

If you have a newborn, it's too early for this idea and you shouldn't obsess about it, since newborns easily and frequently fall asleep while sucking. However, it can't hurt to stay aware so that it doesn't become the way your baby falls asleep 100 percent of the time, since the pattern becomes ingrained and suck-to-sleep dependence is by far the most common problem among parents of babies older babies.

If your baby is already over four months old and firmly established in this ritual, you can read through the following section for a more detailed description of the Gentle Removal Plan.

Pantley's Gentle Removal Plan — The Details

This plan is simple once you understand it, but I know you're sleep-deprived and likely frustrated with this sleep issue, so I'm going to provide more details and information to help you through the Gentle Removal, or as my readers call it: The Pantley Pull-Off.

When your baby wakes up, go ahead and follow your usual pattern: pop in the bottle or breastfeed your baby. But, instead of letting your baby fall fully asleep at the breast or bottle, let them have a feeding and then suck for a few minutes until the sucking pace slows and your baby is relaxed and sleepy. Then break the seal with your finger and gently remove the nipple. This allows your baby to begin to separate the process of feeding versus sleeping. You're letting your baby have a meal, and suck a bit to relax, but then releasing the nipple so they can finish the actual falling asleep without having anything resting in their mouth.

This is a big change so, especially at first, your baby then will startle and root for the nipple. Your baby is accustomed to falling asleep with something resting in their mouth, so the vacant space when you remove the nipple can be unsettling. Help your baby out with this transition. Try cupping your baby's face very gently as you hold their mouth closed with your hand or finger under their chin, or apply a small amount of pressure to the top of the chin, just under the lip, at the same time rocking, or swaying, or patting your baby. The feeling of your hand on your baby's face can be a soothing substitute. (Use your key words if you have developed them.) If your baby struggles against this and roots for you or the bottle, or cries, go ahead and replace the nipple, but repeat the removal process in a minute or so, and as often as necessary until your little one falls asleep.

How long between removals? Every baby is different, but about ten to sixty seconds between removals usually works. It's not so long that your baby settles to sleep, but long enough to allow them to relax. You also should also watch your baby's sucking action. If a baby is sucking strongly or swallowing regularly, this indicates feeding, so wait a few minutes until they stop eating and slow the pace. By paying attention to your baby's swallowing, you can also tell when you have had a letdown reflex. You can try to get your baby to release at that time, but you'll need to stop the flow of milk with your hand, or wait a minute for the flow to subside. Usually, after the initial burst of activity, your baby will slow to a more relaxed "fluttery" pace; this is a good time to begin your removal attempts.

> ## Mother-Speak
> "We got to calling this the Big PPO (Pantley Pull-Off). At first Joshua would see it coming and grab my nipple tighter in anticipation—ouch! But you said to stick with it, and I did. Now he anticipates the PPO and actually lets go and turns and rolls over on his side to go to sleep! I am truly amazed."
> **Shannon, mother of nineteen-month-old Joshua**

It may take two to five (or even more) attempts, but eventually your baby will fall asleep without the nipple in their mouth. When your baby has done this a number of times over a period of days, you will notice the removals are much easier and awakenings are less frequent.

An Example of the Removal in Action

Many of my readers have asked for a more specific example, so the following is just to give you an idea, as every baby is different. The Pantley Pull-Off could look something like this. (This example shows a breastfeeding baby, but the plan is the same whether your baby is breastfeeding or using a bottle.)

Baby is awake and nursing vigorously.
Baby's eyes close, and his sucking rate slows.
You gently remove your nipple.
Baby roots (moving his open mouth toward you).
You try holding his chin, but he'll have none of that!
You put him back to the breast.
Count: one thousand, two thousand, . . . ten thousand.*

---

*The counting is really more for you, to give you a gauge to measure your time and a way to keep yourself calm during your repeated attempts. You can be flexible as you figure out what time spacing works best for you and your baby.

You gently remove your nipple.

Baby roots.

You try stalling, your baby starts to fuss. You nurse again, just long enough to settle your baby.

Count: one thousand, two thousand, . . . ten thousand.

You gently remove your nipple.

Baby roots.

You put him back to the breast.

Count: one thousand, two thousand, . . . ten thousand.

You gently remove your nipple.

Baby moves a little, and you gently cup his face and very softly hold his mouth closed. (The feeling of your hand on your baby's face can be comforting.) Baby is settled and doesn't resist; he is nearly out!

You place Baby in bed.

Bliss! He goes to sleep.

Repeat this process every night until your baby learns to fall asleep without nursing or sucking on a pacifier. If your baby is a "good napper," you can use the technique at naptime, too.

If your baby doesn't nap well, don't trouble yourself with trying too hard to use the removal technique during the day for naps. Remember that good naps mean better nighttime sleep—and better nighttime sleep means better naps. It's a circle. Once you get your baby sleeping better at night, you can then work on the naptime sleep—although once you solve the nighttime association, the naptime sleep may solve itself.

Using the PPO for Pacifier Weaning

You can easily adapt this process when the time comes to wean your baby from a pacifier. You may want to wait until after twelve months of age as some studies show that pacifier use for falling asleep can provide some protection against SIDS.

As mentioned in the information about pacifier use on page 351, you don't need to re-insert the pacifier after it falls out of your baby's mouth to achieve this SIDS protection. You also don't want to create a situation where your baby relies on the feeling of the pacifier in their mouth to sleep after their first birthday.

The First Falling Asleep of the Night

The most important time to use the Pantley's Gentle Removal Plan is usually the first falling asleep of the night. Often the way your baby initially falls asleep will affect the rest of their awakenings for the night. I suspect that this is because of the sleep-association effect that I explained earlier when we discussed basic sleep facts. It seems that the way in which your baby falls asleep for the night is how they expect to remain all night long. So, if your little one falls asleep with the nipple resting in their mouth it is what they expect to feel throughout the night; they'll wake up if it's missing.

Patience During the Process

Because we are using a gentle, respectful no-cry solution, this is not a one-day solution. (Such a thing doesn't exist in any realm.) But within ten to fourteen days, as you gently break this strong sleep association, you should see a major reduction in the number of your baby's night wakings.

Ask any parent who is still struggling with their *toddler's* strong suck-to-sleep association and they'll tell you that ten days—or even a few weeks—is a blink of time. For most people it's well worth the patience to be able to avoid a nightly, heart-wrenching tear-filled drama.

Changing Your Routine

Very often we parents have a routine we have followed with our babies since birth. The final step before sleep is often nursing or having a bottle. Some babies can continue this pattern and still sleep through the night. Others, though, need to have the final step in their routine changed before they begin to sleep all night without needing your help to fall back to sleep. What you'll want to do is take an objective look at your final steps in putting your baby to sleep and make some changes if necessary.

You may want to use massage, cuddles, white noise, or the key words idea to help get your baby back to sleep. Eventually the key word, soft sounds or a loving pat will take over from nursing or bottle-feeding. Gradually the reliance on that cue too will fade away, and your baby will be sleeping longer. Here's what one test mommy reported:

Mother-Speak

"I have changed the way I'm putting Carlene to sleep and it's working! Instead of nursing her down, I just feed her until she is relaxed and then I just let her do whatever she wants in the very dim room with me. When she rubs her eyes and looks sleepy, I put her in her crib. I used to go out of the room, hoping she would drift off herself, but she would just get agitated and work herself up until I came back. But now, I just stay there. I stand next to the crib, and encourage her to sleep. I say my key words, 'Shhh, it's night-night time, close your eyes sleepy girl,' and I tell her that it's OK to go to sleep. I rub her head or her tummy. She shuts her eyes right when I do this. She'll open them back up a few times, but eventually she settles. Since I'm not nursing or rocking, she is falling asleep without these, so when she lightly wakes during sleep cycle transition, she is finally able to go back to sleep without me. It's been a major breakthrough."

Rene, mother of seven-month-old Carlene

Help Your Baby Fall Back to Sleep Without Help— While You Continue to Breastfeed and Bed-Share

Research shows that when you breastfeed and bed-share, you may find that your baby will wake more often than if they were in a crib down the hall. But like many families who bed-share, you may feel that the reasons that you keep your baby in your bed outweigh the inconvenience of a few night wakings. Like you, I chose to breastfeed and bed-share for many reasons that are important to me—and I've done it with all four of my babies.

One important thing to keep in mind when it comes to night-waking is that "this too shall pass." All of my children eventually slept through the night, and your baby will too. However, there are ways that you can speed up the process of your baby sleeping all night—even while keeping your little one in bed with you.

Make sure that you've read the safety list in Part V. Much of what we've learned about the dangers associated with bed-sharing point to unsafe sleeping environments as the real issue. Read up on the topic and make a wise and informed decision, and religiously follow all safety measures.

The challenge with breastfeeding, bed-sharing mother-baby pairs is that each partner is so in tune with the other that the slightest movement or noise will have both awake. You can end up generating additional wakings in between the baby's natural ones, thus creating an all-night wake–sleep pattern.

Nico, six-months-old, and Mami

The trick is to get your baby accustomed to sleeping beside you but able to go back to sleep without your help (typically in the form of nursing). You can do this by shortening your nighttime help routines. I know that this is possible because I am living proof that you don't have to give up a sleeping ritual that you love just to get some sleep. Not all babies will respond as mine did, of course. But many of my test mommies practice breastfeeding and bed-sharing, and many found their own sleep success without having to move their babies out of their beds. Some stubborn little ones do require a move to another room before they will give up the luxury of nighttime nursing, but do try all of my ideas for a few weeks before you assume this to be correct for your baby. (If you decide it's time to move your baby out of your bed, you'll find ideas for a gentle, peaceful transition in the section beginning on page 247.)

Mother-Speak

"I am not ready to move Atticus out of my bed. I enjoy having him near me at night and snuggling with him. I slept with my daughter, Gracie, when she was a baby and she transitioned quite easily when we were both ready. Bedtime has always been a time of comfort for her and I feel that when the time is right for Atticus he will be much the same. Even so, it would be nice to have him waking up less often to nurse."

Pam, mother of eleven-month-old Atticus and five-year-old Gracie

---

When your baby wakes, you probably have a routine to get them back to sleep. Many nursing mothers rely on breastfeeding. I used to nurse my youngest child until he was totally asleep; the nipple literally would fall out of his mouth. Every hour, we had a very exact pattern. My baby sniffed and snorted, I shifted him to the other side, I kissed his head, he nursed—a beautiful, soothing ritual. As sweet as this ritual was, after twelve months of this hourly ceremony, I desperately needed a change, and the Gentle Removal idea was created.

Stop Feeding a Sleeping Baby

Learning how to break the suck-to-sleep association is a gradual, thoughtful process that requires much self-examination. I found I was responding to my baby so quickly and intuitively that I'd put him to the breast before he even made a real noise—he would just fidget, gurgle, or sniff and I would put him to the breast. I began to realize that, on so many of these occasions, he would have gone back to sleep without me!

As you know, I am a follower of the "never let your baby cry" rule, and I took it very seriously. What I didn't understand, though, is that *babies make sounds in their sleep*. And these sounds do not mean that your baby needs to nurse. Babies moan, grunt, snuffle, whimper, and even cry in their sleep. Babies can even nurse in their sleep!

The first step to helping your baby sleep longer is to determine the difference between sleeping noises and awake noises. When your baby makes a noise, stop. Listen. Wait. Peek. As you listen attentively to their noises and watch carefully, you will learn the difference between sleeping snorts and "I'm waking up and I need you now" noises.

When I learned this eye-opening piece of information, I started "playing asleep" when my baby made a nighttime noise. I would just listen and watch—not moving a single muscle—until he began to make actual wakeful noises. Some of the time, he never did; he just went back to sleep without my having to do anything at all! And over time my baby relied less and less on my help to fall back to sleep until he was sleeping straight through every night.

Mother-Speak

"Last night he was nursing and I pulled him off and put my finger under his chin like you suggested. I was thinking 'this will never work, he'll be mad!'—but it worked, he went to sleep! The other trick is helpful too. When I take him off and then roll over, he thinks I'm asleep, then he goes to sleep, too!"

Carol, mother of nine-month-old Ben

Shorten Your Nighttime Nursing Times

You may be following the pattern that we were—putting your baby to the breast and then both of you falling back to sleep. It's very easy to do, because the act of breastfeeding releases hormones that make Mommy sleepy, just as much as the milk makes your baby sleepy. The problem is that your baby falls soundly asleep at the breast, and begins to believe that having the nipple in their mouth is the only way they can sleep. Therefore, every time your baby reaches a brief awakening, they look to re-create the sleep-inducing condition. You can help your baby learn to fall asleep without this aid by shortening your nighttime nursing intervals.

When you are sure your baby is awake and looking to nurse, go ahead and breastfeed. Stay awake! And as soon as your baby is done eating and slows the pace from the gulping, drinking mode to the slow fluttery comfort nursing, you can gently disengage while patting, jiggling, or rubbing or rocking. (See more about Pantley's Gentle Removal Plan on pages 231–237.)

Sometimes you can put your baby's hand on you during the removal, since many babies will accept this touch as a substitute for nursing; it seems to keep you "connected," and they know that the milk is nearby if needed.

Another option, if your baby is past the infant stage, is to make the latch-on a little less comfortable and convenient for your baby. So, instead of lying tummy to tummy with your baby cradled in your arm, once your baby is done actively eating and is just pacifying, you can shift them slightly onto their back so that they have to work a bit to keep hold of the nipple. (Back-sleeping is the most important protection against SIDS, so it's a good way for them to fall asleep.) Babies often decide it's too much effort, so they let go and go back to sleep.

If your baby whimpers at any point during this removal process, or lets you know that distraction is not an option (by crawling onto your chest, for example!), go ahead and breastfeed again. Then repeat the process to keep the nursing session short, and most important—disconnect before your baby is deeply asleep.

Sometimes, it may take three to five times or more before your baby will settle into sleep. Just like many of my test mommies, after a week of using this technique with my own baby, he began to disengage himself, turn over onto his back, and fall asleep! It was wonderful; perhaps only a bed-sharing, breastfeeding mommy can understand just how sweet this moment can be! In fact, by eighteen months of age, my son nursed until he was comfortable, then rolled away from me and fell asleep and then slept ten hours through the night. I left him in the bed with his big brother in our sleeping room, and I was free to join my husband in our own bed for baby-free sleep and couple time.

Move the Milk

Here is another idea especially for bed-sharing breastfeeders, particularly for those with babies who stay glued to your side all night. After you nurse your baby, scoot yourself away. If your baby is snuggled right up against you, they will awaken and want to nurse more often—sometimes, as I mentioned earlier, even in their sleep. If your baby is used to feeling you against them, then you may want

Mother-Speak

"I finally realized that I had a hidden fear that if I night-weaned her she would day wean too. I didn't want that to happen, so I was nursing her no matter the time of day or night. I've modified my thinking, and now I nurse her for a long prebed session and a leisurely morning session instead of thinking we need to nurse all night long."

Becky, mother of thirteen-month-old Melissa

to try a tactile replacement. A small stuffed animal is perfect for the job. (See pages 213–216.) Simply place the toy next to your baby's body or legs (away from their face) when you move away, so that they feel the company closeby.

For persistent night nursers, you may even want to change your sleeping arrangement for a few weeks until you get the frequent night waking under control. Many parents put two mattresses on the floor next to each other. During the period of change, nurse your baby on one bed; once they are asleep, move yourself over to the other. Granted, it is only five feet away, but it's far enough away that you don't cause any additional awakenings with your own nighttime movements. If you have a crib, you can try the side-car arrangement—pushing the crib up next to your bed and letting your baby have their own sleeping cubby. (At the risk of sounding like a nag, follow good safety measures, such as firmly securing the crib in place and checking for gaps, if you do this.)

I must tell you though, that some very persistent bed-sharing night wakers have "Mommy radar" and may continue their

Audrey, twelve-months-old, and Momma

numerous wakings until Mommy and Baby sleep in different rooms. If you try all of my other ideas, and find that your baby is still waking frequently, you'll need to make that ultimate decision—what's more important right now, sharing sleep or just plain sleep? I cannot answer that question for you, and there is no right answer. You'll need to examine the needs of every member of your family to determine just what path you should take. Even if you decide to move your baby to a different sleeping spot, remember that once they begin sleeping solidly through the night, you can welcome them back into your bed anytime.

Mother-Speak

"Chloe now starts the night in her crib and when she wakes I bring her to bed with us. Since we have been co-sleeping from the beginning, I'm so used to having her there that I 'want' her to wake up and come into bed with us! I know it sounds strange, but I just wanted to let you know your program is transitioning me as much as it is Chloe."

Tanya, mother of thirteen-month-old Chloe

You may also want to use your white noise sounds and key words to help get your baby back to sleep. (See pages 218–226.) Eventually, the sounds, key words, and loving touch will take over for nursing, and then that too will fade away, and your baby will sleep longer without waking you.

Just like most of the ideas in this book, the one here is based on gradual, gentle changes over time—no quick fixes or tearful transitions.

☆ *Help Your Baby Become an Independent Sleeper*

Whether you've had your baby in bed with you full-time or part-time, one month or two years, a time may come when you're ready to move your baby out of your bed and into their own. The following is a list of ideas for making this transition. After reviewing them, formulate your strategy by choosing those that best fit your family's unique situation.

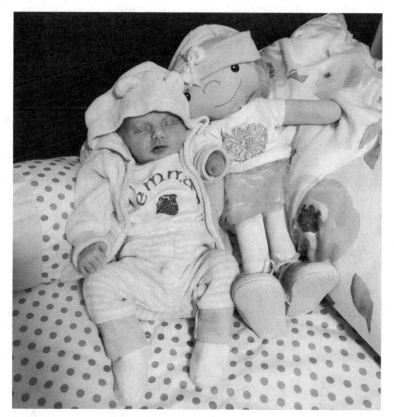

Emma Rose, one-week-old

Some parents decide to wait until their children are ready to make the move on their own. This is perfectly fine; if you are in no hurry to make a change, then, by all means, enjoy this time! Let the process happen naturally. These ideas are not meant to imply that your baby should be in their own bed if this is not what you want; rather, they are here for those parents who have decided that they would like their baby to move on to their own bed.

Keep in mind that, in most cases, you don't have to make the change overnight. Often, taking a few weeks, or even a few months, is the most peaceful route. On the other hand, if one or both parents don't have the desire or patience to wait, or if you have a reason you must make the change, you can make the move quickly, and still be sensitive to your baby's needs.

No matter what you decide, keep in mind that your baby has truly enjoyed nights in your bed, and won't like sleeping alone at first. Try to make the transition as easy as you can for your little one.

I'll provide here a list of possibilities; these have been used by many other parents successfully. Make a check by those ideas that appeal to you. Review them and think about them, and then create your own plan to move your baby out of your family bed.

Staying Close but Not Too Close

Place a mattress or pad on the floor near your bed. Put your baby to sleep on the pad, and then climb back up into your bed. If your baby wakes to breastfeed or needs a cuddle, bottle, or reassurance, Mommy or Daddy can move down to the baby, parent the little one back to sleep, and get back up in the big bed—so the child gets used to sleeping alone. After a week or so of this arrangement, move this same pad or mattress to your baby's room, if your child is over a year old. (You can also do this in reverse, leaving baby in the big bed while you sleep on the pad or mattress.) Again—follow all safety precautions.

Create a Miniature Family Bed

Most babies who are accustomed to sleeping with their parents will sleep fine anywhere with Mommy or Daddy sleeping along-side. You can use this to your advantage when moving your baby toward independent sleeping.

If your baby is old enough—more than a year old or so—place a mattress on the floor in your baby's bedroom. Make sure the room is perfectly childproof and follow all the precautions in Part V.

Use your usual going-to-sleep routine, but instead of sleeping in the big bed, go to sleep with your baby in this newly arranged room. For the first few nights, or even a week or more, you might want to stay there all night long, so your baby gets comfortable with the change.

After you've established this new place as a safe, secure spot for sleep, you can get up and go to your own room after your baby is asleep. If your baby has a lovey or small stuffed animal, place it in your spot when you leave. Keep a baby monitor turned on, and when your baby wakes during the night, quickly go to them. Your child will discover that you're never very far away and will adapt to the new sleeping arrangement and begin to wake less at night.

The Traveling Crib

If you have a crib for your baby and your goal is for your little one to sleep there, try this step-by-step approach to independent sleep. Follow each step from two nights to a week or more, depending on how comfortable you and your baby are at each step, and how quickly you want to make the change. There are no rules: feel your way through the steps and modify them to fit your family.

1. Place the crib right next to your bed in a sidecar arrangement. You can keep the rail that faces your bed down to its lowest setting, or remove it all together. (Important: keep the crib tightly secured to your bed so that it doesn't shift

and create a gap that could trap your baby.) Special cribs are available for this purpose—for example, the Arm's Reach co-sleeper, available through many baby furniture sources.

If your baby has always slept nestled against you, you can make this transition a bit easier if you put your scent on the baby's crib sheet. You can sleep on the crib sheet for a few nights, perhaps using it as a pillowcase, or tuck it inside your nightgown or T-shirt for a few hours before bedtime.

2. Once your baby is comfortable with this new arrangement, you can put the fourth side up on the crib and move it just a foot or two away from your bed. Your baby will hear, smell, and see you, but you won't be waking each other with your nocturnal movements, and they will begin to get comfortable sleeping alone. You can even keep the crib close enough to reach over and put your arm through the bars for a midnight patting if that helps.

3. Move the crib to the other side of your bedroom, as far away from your bed as your room allows. Go quickly to your baby for any awakening, and your child will begin to realize that even when you are farther away you will always be there if they need you.

4. Finally, when you and your baby are ready, and your little one has passed their first birthday, move the crib to your baby's bedroom, keeping a monitor turned on so that you can go to your baby quickly if necessary. After you respond quickly to any calls the first few nights, your baby will be confident that you will be there to provide your normal loving care in the night, and will begin to confidently sleep longer stretches.

The Sneaky Way

If your baby can be moved easily after they fall asleep, you can try this approach. Let your baby fall asleep in your bed as usual. As soon as your little one is completely asleep, gently transfer them to the crib. If your baby is over a year and in their own room, have a baby monitor turned on so that you can go to them quickly when they wake up. When your baby wakes to be fed, feed your baby in a chair, or bring your baby to your safely arranged family bed to nurse, but then stay awake and return your baby to the crib once they are again asleep.

If you use this technique, you can expect to be up and down, or traveling the hallway between rooms for a while until the transition is complete. Many babies will adjust rather quickly and will sleep much longer stretches than when they were in bed with another person whose night movements caused extra awakenings. You might even set a time that you'll stop the transfer. For example, move baby to the crib for every awakening until 3:00 A.M., and then just keep your child in bed with you after that time so you can get some sleep.

Like all of the No-Cry solutions, this is not meant to be a rigid, do-it-or-else proposition. You can work with this idea for a few weeks, making the change more peaceful for both you and your

Point to Remember

To help your baby become accustomed to their crib, spend a few pleasant playtimes each day entertaining your baby while they relax in the crib. Sing, talk, read, give a puppet show, or play with toys. If they are happy playing on their own, just sit quietly beside them and let them absorb the atmosphere.

Take a look around at what your baby sees from the viewpoint of the crib and make sure that what they see is pleasant. This will all help your baby to be more comfortable in the crib setting so that it will become a familiar place to happily sleep, both during the night and for naps.

baby. (Of course, if you want baby moved pronto, you could be very persistent and move through the transition more quickly; that's of course entirely up to you.) More ideas on page 256.

For Your Walking, Talking Toddler or Preschooler

If your little one is old enough to understand, and sleeps in a bed (rather than a crib), you can begin the night by putting your child to bed in their own room and explaining what will happen if they wake up. Set up a "special sleeping spot" in your room: a mattress or pad on the floor near your bed. Explain to your child that if they wake up during the night, they can come to their special little bed and go right back to sleep. Explain that Mommy and Daddy will be sleeping, so they should tiptoe in as quiet as a mouse and get settled without waking you. If they do succeed with this plan, make sure that you heap on the praise the next morning.

When you first use this idea, make a big production about setting up the "big kid" bedroom. You may want to rearrange the room, buy new sheets or pillows, add some glow-in-the-dark stars and moons on the ceiling, and line up lots of friendly stuffed animals. You can leave a sippy cup of water on the nightstand and a flashlight or anything else that might provide comfort in the middle of the night. A quiet nighttime pet, like a goldfish, might provide a bit of company.

As part of this process, make sure that your bedtime routine is long enough to be relaxing, and that it includes pleasant activities like book reading and a back rub. Your child should land in bed feeling peaceful and ready to sleep, with the knowledge that they can come into your room if they need to.

Some children can be convinced to stay in their own beds if promised a reward at the end of the week. A small wrapped gift (like a toy car or plastic dinosaur) can be a great motivator. You might also use a situational prize, for example, "If you stay in your bed all week, you can sleep with Mommy and Daddy on Saturday night." Granted, like many parenting ideas, you need to think about this before you try it. This one may not work for your child in particular, and may even backfire, causing your little one to crave the family bed every night.

This is a good time for me to remind you that you should not only take into account your particular child's disposition and family situation, but that you should feel free to take bits of my ideas here and formulate your own. Use your creativity. You know your own family best, and I know sleep—together, we can help your child sleep all night!

Create a Sibling Bed

If your baby is more than about eighteen-months-old, and if you have an older child close in age who would welcome the idea, move your baby from your bed to the sibling's bed (being sure, of course, to take all safety precautions outlined on pages 353–354).

Amelia, one-year-old, and Charlie, two-years-old

We used the sibling bed idea in our family and found that our children truly enjoyed sleeping together when they were young. Other parents who use this arrangement agree that it helps decrease sibling rivalry and fighting. I suspect that those late-night and early-morning cuddles and chats keep siblings close.

A sibling bed arrangement can also include some "bed hopping." The kids can decide each night where they would like to sleep, taking turns being the host for the evening. If you do use the sibling bed idea, you'll find that over time your children will begin to sleep separately—first one night, then two, and soon they'll settle into their own beds, on their own. (Many will continue to have "sleepovers" in each other's rooms for years after that, maintaining the special connection that a sibling bed creates.)

Help Your Breastfed Baby Fall Back to Sleep with Another Person's Assistance

In most cases, breastfeeding, bed-sharing babies wake up frequently to feed throughout the night because they love having access to Mommy all night long. Anytime they wake up, they see, hear, smell, and feel you and think, "Aha! Lovely warm milk and a cozy mommy. Gotta have it!" So, if you have a husband, partner, mother, or someone else who is willing and able to help for a week or so, you might want to ask that person to sleep near your baby in your stead.

If your baby is younger than about eighteen months, set up a crib, cradle, or mattress right next to the helper's bed, as it's never a good idea for someone other than Mom to sleep right next to a baby (See the safety chapter). This should be a person your baby is very close to and comfortable with. If possible, have him or her start this process with naps for a few days first to make it easier on both of them. (If not, that's OK—start right in with bedtime.)

Mother-Speak

"I found it virtually impossible to soothe my daughter back to sleep without the breast. She would just get agitated and angry. After she turned a year old, our answer was to have Daddy go to her when she woke up to resettle her. The first few nights she was quite irritated that it was daddy and not Mommy coming to her beck and call. But, by the end of the week, she was totally in love with her Daddy. My husband still says that helping night-wean her (though he was sleep deprived at the time) was one of the most important ways he has ever bonded with his little girl. I noticed that closeness in their relationship immediately, and it still hasn't gone away, even though we're long past that time."

Deirdre, mother of nineteen-month-old Violet

When your baby awakens, and it's not yet time for a feeding, have your helper rock, walk with, hum to them—anything that helps your little one go back to sleep. It's fine if your helper uses a pacifier to calm your baby. Keep in mind that at some point down the road you'll probably have to deal with weaning from the pacifier, but since it can be a helpful sleep aid, many parents find that they are comfortable with that scenario.

Tell your "sleep assistant" that there are no absolute rules here, and they can find their own best ways to handle the night waking. If at any time your baby starts to cry and gets upset, or if your helper is losing patience, tell him or her that it's OK to bring them to you, if they wish. Let them decide when to give up, and don't interfere if that person is trying their loving best with your baby. They may have to give up the first few times, and that's normal. Just try again with the next waking or the next night. When your baby comes to you (notice I said "when," not "if"), follow the ideas in the previous sections of this book dealing with breast-feeding to sleep.

⭐ Help Baby Fall Back to Sleep in the Crib

If your baby sleeps in a crib and wakes up for your attention many times throughout the night, the all-night up-and-down is beyond exhausting. It's likely that every time your baby is crying or calling out to you during the night you are doing something to help them to fall back to sleep. To gradually get your baby to go back to sleep without your assistance, you need to shorten these helping routines during the night.

When your baby wakes, you probably follow a specific sequence of events to get them back to sleep, such as picking them up, rocking, nursing, or giving a bottle or pacifier. As you read in Chapter 2, it's

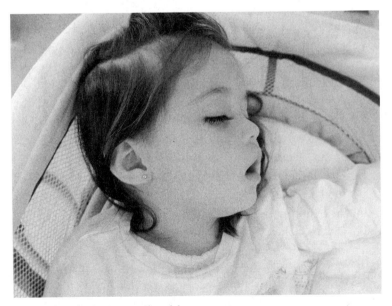

Fernanda, nineteen-months-old

likely that your baby thinks that these things are necessary in order to go back to sleep. We don't want to go cold turkey and cut out the familiar, nurturing pattern that you have established; that's a sure way to cause stress and tears. Instead, you can very gradually modify the length of your help routine so that you are doing less each night. Eventually, your baby will develop a new routine that doesn't require your presence.

When your baby wakes up, go ahead and use your regular means of getting them back to sleep, but gradually shorten the duration and vary the technique. So, instead of letting them completely fall asleep, encourage drowsiness and then see if they'll finish falling asleep on their own in the crib. If your baby starts to cry, you can pick them up until they settle, and then repeat the process. This may take three, four, or more attempts the first few nights; and you may even have to abort your mission on some nights. Over a period of a week or two you will see definite progress.

Your nights might currently look something like this:

- Baby wakes up.
- You pick her up; sit in a chair; and rock, nurse, bottle-feed, or take her to bed with you until she's soundly asleep.
- Then you probably ease her gently into the crib without waking her. When you move Baby from your arms to the crib, you do it very slowly and carefully, without waking her, so she has no idea she's changed places from your arms to the crib.
- Then you creep out of the room and await your next call, which undoubtedly will arrive as soon as your baby moves between sleep cycles and realizes she is now alone in her crib.

If you are going to use this suggestion, and if your baby uses breastfeeding or a bottle at every night waking, then you will want to incorporate Pantley's Gentle Removal Plan (pages 231–237) along with the ideas that follow.

I have found that many parents have been told to respond to their babies immediately and never let them cry, and they rigorously obey this edict. Of course, it's important not to leave your baby to cry, but there's one problem with this practice that typically isn't explained: *babies make sounds in their sleep.* Babies moan, grunt, snuffle, whimper, and even cry in their sleep. Loving parents often run to their little ones at the first noise and scoop their babies out of their cribs. I did this with my first baby, and I can still remember that sometimes she was asleep in my arms before I even got to the rocking chair to sit down. What I didn't know was that she had never really been awake.

Mother-Speak

"Last night when I heard Lauren making sounds I just waited and listened, instead of running in to her. I am amazed. Twice, by the time I was down the hall to peek in at her, she'd gone back to sleep!"

Christine, mother of thirteen-month-old Lauren

The first step to helping your baby sleep better in the crib is to determine the difference between sleeping noises and awake noises. I'm not suggesting that you ignore a baby's true cries by any means; your baby may need you, and this is the only way they can communicate this. In fact, when you wait too long and your baby wakes up fully it's much harder to fall back to sleep. Rather, be wise about determining if your baby is actually awake: If your baby is in another room, keep the door open or use a baby monitor. When your baby makes a noise, stop. Listen. Wait. As you listen attentively to these noises, you will learn the difference between sleeping snorts and "I'm waking up and I need you now" noises.

Once you have confirmed that your baby is truly awake and needs tending, pay attention to how much time you spend and how intense your helpfulness is. You may be providing more help than is needed and for a longer period of time. You can gradually reduce this until it naturally fades away to nothing.

The following sample shows the duration and type of nighttime help being shortened. This is by no means an exact plan, your own method may be quite different, but this will give you an understanding of the concept.

Phase One: Comfort Until Baby's Almost Asleep

Once you determine that your baby is really awake, go and get them. Sit in a chair and rock, nurse, or bottle-feed your baby but only until their eyes close and sucking rate slows. (Be sure to stay awake yourself.) Do not wait until your baby is totally asleep, just until they are fed, settled, and relaxed. Stand up with your baby in your arms and rock or sway gently. When you lay your baby down, keep your arms in place for a few minutes, making gentle rocking motions. (Yes, this can be tough on your back, but it's only temporary.) Your baby will accept the change from your lap to bed if you don't abruptly "dump" them there. Touch down with Baby's feet first, since head first can feel like falling. Keep in mind that when they fall asleep on you, you are moving and breathing, while the bed is still and silent. So gentle movement during the transition helps. You might even put a warm-pack or towel warmed in the dryer on the mattress to warm up the space before you lay your baby down. Remove the pack or towel and test the area before you place your baby there.

Once your little one is settled in the crib, gently slip your arms out. If your baby stirs, put your hand on them; whisper your key words or turn on some white noise; and rock, pat, or touch them gently until they're asleep. If your baby wakes and cries, pick them up, and repeat this process. You may have to do this two, three, four, maybe five times, but that's OK—really. It's just temporary.

If you or your baby get truly upset at any point, just go ahead and put them to sleep in your usual way and ditch the plan for the moment. Eventually they will get more comfortable with your new routine and go to sleep. They will still be depending on you to help get back to sleep, but because they are finishing the falling-asleep process in the crib, they will be one step closer to being able to go back to sleep after waking up in the night.

Remember, you are making a major change. It may take a while for this to work, but this beats spending another year or more in a sleep-deprived stupor!

When you feel that your new routine is working, go on to Phase Two. Depending on your baby's sleep personality, your dedication, and your goals for how quickly you want things to change, this could be days or it could be weeks.

Mother-Speak

"The first night I tried the 'Pantley Way,' it worked like a charm. I had to take him out of the crib four times and hold him, but after the fourth time he fussed a bit, I rubbed him and used my key words—he never cried—and he went to sleep until almost 5:00 A.M. That's another success, because it is usually 3:00 or 3:30 A.M. Getting him back to sleep after that early waking is another battle we are working on. I know—patience and baby steps!"

Kim, mother of thirteen-month-old Mathieau

Phase Two: Comfort Without Pickups

Once you have most mastered Phase One, you can move on to the next step. Continue your bedtime routine as you have been, but begin to work on reducing your assistance when your baby wakes up during the night, specifically when feeding is not needed—for example, a ten-month-old who is still waking up every hour or so almost never needs that much feeding! When your baby makes waking sounds, go immediately to them, but try not to pick them up unless they clearly need to be fed; instead, play your white noise sounds, pat, touch, or put your arms around them in the same ways you have been, until they are back to sleep. While your baby is falling asleep, say your key words. If they actually cry, you can go ahead and revert back to Phase One if you need to—but try to make it brief. And repeat this process throughout the night. Keep your helping episodes short.

When you feel that your new routine is working, go on to Phase Three.

Mother-Speak

"We had good success at Phase One and Phase Two, but there's no way she'd have Phase Three. We kept trying though, and just when I was about to give up, lo and behold! One fine night she actually went back to sleep without my taking her out of the crib! That was the turning point. We never made it to Phase Four, because a week later she stopped waking up at all."

Heidi, mother of ten-month-old Elise

Phase Three: Soothing Pats

Go immediately to your baby when you hear waking noises, but try very hard not to pick them up (unless, of course, they need feeding). Play your white noise sounds and provide a bit of patting, rubbing, or gentle touch. Stand by the crib and say your key words, or hum quietly. If your baby cries, revert to Phase Two as needed, but try to make your interactions brief. Repeat this process throughout the night.

When you feel that your new routine is working, go on to Phase Four.

Phase Four: Verbally Soothing Baby

When your baby wakes in the night go immediately to the side of the crib. Turn on your white noise sounds, and say your key words or hum softly. If they wake up fully and start crying, revert back to previous phases, but try to make your interactions very brief. Repeat this process throughout the night. When your baby needs feeding, of course you will pick them up to do so.

Summary of the Phases Sleep Solution

The idea with this process is to take small, gradual steps toward your goal and settle comfortably at each phase before moving on to the next one. The previous example is not meant as a blueprint for every baby; rather, it's one demonstration of the idea. You'll need to examine your own bedtime rituals and modify them slightly every few nights until you reach your sleeping goal.

Keep in mind that the phases are not meant to be rigid, inflexible steps. Watch your baby. Stay in tune with your own feelings. Follow your heart. Modify your plan and be flexible as you move through the steps. As long as you are gradually moving toward your goal of having your baby sleep all night without your company, you will eventually get there. Unless there is a major reason, such as illness, that requires a rapid change in routine, usually the only harm in taking longer is a strain on your patience. But focus on celebrating every small victory along the way and you'll find improved sleep is the pot of gold at the end.

⭐ Write a Family Bestseller

If your baby is older than about eighteen to twenty-four months, your little one can now understand more things about life. You have most likely begun to teach the words "please" and "thank you." Your child is probably able to follow simple instructions, such as, "Put this on the table." Most babies at this age enjoy reading books, especially books with pictures of real babies. Reading books about sleep to your child at bedtime can be helpful. I've found that most of these stories depict a predictable, typical bedtime routine: play, bath, pajamas, story, breast or bottle, bed. Learning that other children go to bed in the same way they do can help your child do the same.

In addition to reading published books, this is a great time to write your child's own book about sleep. Here's how to do it.

Use poster board or very heavy paper. Your book should be large—8.5 inches by 11 inches or bigger. Tape the pages together with heavy tape (but don't do so until you've created the entire book so that you can easily replace any pages that you mess up).

Here I'll describe making two different types of books. Make either one, or even both!

Book One: My Sleep Book

Cut out many pictures of children from magazines, advertisements, or print images you find online. Look for pictures that pertain to your routine, such as a child getting a bath, brushing their teeth, reading a book, or putting on pajamas.

Use your pictures to create a custom storybook that demonstrates your exact bedtime routine, step by step. Write a story on the pages to go along with the pictures.

Read the book every night just before you begin your bedtime routine.

Book Two: The Personalized Growing-Up Book

A more personalized book can be used to go beyond a simple bed-time routine—it can also help to wean your child from the family bed, breastfeeding, using a bottle or pacifier, or for that matter, to help your child adjust to any major change in life, such as intro-ducing a new pregnancy or sibling, dealing with starting daycare, or a parents' divorce.

Title your book *All About [insert Baby's name]*. It will depict the story of your child's life, with the focus on sleep (or whatever top-ics you are addressing).

Gather pictures of your child. Start with a shot of her as a new-born, and progress through her life, finishing up with those pic-tures that feature actions and items in your bedtime routine (or addressing your chosen topic). Pictures of Baby breastfeeding, drinking a bottle, using a pacifier, wearing pajamas, having a bath, reading a book, lying in bed, and sleeping, are the most helpful. If possible, take photos of your baby during every step of your desired bedtime routine—including several of your child sleeping soundly—perhaps with a favorite stuffed animal nearby.

Each page of your homemade book will show a picture of your child and explain what is happening. The book will show your goals in action. In other words, the book will portray the results you are aiming for.

This book will be customized to fit your family.

Don't make the book so long that your little one will lose inter-est, because the ending is, after all, the real goal of the book. You know your own child's reading attention span, so stay within that length. Read this book every night. (Your child may like it so much that they want to read it during the day, too—and that's per-fectly fine!) Talk about what you read. Help your little one to do the things you talk about in the book.

⭐ Make a Bedtime Poster for Toddlers and Preschoolers

After the second birthday, most children thrive on predictability and routine. They like it when the same things happen in the same way every day. This can be somewhat frustrating for you when your schedule happens to conflict with your child's regular naptime; you may be set on completing the day's errands, but your child is ready to sleep and letting you know it with fussy, whiny behavior. You can use this desire for routine to your advantage when it comes to creating a healthy bedtime ritual.

We have already discussed the importance of a bedtime routine for babies. Since your little one is older, you can involve them in the process. The most effective way to do this is to create a bedtime poster. Here's how:

- Get a large piece of poster board.
- Gather colorful markers or crayons.
- Follow the photo- or picture-gathering instructions from the previous section on making a bedtime book.
- Use the pictures and markers to create a fun, colorful poster that clearly demonstrates the steps to bedtime.
- Hang the poster on your child's bedroom door or wall at their eye level.
- Have your child help you follow the chart each night by asking, "What's next?"
- Give lots of praise for following the steps ("Good job!").

Here's a sample bedtime chart:

My Bedtime Chart

1. Have a snack.
2. Put on pajamas.
3. Brush teeth.
4. Read three books.
5. Get drink of water.
6. Go potty.
7. Turn on white noise and night-light.
8. Kisses, hugs, and back rub.
9. Go to sleep.
10. Mommy and Daddy go to sleep.

For many children, the chart alone will provide the consistency and routine that will ease them into bed each night.

If you have a child who wakes during the night crying for you, you can add your own preferred way to handle the issue to your chart. For example:

- When Jenna wakes up, she goes to her sleeping place in Mommy and Daddy's room—quiet as a mouse.

Or, here's another example:

- When Santiago wakes up during the night when it's dark outside, he can go potty, get a drink of water, and go back in bed. When Santiago wakes up and it is light outside, he can climb into bed with Mommy and Daddy.

This is a good time for you to think about exactly what you expect of your child and commit it to paper. Then help your little one to follow the steps. Try to patiently remind your child—even during the night, "Remember your bedtime chart? This is what you need to do now."

When Your Child Won't Stay in Bed

If you have a preschooler who is a little yo-yo who likes to get up after your routine, asking for a drink of water, a hug, or whatever, you can add this step to your chart to help eliminate this exasperating process:

- Alexander will get two Get-Out-of-Bed-Free cards. He may come out for potty, water, kisses, or hugs two times. When Alexander's tickets are gone, it is time to stay in bed and go to sleep.

These "cards" are simply pieces of paper that you create with your poster supplies. At the end of your routine, give your child the tickets. He has to give you a ticket each time he gets out of bed. Base the number of tickets on his current number of bed escapes, minus a few. That is, if he normally climbs out of bed five or six times, start with four tickets. After a week or so, change to three, and then two, and eventually, one. You may even want to let your child turn in any unused tickets in the morning for a small reward like a sticker.

Always remember to praise your little one for following the bedtime routine.

Be Patient

One trait I noticed among many of my test parents was an incredible eagerness to obtain results. That's absolutely understandable! But an extra dose of patience will make the process tolerable.

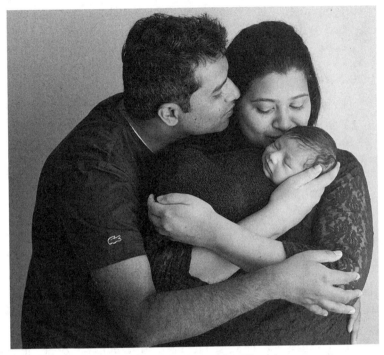

Samarth, three-weeks-old, with Mommy and Daddy

Some test parents ambitiously created daily logs hoping to see change day by day, and got frustrated if success was not immediately evident. The logs have a time and place. Complete one every ten days, two weeks, or even once a month to see how far you have progressed, but none in between. Similarly, don't watch the clock all night. Simply create and follow your plan, and soon enough, both you and your baby will be sleeping blissfully.

Part III

Special Situations

Teething

The process of teething is a common reason that babies have trouble falling and staying asleep. Think back to the last time you had a toothache, headache, sore back, or stiff neck. Discomforts can disrupt your ability to sleep. Babies can't tell us what the problem is; they can only cry or fuss. Often this behavior starts long before we see a tooth pop out, so it can be hard to tell that teething is responsible for your baby's fussiness.

Symptoms of Teething

Babies can begin the teething process as early as three months old. These symptoms typically accompany the teething process:

- Difficulty falling asleep or staying asleep
- Fussiness
- Drooling
- Runny nose
- Rash on the chin or around the mouth
- Biting

- Red cheeks
- Rejecting the breast or bottle
- Increased need to suck
- Swollen, discolored gums

Some parents report that a slight fever, diarrhea, vomiting, or diaper rash accompany teething, but because these symptoms also may signal an infection or virus, they should always be reported to your doctor.

How to Help Your Baby Feel Better

If you suspect that your baby is teething, the following interventions might relieve their discomfort so that they can relax enough to sleep:

- Provide a clean, cool washcloth to chew on.
- Let your baby chew on a teething ring that is either room temperature or chilled in the refrigerator (not frozen).
- Frequently and gently pat your baby's chin dry.
- Offer a sip of cold water.
- Rub their gums with your clean, wet finger.
- Use a specially made baby toothbrush to clean the gums.
- Dab petroleum jelly or a gentle salve on the drool area.
- Breastfeed often, for comfort as well as nutrition.

The teething pain relief ointments that are available over the counter can be quite potent (put a dab on your lip and you'll notice a tingly, numbing feeling). So, use these sparingly and only with the approval of your doctor.

Separation Anxiety

As babies get older, they will begin to become aware of their "separateness" from you. They live in the present, and have a limited experience of time and memory; so when you leave, your baby wonders where you've gone and worries that you may not come back. This is called separation anxiety. According to Dr. Avi Sadeh, in *Sleeping Like a Baby* (Yale University Press):

> Separation anxiety is one of the main causes of sleep disorders in early childhood.
>
> The rise in the frequency of sleeping disorders during the first year of life may be linked to the appearance of the separation anxiety that is a normal developmental occurrence at this age.
>
> A change such as the mother's return to work after maternity leave, a new caretaker, the transition to day care, or any change that

Raylan, four-years-old, and Conor, five-days-old

signifies separation and a new adaptation is frequently expressed immediately in the form of a significant sleep disorder.

Dr. Sadeh explains that even a temporary separation, such as the mother going to the hospital to give birth to a new sibling or a parent leaving for an overnight event, can have a powerful impact on a baby's sleep pattern. His research showed that even after the separation, babies woke up more often, cried more often, and spent less time sleeping in general.

Many parents find that as their baby enters the developmental stages of crawling and walking, separation anxiety peaks. This is because babies learn that they can move away from you—and you can move away from them.

Help for Separation Anxiety

When separation anxiety hits, let your child know that you, or another loving caregiver, is always nearby. Here are some ways to send this message to your little one:

- Increase your daytime nurturing by giving your baby more hugs and cuddles.
- Follow a peaceful, consistent routine in the hour before bedtime.
- Keep a large photo of Mommy and Daddy, or other important people in your baby's life, near your baby's bedside.
- When your baby is awake, don't sneak away when they're not looking. Always say good-bye or good night on your way out.
- Show confidence and joy when you leave your baby, not insecurity or fear. Respond quickly to your baby's nighttime calls or cries, even if it's just to say, "I'm here and everything's OK."

- Help your child develop an attachment to a lovey (see pages 213–216) so that they'll have something to hug when you're away.
- During the day, periodically step away from your baby and go into another room while talking, singing, or whistling, so that your baby knows that while they can't see you, you are still there.

Developmental Milestones and Growth Spurts

Commonly, a baby who is learning a new developmental skill awakens in the night with a sudden need to practice it. This is usually a short-lived sleep disruption and tends to go away as soon as the new skill is mastered.

Camden, one-week-old

Mother-Speak

"I've noticed with my babies that the first few days after they learn to do something new, like crawling or pulling up to standing, they sleep restlessly. When they wake up in the middle of the night, they immediately want to do their new 'trick.' If I weren't so tired, it would be funny to see Thomas or Rebecca go straight from sleeping into crawling or standing! After a while, they seem to get used to their new abilities, and then they sleep better."

Alice, mother of ten-month-old twins Rebecca and Thomas

Similarly, your baby might suddenly be eating more, sleeping less, and growing out of their clothes almost before the price tags are cut off. This is a growth spurt, and your baby is doing some serious growing—day and night.

The key to handling these types of night wakings is to help your baby lie back down and get resettled with a minimum amount of time and fuss involved. Often, using white noise, your key words, and gentle patting or rubbing will help, because your baby won't even be fully awake.

Mother-Speak

"It never occurred to me that Kyra's new skills could be making her restless at night. Every morning for the past two weeks I've found her standing up in her crib in the wee hours. Now that you mention this, I realized that she has been pulling herself up to stand on anything she can during the day for the same two weeks!"

Leesa, mother of nine-month-old Kyra

Common Illness and Discomfort

Just like an adult, a baby who does not feel well will not sleep well. However, unlike an adult, they don't know why they feel bad, nor do they know how to help themselves feel better. When your baby isn't feeling well, do what you can to make them comfortable. Back off a bit on your sleep plan for a few days.

Here are some suggestions that might help your baby feel better:

- **Let your baby rest.** Put off running errands, having visitors, or doing anything else that disrupts your baby's quiet recovery time. This also helps *you* stay calm and peaceful so that you can help your baby to recover.
- **Give lots of fluids.** No matter what the illness, your baby will feel better if they are well hydrated. If you are breastfeeding, nurse frequently. If your baby drinks from a cup or bottle, provide lots of breast milk, formula, juice, and water. For older babies, add popsicles, soup, and ice chips.
- **Pamper and cuddle.** You may have to put everything else on hold for a few days. The more you try to accomplish when your baby is sick, the fussier they will be.
- **Clear your baby's nose so that they can breathe easily.** Do this by using saline nasal spray mist (ask your pharmacist for a recommendation) followed by suction with a nasal aspirator made especially for babies.
- **Keep the air moist.** During sleep times, use a humidifier or vaporizer with clean distilled water.
- **Encourage as much sleep as possible.** Do those things that work best to help your baby nap and sleep well.
- **Talk to a doctor anytime your baby is sick.** Someone at your health care provider's office or your local hospital is always available to give you advice on how to treat your baby's illness.

Gas and Colic

All babies have gas, but some babies struggle more with releasing it from their systems. Your baby may swallow air when feeding or crying, which can result in an uncomfortably full feeling, gas, or even stomach pains.

You may have heard the term *colic* applied to any baby who cries a lot. Not all crying babies have colic, however—but all colicky babies cry. Though researchers are still unsure of its exact cause, most believe that colic is related to the immaturity of a baby's digestive system. Some also think that a baby's immature nervous system and inability to handle the constant sensory stimulation that surrounds them might cause a breakdown by the end of the day. Whatever the reason, it's among the most exasperating conditions new parents face. Symptoms include:

- A regular period of inconsolable crying, typically late in the day
- Crying bouts that last one to three hours or more
- Age range of three-weeks to four-months-old
- Healthy and happy at all other times of the day

It's Not Your Fault

Because colic occurs when a baby is so young, new parents often feel that they are doing something wrong to create the situation. Their vulnerability and lack of experience puts them in the position of questioning their own ability to care for their baby. Because you are a parent who doesn't believe in letting a baby cry to sleep, I know that hearing your baby cry with colic is especially painful for you, as it was for me when colic struck our home.

Although I've handled all of my babies similarly, only one of my four had colic. It was a dreadful experience, but I learned a lot about myself and my baby through the process. Please

Kayden, one-week-old

allow my personal experience with colic, as well as my research and discussions with other parents, to put your mind at ease. *It's not your fault.* Any baby can have colic. The only good thing about colic is that, by the time your baby is three- to four-months-old, it will magically disappear and become just a blip in your memory.

Help with Colic

There is no simple, effective treatment for colic. By using their experience, parents and professionals are able to offer suggestions that may help your baby though this time period. Experiment with everything on this list until you find the interventions that help your baby best. Keep in mind that there is no magical cure, and nothing you do will completely eliminate colic until your baby's system is matured and able to settle on its own. Until then, do what you can to help calm your baby and yourself.

- If breastfeeding, feed on demand as often as your baby needs to stay calm.
- If breastfeeding, experiment to see if any of the food you are eating add to your baby's discomfort. See if it helps to avoid eating foods that may cause gas in your baby, such as dairy, caffeine, cabbage, broccoli, and other gassy vegetables.
- If bottle-feeding, offer frequent smaller meals; experiment with different formulas.
- If bottle-feeding, try different types of bottles and nipples that prevent air from entering your baby's system.
- Hold your baby in a more upright position for feeding and directly afterward.
- Offer meals in a quiet setting.
- If your baby likes a pacifier, offer after meals.
- Burp your baby more often.
- Invest in a baby sling or carrier, and use it during colicky periods.
- Bring your stroller in the house and use it to walk baby around, or take a walk outside during colicky times.
- Give your baby a warm bath.
- Place a warm towel or wrap a warm water bottle and place it on your baby's tummy (taking caution that the temperature is warm but not hot).
- Hold your baby in a curled position, with legs curled up toward belly.
- Massage your baby's tummy.
- Swaddle your baby in a warm blanket.
- Lay your baby tummy down across your lap and massage or pat their back.
- Hold your baby in a rocking chair, or put them in a swing.
- Walk with your baby in a quiet, dark room.

- Lie on your back and lay your baby on top of you, tummy down, while massaging their back. (Make sure another adult is watching you if you fall asleep.)
- Play soothing music or turn on white noise.
- As a last resort, ask your doctor about special medications available for colic and gas.

Tips for Parents with a Colicky Baby

Use the following suggestions to help you cope with the stress of having a colicky baby. Remember that if you're taking care of yourself and simplifying your life, you'll be available to offer comfort to your baby during these unhappy periods.

- Plan outings for the times of day when your baby is happy.
- Know that your baby *will* cry during the colicky times and while you can do things to make your baby more comfortable, nothing you can do will *totally* stop the crying.
- Take advantage of another person's offer to take a turn with the baby, even if it's just so that you can take a short walk or quiet bath or shower.
- Keep in mind that this is only a temporary condition; it will pass.
- Try lots of different things until you discover what works best.
- Avoid keeping a long to-do list right now; only do what's most important.
- Talk to other parents of colicky babies so you can share ideas and comfort each other.
- If the crying is getting to you and making you tense or angry, put your baby in the crib, or give them to someone else to hold for a while so that you don't accidentally shake or harm your baby.

- Rest assured that babies do not suffer long-term harm from having colic.

When Should the Doctor Be Called?

Anytime you are concerned about your baby, put in a call to your baby's medical care provider. In the case of colic, you should definitely make that call if you notice any of the following:

- The crying is accompanied by vomiting.
- Your baby is not gaining weight.
- The colicky period lasts longer than four months.
- Your baby seems to be in pain.
- Your baby doesn't want to be held or handled.
- The crying spree isn't limited to one bout in the evening.
- There are no regular bowel movements or wet diapers.
- You notice other problems that don't appear on the previous list of symptoms.

Ear Infections

If your baby has been very fussy, is waking up more than usual, wakes up crying as if in pain, or pulls at their ears, your baby may have an ear infection. Ear infections are very common in babies because their ear tubes are short, wide, and horizontal, giving bacteria from the nose and throat a fast, easy path to the ears. As babies get older and their ear tubes mature, they will no longer be so susceptible to ear infections. In the meantime, an untreated ear infection will prevent your baby from sleeping well because the pain increases when lying flat—in the position for sleep.

Causes and Symptoms of Ear Infections

Ear infections occur when bacteria and fluid build up in the inner ear, often after a cold, sinus infection, or other respiratory illness. The fluids get trapped in the ear, causing a throbbing pain. Ear infections are not contagious, although the illnesses that typically precede them are.

Your baby may exhibit all of these, some of these, or even none of the symptoms. It's always important to see your health care provider if you even suspect an ear infection. A gut feeling that something isn't quite right is justification enough for a call or a visit to the doctor. Listen to your instincts.

These symptoms *might* indicate an ear infection, or another health issue that should be addressed:

- A sudden change in temperament: more fussiness, crying, and clinginess
- An increase in night waking (as if you need this!)
- Waking up crying as if in pain
- Fever
- Diarrhea
- Reduced appetite or difficulty swallowing (your baby may pull away from the breast or bottle and cry even when hungry.)
- Runny nose that continues after a cold
- Drainage from the ear
- Fussiness when lying down that goes away when your baby is upright

These symptoms almost always indicate an ear infection:

- Frequent pulling, grabbing, or batting at the ears that is not done playfully, but rather with apparent discomfort
- Green, yellow, or white fluid draining from the ear
- An unpleasant odor emanating from the ear
- Signs of difficulty hearing

What to Do About an Ear Infection

If your baby is exhibiting any symptoms and you suspect an ear infection, make an appointment with your doctor right away. Hearing a doctor say, "Everything looks fine" is far better than letting your baby (and you) suffer through an untreated infection. Seeing your doctor is also important because an untreated ear infection can lead to speech difficulties, hearing loss, meningitis, or other complications.

Your health care provider may suggest some of the following if your baby does have an ear infection (but don't try to solve this problem on your own without a medical professional's direction):

- Give a pain reliever, such as acetaminophen (Tylenol) or ibuprofen. (Do not give your baby aspirin unless a doctor tells you to.)
- Keep your baby's head elevated for sleep. You can do this by raising one end of their mattress (try taping tuna cans under one end or some of the ideas on page 285).
- Let your baby fall asleep in your arms or in a sling or soft carrier.
- Place a warm compress over the affected ear.
- Keep the ears dry and out of water.
- Offer plenty of liquids.
- Use prescribed ear drops.
- Administer prescribed antibiotics.
- Keep your baby home from daycare or baby-sitters.

Reduce the Chance of Ear Infections

Any baby can get an ear infection, but you can take a few measures to reduce the likelihood:

- **Prevent the colds and flu that introduce the bacteria into your child's system.** Wash your baby's and your hands frequently. Encourage anyone who holds your baby to wash their hands first, particularly if they or anyone in their family has a cold. Keep your baby away from anyone who is obviously sick with a cold or flu.
- **Keep your baby away from cigarette smoke.** Just one afternoon spent with secondhand smoke can increase your baby's chances of developing an ear infection.
- **Breastfeed your baby for a minimum of six months.** The antibodies and immune system boosters in breast milk discourage bacterial growth. In addition, the way your baby drinks from the breast (vigorous sucking and frequent swallowing) helps prevent milk from flowing into the ears. Breastfed babies are far less prone to ear infections than those who are bottlefed.
- **Never prop a bottle for your baby, or leave your baby to sleep with a bottle.** This can cause milk to pool in the mouth and seep into the ear canals. (It may also cause decay in your baby's teeth.)

Reflux (Gastroesophageal Reflux—GER)

Gastroesophageal refers to the stomach and esophagus. *Reflux* means to return or flow back. Gastroesophageal reflux is when the stomach's contents flow back up into the esophagus. A baby with reflux suffers from heartburn-like stomach pains, which will tend to be most uncomfortable when lying down for sleep. This makes it hard for them to fall and stay asleep. Reflux is most often caused by an immature digestive system, and almost all babies with reflux will outgrow the problem.

The following are the most common symptoms of reflux:

- Spitting up or vomiting frequently
- Difficulty feeding or fighting feeding even when hungry
- Guzzling or frantic swallowing
- Crying that appears to be a sign of pain
- Waking in the night with a burst of crying
- Fussiness and crying after eating
- Increase in fussing or crying when lying on their back
- Decrease in fussiness when held upright
- Frequent colds or recurrent coughing
- Spitting up when straining to have a bowel movement
- Frequent hiccups
- Sinus and nasal congestion
- Losing weight

If your baby shows some of these symptoms, you should talk to your health care provider about the possibility of reflux. Once your suspicion has been confirmed, they may suggest some of these remedies:

- Offer your baby frequent, small meals as opposed to fewer, larger feedings.
- Hold your baby upright for thirty to sixty minutes after feeding.
- Have a supervised period of tummy-down time with baby on a thirty-degree angle after feeding. Remember that most babies should sleep on their backs—according to the American Academy of Pediatrics, even those babies with reflux. If your baby has severe reflux, talk to your doctor about a possible alternative for your baby.
- Avoid putting baby in a sitting position (such as in an infant seat) that could result in their becoming slumped over directly after eating.

- Elevate the head of your baby's bed by using a higher setting on one end of the crib mattress, by placing something stable under the legs of the bed or crib, or by placing a block of wood or books under the mattress.
- For a bottle-fed baby, switch to a different brand of formula, or try a thicker variety. Experiment with different bottle types and nipple styles to reduce excess air.
- For a breastfed baby, give frequent, smaller feedings.
- If your baby is ready for solid food, add a small serving of rice cereal after nursing.
- Avoid putting your baby in clothing that is tight around the belly.
- Avoid letting your baby cry for any length of time, as crying can make reflux worse. Carry your baby as much as possible to decrease crying.
- Avoid any exposure to secondhand smoke.

If reflux is severe, talk to your doctor about medical remedies, such as using a children's antacid.

Allergies and Asthma

If a baby has a condition that affects their breathing, it usually affects their sleep, also. Parents may be struggling with a baby who wakes frequently at night and they might not be aware that the cause is allergies or asthma.

Symptoms of Allergies and Asthma

Sometimes it's hard to tell the difference between a common cold and a more serious condition. Here are the signs of allergies and asthma to look for:

- Runny nose
- Coughing, especially at night
- Sniffling
- Sneezing
- Stuffy nose, especially upon waking
- Itchy eyes, ears, or nose
- Watery eyes
- Sore throat
- Difficulty breathing
- Skin rash
- Diarrhea
- Cold symptoms that last more than two weeks
- Persistent, chronic ear infections
- An increase in these symptoms after contact with animals or being outside near plants and flowers

Only a doctor can tell if your child truly has allergies or asthma, because many of the symptoms resemble those we normally attribute to a cold, respiratory congestion, or other normal childhood conditions, like teething. If you suspect that your child may have either condition, it's important to talk to your health care provider about your concerns.

Nightmares, Night Terrors, and Sleepwalking or Sleep-Talking

Older babies may have their sleep interrupted by a variety of common sleep disturbances. Your baby may occasionally wake up crying or talking in their sleep, or they might move around, sit up, or even crawl or walk in their sleep. The majority of these incidents are infrequent and short-lived.

What Should You Do About Nightmares?

As an adult, when we wake up in bed, in the dark, from a dream—no matter how vivid—we immediately identify the experience as a dream. A baby, on the other hand, hasn't mastered the understanding of life versus dream, reality versus fantasy, real versus pretend. When your child wakes with a nightmare, they will likely be confused. For young children telling them, "It was just a dream" doesn't explain what they just experienced. Keeping this in mind, it only seems fair to comfort children in the same way we comfort them when they face a tangible fear or danger, since the emotions they feel are likely the same.

The following are things you can do if your baby wakes with a nightmare:

- The most important thing you can do is be there and offer comfort, just as you would in any other situation when your child is feeling afraid.
- Stay with your child until they feel relaxed and ready to go to sleep, or you can go ahead and stay with them until they are actually sleeping.
- Stay calm. Your attitude will convey to your child that what's happening is normal and that all is well.
- Reassure your child that they're safe and that it's OK to go back to sleep.

What Are Night Terrors?

Night terrors are completely different from nightmares. During a night terror your child will wake suddenly and may let out a panicky scream or a fearful cry. Their eyes will likely be open with pupils dilated, but they won't be seeing. They may hyper-

Tyler, eleven-months-old, and Mummy

ventilate, thrash around, or yell. Your child might be sweating, their face may be flushed, or their heart might be beating rapidly. If your child is a walking toddler, or preschooler they may climb out of bed or even run around the room. They may appear to be terrified by a horrible nightmare.

Actually, your child is not frightened, not awake, and not even dreaming! They are sound asleep and in a zone between two sleep cycles, somewhat stuck for a few minutes. Your child is unaware of what's happening and won't remember the episode. So the *terror* part of night terrors is named not for the child, but for the parent who watches the disturbing scene.

While it may still be difficult and unsettling to watch your child during an episode, you can rest assured that your child is neither awake nor frightened.

What Should You Do About Night Terrors?

This is the hard part! A parent's natural response upon seeing their child acting frightened like this is to comfort them. However, during a night terror your child is not awake or aware of your presence. Often, trying to hold a child during his thrashing will result in them pushing you away—making the whole thing even more frightening for you. In this case you can try a gentle pat or touch along with a series of comforting words, shhh shhh sounds, but realistically these might be more to give you a sense of doing something to help than achieving any real purpose.

There is no value in waking your child up, and in fact, trying to wake him may just prolong the episode. Your goals are to keep your child safe by preventing them from falling out of bed, down the stairs, or otherwise getting hurt.

Can You Prevent Your Child from Having Nightmares and Night Terrors?

To a certain extent you can't prevent your child from having nightmares or night terrors. However, some things have been found to reduce the number of episodes or the severity of the episodes:

- Monitor the movies and television that your child sees, since scary images can show up in your child's nightmares. Pay attention not only to the shows they are watching, but whatever is on the screen when they are in the room. Just because it's a program created for children doesn't make it safe to watch, so choose carefully what you allow your child to see. Young children can be scared by things that we adults might find amusing, so watch your child's reaction, more than what's on the screen.

- Avoid books that have pictures or stories that disturb your child. Again, watch your child for cues to his feelings, as they can find the oddest things frightening. For example, many babies are afraid of clowns, human-looking dolls, or distorted images of real things.

- A child who is overtired or sleep-deprived will have more episodes of nightmares or night terrors, so as you see more sleep success these episodes should lessen.

- An erratic sleep schedule can contribute to sleep terrors and possibly to nightmares as well. Aim to have your child in bed at the same time every night and see if this reduces these nighttime problems.

- Make sure that you follow a calm and peaceful routine the hour before bedtime. This will ensure that your child falls asleep while feeling happy and safe.

- If your child is taking medication, ask a pharmacist or your health care professional if the medication could be disturbing your child's sleep.

- Children with special needs or those with ongoing medical ailments may have more frequent or severe nightmares or night terrors. If your child has any special health conditions, talk over this possibility with your health care provider, or chat with parents of children with similar health circumstances to share ideas.

- Some children have more night terrors if they are new to nighttime dryness and go to sleep with a full bladder. Remember to have your child use the toilet just before they get in to bed.

- Examine your child's life situation to see if stressful conditions may be promoting nightmares. Stress can manifest itself into nightmares. If you can pinpoint a problem and find ways to reassure your child, it may help reduce the intensity or frequency of nightmares.

Is There a Time to Call a Professional?

Don't ever hesitate to call a medical professional if you have concerns about your child's sleep. There are a variety of ways a professional can help you. These include techniques that can be used to control episodes of sleep terrors or nightmares without the use of medication.

Snoring and Sleep Apnea

If your baby is a very restless, noisy sleeper; breathes through the mouth; and snores or snorts loudly, they may be suffering from sleep apnea. *Apnea* means "absence of breath." The most disturbing symptom of this sleep disorder is that the sleeper actually stops breathing for up to thirty seconds, occasionally longer. This is very frightening for a parent to witness and should be taken very seriously, but in general, it is not life threatening and can be treated. Up to 10 percent of children have significant sleep apnea. The main causes include a narrow throat or airway, enlarged tonsils or lymph nodes, obesity, and facial abnormalities. Additional symptoms that may appear in older children are daytime sleepiness, nightmares, bed-wetting, sleep terrors, sleepwalking, sweating profusely while asleep, and morning headaches.

Not every child who snores has sleep apnea. However, if snoring is loud or is combined with the other symptoms, apnea could be the problem. Conversely, not all children with narrow airways, enlarged tonsils, or excess weight have sleep apnea.

Untreated apnea can cause heart problems and high blood pressure, in addition to significant sleep deprivation.

What Is the Cure?

The most common remedy for childhood sleep apnea is removal or reduction of the tonsils or adenoids. Other typical treatments are enlarging the air passage, holding the passage open during sleep, or (when the condition is caused by obesity) weight loss.

Checking Baby for Sleep Apnea

All parents should check their sleeping babies from time to time. In a quiet room, your baby's breathing should be barely audible; it should be through the nose and appear effortless and regular. (This does not hold true if your baby has a cold or stuffy nose, although it's important to know that children with sleep apnea often have exaggerated symptoms when they have colds.)

If your baby's breathing during sleep is through the mouth, loud, accompanied by snoring or wheezing, or if they appear to be struggling to breathe, talk to your pediatrician; an ear, nose, and throat specialist; or a sleep disorders clinic about the possibility of sleep apnea. If your baby is a newborn, these signs can be extremely serious and should be reported immediately.

Sleep Regressions and Setbacks

Very often, things have been going well, and you've enjoyed improvements in your baby's sleep, and then suddenly, you seem to be going backward. What's happening?

Oh, the amazing twists, turns, and surprises of parenthood! Children grow and change from day to day; they can be unpredictable, irrational, illogical, and downright baffling at times. On any given day, just when you feel you've figured it all out, your child changes the whole program on you, sending you back to square one.

The journey to a good night's sleep is almost never a straight path. It's more like a dance: two steps forward, one step back, and even a few sidesteps in between. It's also as much a process of learning about your child as it is about learning sleep facts, and then applying what you've learned about both to bring about the best results.

Identify the Reason for a Setback

When sleep setbacks occur, it can be helpful to try to identify the reasons, if you can. Check your child's gums for telltale signs of teething, consider new physical milestones, review the changes that have occurred in your household, do another log to pinpoint more clearly what's happening. If you're able to identify the issues, take steps to handle those things first, and then return to your sleep plan. Sometimes you'll just be left scratching your head, unable to discern exactly what's up. If that's the case, simply start from the beginning and organize a sleep plan incorporating any of the solutions that have brought you success in the past, or try something new that you may have missed before.

Is Your Baby Sick or Teething?

The first order of business is to be sure your baby is well. An ear infection, difficult teething, allergies, or other sickness almost always disrupts sleep. So, the first order of business is to make sure that your baby is well.

Is a Sleep Regression Really a Milestone Progression?

Disruptions in your child's sleep routines often occur during times of milestone jumps, growth spurts, or leaps in brain development. Any major adjustments in your child's physical and mental development can disrupt sleep.

There are common sleep regressions around three to four months, eight to nine months, twelve months, eighteen months, and twenty-four months: all times when there are often great jumps in a baby's development.

Point to Remember

In reality, it often feels like the first two years are just one sleep regression after another! Don't take it personally—sleep regressions are a normal part of development, and your child's sleep will eventually even out into a more pleasant and predictable pattern.

Has Life Thrown You a Curveball?

Life's many challenges can disrupt your efforts. Illness, vacations, visitors, schedule disruptions, the birth of a sibling, starting daycare, and teething are just a few examples. When these things happen, and your baby responds with difficulty falling asleep, more night wakings, and shorter naps (or heaven forbid, no naps!), you may find yourself giving up and then berating yourself for abandoning your plan—an exercise in frustration that just adds tension and stress, which further prevents your success. But, please, keep in mind: life happens, and therefore setbacks happen, and they happen to everyone.

Has Your Commitment Had a Setback?

You may have started out motivated to follow your sleep plan, and even seen some success, but then, you didn't have the time, ability, or heart to organize and follow that plan. You may realize that the reason that things were going so well before is that you were consistent, and now that you've become lax with the bedtime routine, daily naps, or other details, that's affecting your child's sleep. A re-commitment to your plan is what you'll need to get back on track.

Is It Really a Setback?

Sometimes setbacks aren't really setbacks at all! Sometimes the only thing that needs adjustment is your expectation. Are you being realistic about what you are expecting from your child? Have you been comparing your child's sleep patterns to another child who happens to be a fabulous sleeper? Every human being is different, and patience is a parental requirement.

Are You Experiencing a New Problem?

Maybe what you're dealing with is not a setback at all, but a brand new problem. For example, both easy-sleepers and challenging-sleepers can be adversely affected by changes in their biological sleep needs. Perhaps your baby's biology is dictating a switch from two daily naps to one, or they're ready to give up naps entirely. Perhaps the 7:00 P.M. bedtime is suddenly too early, and your child isn't tired when pajamas get put on, or the days have become busier and your child is overtired by 7:00 P.M. and too wired up to sleep. So, while it may seem like a step backward, it's just one of those sidesteps that happen during your dance toward great sleep. Once you identify your child's new sleep requirements and adjust to them you should find sleep time easier.

Do You Need to Refocus?

Have you taken the time to celebrate the sleep successes you've had so far? Oftentimes it takes a year of various sleep plans and changes before you finally settle into a great sleep pattern because of all the ups and downs and setbacks and regressions. Sometimes being focused on the things that bother you, or setting your sights on the ultimate end goal, will get in the way of your seeing that overall, things really are changing for the better. Give yourself—and your child—a pat on the back for the good changes that are occurring.

Is Focusing on Sleep Problems Preventing Daily Joy?

At times your child may be having wonderful successes and leaps in development in other parts of his life, but you've become so focused on sleep issues that you're not open to enjoying the other daily triumphs that your child is demonstrating. Stop for a minute and smell the roses. If you've been too stressed about the sleep issues in your home, you may even want to back off from your plan for a day or two, or even more, and catch your breath.

Should You Use This Time as a Running Start?

Regardless of the details or reasons for sleep setbacks or regressions, keep in mind that even if you only follow part of your plan, and even if you can't be 100 percent consistent, you will still see sleep *improvement*. Even a few changes in your routines and habits can bring better sleep; then, when things settle down around your house, you'll have a running start to really focus on your sleep plan. Take a deep breath, go back over all the successes that you have experienced, and slide through these inevitable setbacks.

> **Point to Remember**
> Have faith in yourself and confidence in your sleep plan. Enjoy all the little successes along the way—you will eventually achieve the goals you are reaching for.

Swaddling: When and How to Wean

Swaddling can be an incredibly useful tool for helping a newborn baby sleep better. There comes a time, though, when swaddling needs to come to an end. You'll need to decide when the time is right for your baby. Every situation is unique, but there are a number of critical cues to watch for in deciding when to end the swaddling.

Most experts say that once your baby begins to move, roll, and squirm around, they could flip over onto their belly while swaddled and then be unable to safely position their head and body, which could affect their ability to breathe. In addition, the loose fabric of a swaddling blanket could become a hazard during the night. Trailing fabric can become entwined around your baby's limbs or face. Also, having mobile babies wrapped up in a swaddle prevents use of their limbs to extradite themselves from an uncomfortable or hazardous position. Therefore, many groups

Sophia, seven-days-old

recommend weaning from swaddling when your baby begins to make efforts to roll (around three to four months) when placed on the floor unswaddled. Other groups recommend that you use swaddling only for the first two months, and then wean your baby before mobility even becomes an issue.

A few experts, such as Dr. Harvey Karp, author of *The Happiest Baby* series, say that swaddling can be done up to six or more months of age, if done properly.

It's important that you discuss this topic with your health-care provider and do your own research into the safety aspects of swaddling older babies if you wish to continue to swaddle your baby after infancy.

Professional-Speak

"Parents should stop swaddling when the potential risks outweigh the potential benefits."

Jennifer Shu, MD, FAAP, medical editor
of the AAP Healthy Children website

Alternatives to Swaddling During Weaning

If you have a squirmy baby who continues to wiggle out of the blanket, yet doesn't sleep well when unswaddled, you might consider a premade swaddling-blanket that uses Velcro, zippers, or snaps rather than tucking long pieces of fabric. Shop carefully, though. Some commercially available swaddling blankets are very thick and warm and could contribute to overheating, depending on the temperature in your bedroom.

Another option for a squirmy baby who still enjoys being swaddled is to wrap your baby snugly (using a lightweight muslin blanket or Velcro swaddler) around only the torso, keeping both arms and perhaps even their legs untucked, so that your little one has freedom to move around, and the ability to push themselves up or shove blankets out of the way.

Step-by-Step Weaning from Swaddling

If it's time to wean your baby from swaddling, you can begin by leaving only one arm out of the swaddle, then, a few days or a week later, leave both arms out. Keep your baby's middle snugly swaddled and legs loosely swaddled as usual for a week or two, and then experiment with letting them sleep fully unswaddled. This gradual approach often works better than just stopping the swaddling suddenly.

Keep in mind that once your baby's arms are free it will be easier for your little one to roll over onto their stomach, particularly if they are trying this feat during the day during tummy time, so always keep an eye open and swaddle only for supervised naps, not when you are all sleeping at night.

A great transitional sleep solution for a baby when you wean from swaddling is to dress your baby in an armless sleep-sack style sleeper (like a sleeping bag with arm holes). These sacks give a little one who likes to be swaddled a similar tactile sensation, rather than going straight to normal pajamas or bare legs. A pair of socks can also help your baby feel more contained.

The time for weaning from swaddling often occurs when other big things are happening in your baby's life—turning over, sitting up, scooting on the floor, and teething. To reduce the stress to your baby when everything happens at once, keep all the other parts of your bedtime routine the same. If you've been using white noise, for example, continue to use it in the same way you have been.

Build a New Routine—Minus the Swaddling

When weaning away from any bedtime-related factor, having a bedtime routine really helps. If you don't already have a specific bedtime routine for your baby, begin using one prior to weaning. Follow the same sequence of events prebedtime for a week or two. It doesn't have to be complicated or long, but a few consistent steps help create an expectation for sleep. (See Key 14, "Develop a Hint of a Bedtime Routine," page 168.) Then keep all the other facets of the routine intact and work on eliminating just this one feature a bit at a time, as described previously.

Any transition related to sleep often takes a few months to really settle in. So please be patient with your baby and with yourself. Also keep in mind that weaning from swaddling may not be the cause of more frequent waking for a baby who is also going through developmental leaps. Teething, rolling, sitting up, and scooting all tend to disrupt sleep patterns as your child grows and masters these new milestones.

Motion-Sleep: When and How to Wean

During the newborn months there is no need to wean your baby from motion-sleep, if it works for your infant and you, and if you are following safe motion-sleep practices whether your baby sleeps in a sling or swing. Establishing your unique bond, keeping everyone calm and happy, and genuinely enjoying your time together should be your priority, and if some motion-naps enhance this, then enjoy them.

Gradually over the early months of life most babies will adjust to a motionless sleeping surface, but some need a bit more time and some help to make the transition. There is no absolute rule for when you must wean your baby from motion-naps to stationary sleep. The right decision is different for every child. The following questions can guide you as you determine if you should continue naps as they are, or if it is the right time to move your child to stationary sleep:

- How do your child's daily sleep hours match up to the chart on page 43? Is your baby getting enough sleep and napping often enough throughout the day?
- Is your baby safe? Is your baby within the stated age and size for the device, or has it been outgrown?
- Is the motion-sleep becoming troublesome or complicated, or is there another reason that your baby must be transitioned now?

How to Wean from Motion-Sleep

If motion-sleep is not working for your family, for whatever reason, it's perfectly fine to transition your baby to stationary sleep. Once you decide it's time to wean your baby from motion-sleep, you can do it gently without any tears. Here are a few ideas to help this along.

Move Your Sleeping Baby

If your baby falls deeply asleep in a swinging cradle and you want sleep to start happening in the crib, try letting them fall asleep and then move them while they sleep. Set up their bedroom to be inviting for sleep: pull down the shades, turn on soft music or white noise, and warm up the soft flannel sheets with a heat pack or warm towel (remove these and test the temperature before you lay your baby down).

It can help to locate the cradle or swing in the bedroom adjacent to the crib so that you aren't traveling a long distance between the two places. This helps your baby get used to the bedroom.

Point to Remember

Any time you change what you are doing at sleep time, your baby may resist the whole idea. This is typical whenever you modify a sleep routine that your baby is happy with. Stay with any new idea for a week or two to allow your baby to adjust before you judge its true effectiveness.

Watch for Tired Signs and Happily Awake Spans

Remember to watch the span of wakeful time between sleep sessions. Be sure your baby has been awake long enough, yet not too long, and is showing some signs of tiredness before you head to naptime. A baby who isn't quite tired enough can be lulled to sleep with motion, a benefit that is lost when moving to a stationary bed and requires that you be more observant regarding tired signs.

The Step-by-Step Plan for Transitioning from Motion to Bed Sleep

If it's time to transition your baby from the swing, stroller, or rocking cradle, try this step-by-step plan.

- First: slow it down. An easy way to begin the transition from motion to stillness is to keep your routine exactly the same, but gradually reduce the speed, intensity, or length of time over a period of several weeks.
- Analyze your current sleep routine. Even if you don't realize it, you do have a "bedtime routine" that precedes nap or bedtime sleep. What actions do you take, and in what order they occur—including feeding and diaper changing? How does the routine need to change?

- Add more sleep cues. Babies who love motion-sleep typically don't need any other sleep cues, except perhaps a full tummy and a dry diaper. It can help to create a bedtime and naptime routine so that your baby expects sleep to follow the steps that you take.

  What are all the technical parts of your sleep arrangement other than motion? These are important. If you don't have them, add them to your routine consistently for a week or two to help create sleep cues other than motion. These might be a darkened room, white noise or soft lullaby music, a pacifier, or swaddling, if your baby is a newborn.

- Set up your baby's new sleeping place. Where would you like your baby to sleep? Is it a bassinet, crib, or your baby-safe family bed? Make sure the location is prepped (see the safety tips on pages 365–373). Do what you can to make the bed cozy, for example, by using soft flannel or fleece sheets.

When it's time for sleep, follow these steps:

- Prepare the room for sleep (dim the lights, turn on the white noise).
- Be sure that your baby is tired, which may include breast-feeding, having a bottle, rocking, or other relaxing actions.
- Follow your exact routine—except when it comes time to place your baby in the swing or other motion device, put your baby in the stationary bed instead.
- When you put your baby in bed, slightly move or jiggle the mattress or bed until your baby's eyes close.

  Stay right beside your baby and begin the jiggle again if necessary. Once your baby is fully asleep, stay close enough to get to her the minute she wakes so she doesn't become startled and have negative feelings about the new location. (Make sure your crib doesn't have any loose screws!)

- Over the next week, continue the routine. As your baby gets accustomed to the new routine you can reduce the amount and intensity of your jiggle. Soon this new location will be a happy napping place!

Be patient, as the transformation from motion to stationary sleep could take anywhere from a week to several months, depending on your baby's age, how deeply ingrained the motion habit is, the actual reasons your baby is attached to motion-naps, and how well the solutions you pick match your baby's personality.

If your baby totally resists all attempts you make to sleep in the crib, or if you are becoming frustrated, then sometimes it's best to leave well enough alone for a week or two, and then try again, perhaps with a different plan. Sometimes a slight change to your approach, along with another week or more of maturity, can make a big difference in the end result. All babies eventually outgrow the need for motion during naptime. Be patient!

Babies with Special Needs

While sleep issues are common among all children, those with special needs are even more likely to have sleep difficulties. Further, they often require a more intense and committed plan in order to solve their sleep issues. "Children with special needs tend to have at least one sleep disorder," says Dr. Stephen Sheldon, director of the sleep medicine center at Children's Memorial Hospital in Chicago, Illinois. He explains that special needs children often have health issues that contribute to sleep disorders such as snoring, sleepwalking, sleep apnea, teeth grinding, night terrors, bedwetting, and insomnia.

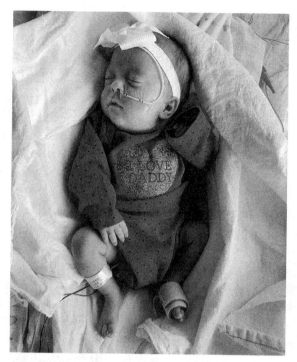

Avelina, three-months-old

There are, of course, a wide range and various degrees of special needs, and therefore it may be helpful to converse with your health professional and parents of children with similar situations. There's tremendous value in sharing ideas with parents who have children who are like your own. Keep in mind, though, that parenting philosophies differ, so find parents who also share your gentle, respectful approach to sleep.

No matter your situation, there are a few general guidelines that will apply to most families when it comes to addressing sleep issues.

Define Your Baby's Sleep Issues

Take the time to complete the logs and worksheets provided in this book. These will help you understand how your child is sleeping now and will assist you in the process to clearly identify the sleep issues that need to be changed. It will also be important as this will help you to identify your feelings about your baby's sleep patterns.

Not all sleep-related issues need to be labeled as problems; some may just require a change of viewpoint, understanding or even acceptance. Many sleep problems are not at all related to your child's special needs, even if you may have thought they were. For example, the majority of babies and young children are not self-sufficient when it comes to bedtime. They require a parent to get them settled into bed. In a National Sleep Foundation poll, less than 1 percent of children in the *toddler* age group, and barely 1 percent of *preschoolers* managed the amazing feat of getting settled for bed on their own. So, if you've been thinking that this situation in your house is in any way unique, it may help to know that it's very normal among all families.

Make a Realistic, Thoughtful Plan

As you put together your sleep plan, be realistic. It would be wonderful if a few minor adjustments would allow you to say "night-night" to your child at 7:00 P.M. and then not hear a peep until 7:00 A.M. when they called out a cheerful "good morning." But this is unrealistic in any situation, and you would just be setting yourself up for frustration and disappointment if you aimed for that goal. Instead, be reasonable as you lay out your sleep plan. Aim for short-term goals, and as you achieve these, then set a few more.

One Step at a Time

You may have a number of sleep issues that you'd like to change. Trying to fix everything at once may be overwhelming to you and your baby. It may be more productive and less stressful to pick one or two issues and work to change those before moving on to the next. With the knowledge that you can make good improvements in time, you can patiently work on a few items and then move on to the next issue.

Choosing the Steps to Address

You have several choices as you choose which issues to begin with. You can either pick the problem that bothers you the most, or choose the one that may be easiest to correct. For example, if your child is waking you up every few hours all night and draining all the energy you have so that your days are a struggle, then address that one issue first, and deal with that one issue alone. Or, you can choose a problem that is relatively easy to fix, such as the early bird syndrome, resistance to napping, or a change in timing or type of a medication that might be causing sleeplessness. Once you've had success with one issue, move on to the next. Keep in mind that gradually applying all that you've learned in this book will bring the best long-term success. However, there's no reason to add stress to your life by trying to do it all at once.

Focus on Routines and Rituals

Your child may respond best when all their sleep-related activities are choreographed to occur in exactly the same way every night.

Design your child's bedtime routine to meet their needs, strengths and developmental capabilities. If something seems difficult for them (or you) don't complicate your bedtime routine. Save new or challenging tasks for the future or the daytime, and do what you can to make the bedtime routine pleasant and stress-free.

Dig Deep for More Patience

As you are struggling with the effects of your child's sleep-related problems, your baby may pick up on your emotions over their sleep problems. "Children can sense if their parent is upset or angry because they have been woken up, have to change the sheets or have to lose sleep to tend to the child," says Dr. Sheldon. "And because special needs children can be more emotional, sensitive, and fragile than others, the effects of their parents' reactions last for hours, days or even weeks." These complex emotions can add even more depth and confusion to your child's sleep issues.

Take a deep breath, and take it one night at a time. While your baby's sleep patterns may be frustrating for you today, and there are many steps that you can take to improve their sleep; it can't be done overnight. If you take a methodical approach, and sprinkle it with plenty of patience and encouragement, it's likely you'll have more sleep successes.

Ask for Help

There are times when problems are due to medical sleep disorders that won't improve until they are identified and addressed. If you've made a sleep plan and followed it consistently for sev-

Mother Speak

"If things aren't working in your house get help—and get it now. There are plenty of people who are ready and willing to give you a hand. Look for these helpers."

Carol, mother and special education teacher

eral months without any positive results, then determine if your child might be served by a sleep professional who can provide a more extensive evaluation and specialized remedies. Even if you don't suspect a sleep disorder, you can still gain wonderful insight and ideas from a professional.

Multiples: Twins and More

Since babies in general are alike in many ways, every topic in this book that applies to one child applies to your babies, as well. The biggest issue, of course, is that you can't be in two (or more!) places at once, and this creates a unique challenge. With knowledge and a plan, though, this is a challenge that you can meet and overcome.

Rely on Routines

Having a dependable bedtime routine and consistent sleep times is important for all children, but can be especially important for parents of multiples, who may already feel pulled in too many directions. A written routine, perhaps displayed as a bedtime poster, can help guide all of you through the nightly process and keep things running smoothly. (See page 265.)

Where Should They Sleep?

Together, apart, same room, different rooms, parent's room? As I researched the best place for twins to sleep I discovered something very interesting. Based on the experience of twin parents and the expertise of numerous specialists, I could easily formulate a credible argument for just about any sleep arrangement. There are those who swear that separating twins from the start

Mila and Lily, three-weeks-old

prevents them from waking each other up, and those who are adamant that having them sleep together allows them to comfort each other so that they sleep better.

The bottom line: Do what feels right to you and what works best for your children.

It's perfectly fine to experiment a bit. If your current sleeping situation isn't working, try something different for a month or so, and see if a new arrangement works better. If it doesn't, try something else. You'll eventually find the right setup for your children. And don't be surprised if this changes over time. Be open to different sleep arrangements for nap versus bedtime, too. Keep in mind that as your children get older their preferences and sleep patterns will change, and it's fine to make adjustments as you go.

Mother-Speak

"What we found is that things change from time to time. At one point the girls will sleep together well; then they won't, so we separate them. Then after a time we start finding them in bed with each other again. My suggestion would be to have the most flexible furniture and room setups, so that you can make necessary modifications throughout these transitions."

Shahin, mother of six-year-old twins, Aria and Rose

Pay attention to your children's needs and be flexible as you apply what you learn. If you take your children's needs into consideration, and combine this with their sleep patterns and your own needs, then you can come up with the right solutions.

Synchronizing Sleep Schedules

Each baby has individual sleep needs. To a certain extent you can't force them to adapt to a schedule just because it would work better for you. However, the good news is that overall most children in the world have similar sleep needs at the same ages, and this can work in your favor.

In order to guide your children towards the same sleep/wake schedule, make your best effort to coordinate all aspects of their daily schedules. They're more likely to respond well to the same naptimes and bedtime if they wake up, and eat at about the same time every day.

You can also encourage them to have the same sleep schedule by keeping their room dark during sleep times, brightly lit upon awakening, and by utilizing white noise as a sleep cue and a way to mask outside sounds that could wake them.

Pick Your Battles

It may be most helpful if you take the time to review each of your children's sleep patterns individually and learn what the most important issues are. The forms in Chapter 3 will help you do this. It might make more sense to choose those that are most frustrating for you, or those that are most disruptive to your family first. Once those things are solved, move onto the next.

You may want to complete separate forms and outline the details for each of your children. Then create two separate sleep plans, thinking only of the one child you are writing out a plan for. Once you have the two plans, look at them together. How can you address both of their needs, while taking into account that you don't have superhuman or magical powers?

Once you have an idea of a family plan, write it down. Create several "phases" so that you have a map of direction. This will also help you to celebrate small successes along the way and give you a glimpse of the nightlight at the end of the tunnel.

Have Realistic Expectations

Everything is twice as challenging when you have multiples, and their sleep issues can doubly affect your own precious sleep. If you are trying to run a perfect household and be a perfect parent, you'll surely set yourself up for disappointment. Take a good look at your daily schedule and adopt these guidelines for yourself:

- Relax your housekeeping standards and/or get help.
- Say "No" more often to outside events that create family stress.
- Ask for help from those willing to give it; accept help when it's offered.
- Take care of yourself: Eat right and exercise.
- Give yourself credit for all the things you do right.

Get Support

There are quite a number of good books and websites written about raising multiples. There are also numerous support groups, both in person and online. Check into getting yourself some reading material and some personal support from other parents. Keep in mind that while all parents of multiples have that one particular thing in common, they have many different philosophies about child-rearing. It's important to align yourself with like-minded parents. When you do find support this can mean the difference between struggling with your problems, or knowing that everything you're facing is normal and developing the confidence that you can solve today's challenges.

Part IV

Let's Talk About You

Your baby doesn't sleep all night, yet somehow wakes up happy and bounces through the day with a joyful exuberance about life that belies any lack of shut-eye. You, on the other hand, may find yourself wandering about aimlessly in a sleep-deprived stupor, longing for that seemingly impossible night when you can stay snuggled in your bed—all night—without interruption. Even worse, you may be waking up on your own in between the baby's stirrings, adding to an already frustrating situation. Many parents find that once their baby is sleeping soundly, they continue their *own* pattern of frequent night waking. If there's anything more challenging than waking for your baby every few hours, it's waking every few hours even when your baby is sleeping peacefully!

This section is about *you.* It's about helping you to get back to a normal pattern of sleep. And it's full of good news: By following these tips, you should be snoozing happily in no time.

This part of the book is about keeping your sanity during this sleepless time. It will nudge you along in your journey toward balance and help you stay focused on the future. It will give you ways to ease your frustration and helplessness and strengthen your resolve to work through your baby's, and your own, sleep plans right now.

11

Take Care of Yourself and Your Own Sleep

It's probably been a long time since you've had a full night's sleep. Almost certainly even longer than you realize! Many parents actually forget what their sleep patterns were like before children entered their lives. Many assume that they used to get eight hours consistently and without interruption. Eight hours *is* the amount of time that sleep experts recommend for most adults. In reality, though, according to the National Sleep Foundation, adults sleep an average of about seven hours per night. Furthermore, at least half of all adults have trouble sleeping—falling asleep and staying asleep—baby or no baby. And remember! No human being sleeps straight through the night—we all have brief awakenings between our sleep cycles. In other words, if you weren't sleeping like a log before baby, you won't be sleeping like a log now, either.

Mother-Speak
"The baby's sleeping better but I'm up every two hours staring at the clock."

Robin, mother of thirteen-month-old Alicia

How to Get a Good Night's Sleep

Everyone has different sleep needs, and you should gauge your sleep requirements according to your own health. Let your own body tell you what it needs, and do your best to listen to it. Learn to recognize the signs that tell you that you are or are not getting enough sleep.

The following are a few helpful tips for improving adult sleep that I've run across in my exhaustive research for this book. Sift through the list and use as many as you wish. Applying even just one or two of these suggestions should prove helpful.

Here's an important point to bear in mind. Sometimes, people who have been sleep deprived for any length of time actually feel *more* tired when they first begin to make changes to improve their sleep rhythms. The good news is that this is short-lived, and as soon as you adjust to your improved sleep, you will feel better emotionally and physically.

Review the following ideas, check off the ones that appeal to you, and create your *own* sleep plan. Soon, you'll be sleeping— like a baby (a baby who *doesn't* wake up every two hours).

Stop Worrying About Sleep

Turn your clock away from your bed, and don't agonize over whether you are sleeping or not. Don't lie there wondering when your baby will be calling out for you again. You'll just keep yourself awake. As a busy parent, you may be compounding your problem by worrying that your sleep time is taking up productive time that could be spent doing other things. You either get yourself to bed much too late, or lie in bed and feel guilty about it, thinking about all those other things you "should" be doing. Give yourself permission to sleep. It's necessary for your body, and important for your health, and good for your soul. Remember that your baby will benefit if you are well rested, too, because you'll be a happier parent. And if you're breastfeeding or pregnant, your improved sleep will be beneficial to both you and your baby.

Pay Off Your Sleep Debt

When we don't get enough sleep, we create a sleep debt that mounts further with each additional sleepless night. If you are still feeling sleep-deprived, try to gather as many additional sleep minutes as you can. Set aside a week or two for a period of sleep recovery, and squeeze in some extra sleep. Make it a priority. Go to bed early whenever possible, take a nap when you can, sleep

Chloe, one-day-old, and Mommy

a few minutes later. Even an extra hour of sleep will help you to pay off at least a portion of your sleep debt. You'll feel much better and can move on to establishing a healthy sleep routine.

If you simply cannot find any time for extra sleep, then bypass this idea and work on developing a healthy sleep routine. You may find that it will take a month or so for your sleep debt to dissipate and your new sleep program to work, but it will. Once you've developed your own plan, you'll find that sleep will no longer be on your list of things to think about. It will instead be just a simple, natural part of your life, the way it is for your baby.

Set Your Body Clock

Your body has what amounts to an internal alarm clock that can be set for sleep time and awake time. The consistency of your sleep schedule sets this clock and makes it work for you, just like it does for your baby. If your bedtime and awake time are different every day, the effectiveness of this amazing gift of nature is undermined; your clock is out of sync. You'll find yourself tired or alert at inappropriate times, sometimes feeling as if you could fall asleep standing up during the day, but then lying wide awake in bed at night.

This explains why many people have trouble waking up on Monday morning. If you have a specific wake and sleep time during the week, you probably find that by Friday morning you are waking up just before your alarm goes off, and on Friday night it's an effort to stay awake during the late-night movie. Come Monday morning, you're groggy and exhausted when your morning alarm goes off. What has happened is that by the end of the week your biological clock has taken control because of your consistent wake–sleep schedule during the week. But come the weekend, we push our bedtimes later, and, if we're lucky enough

to manage it, we sleep late in the morning as well. This effectively cancels the setting on our clocks, and by Monday we have
to start all over again.

This imbalance is an easy one to fix—and a solid, consistent
sleep plan is the handy tool that will do the trick. Choose a specific bedtime and time to wake up; stick to it as closely as possible, seven days a week. Obviously, your busy life will alter this
routine sometimes. You can deviate from your plan once in a
while without doing too much to upset things. But on the whole,
if you adhere to your schedule as consistently as possible, your
sleep will be more refreshing, and you'll be more energetic and
alert. Your body clock will function as it should, allowing you to
tick through your day productively and wind down at night
calmly.

Naturally, a few lucky people can function perfectly with a
varying sleep schedule, but they're the exception. Most people
are helped immensely by this simple, effective suggestion.

Get Organized

When your days are hectic and disorganized, your stress level
increases; the natural physiological and emotional responses to
this stress hamper your ability to sleep. So we can attack this
kind of sleeplessness by getting at the root of it—becoming more
organized and purposeful during the day.

A formal daily to-do list or calendar can help you feel more
in control of your days. With the myriad critical details of each
day written down, you'll be able to relax somewhat. Think of it
as moving all the dates and times and tasks out of your head and
onto your list, freeing up a little breathing room upstairs. And
late at night you won't wonder, "What do I need to do? What
did I forget?" It's all right there in your lists and on your calendar.

Keep a pad and a pencil near your bed in case an important idea or task *does* pop into your mind as you're trying to drift off. Don't use your your phone or other device for your midnight notes—the light from the screen can be alerting to your brain and prevent you from falling back to sleep easily. Write your thought down—then *let it go for now.*

Avoid Caffeine Late in the Day

Here's an interesting tidbit. Caffeine stays in your bloodstream between six and fourteen hours! The caffeine in that after-dinner cup of coffee is still hanging around in your system at midnight and beyond. Caffeine causes hyperactivity and wakefulness, which is why many people find their morning coffee so stimulating. Tolerance levels for caffeine vary; so you'll need to experiment and find out how much you can drink and how late you can drink it without disrupting your sleep.

If you are a nursing mother, watch your baby carefully to see if your child is being affected by caffeine. While no study has proved the connection between caffeine and a baby's sleeplessness, we do know that diet affects the quality, quantity, and palatability of breast milk, so a connection is not exactly far-fetched. (Many a breastfeeding mother has reported a perceived effect of caffeine on her baby, so it's worth taking a look at your own situation.)

Keep in mind that caffeine is an ingredient in more than just coffee. Tea (all types unless labeled caffeine-free), cola, some other soft drinks (even root beer and orange; check the labels), chocolate, even some over-the-counter painkillers contain it, although in smaller amounts.

Better choices for prebed drinks are warm milk or herbal teas that will bring on the relaxed state needed for sleep.

Watch Out for the Effects of Drugs and Alcohol

If you are taking any medication, ask your doctor or pharmacist if it has any side effects. We often are aware of what medications make us drowsy, but we don't realize that some have the opposite effect—acting as a stimulant.

Likewise, an evening glass or two of wine or beer usually won't affect sleep and might bring it on. But more than that can have a rebound effect, causing an episode of insomnia a few hours later, in the middle of the night. Alcohol can also disturb the *quality* of your sleep, making it shallow and disrupting normal dream cycles.

Make Exercise a Part of Your Day

There are many benefits to fitting regular exercise into your day, and improved sleep is at the top of the list. Many studies (not to mention common, everyday experience) have shown that moderate, regular exercise reduces insomnia and improves the quality of sleep.

The key to using exercise to improve sleep is to maintain a regular pattern: thirty to forty-five minutes of moderate aerobic exercise, three to four times a week. For best results, make sure you complete your exercise at least three hours before bedtime; exercise leaves most people too energized for sleep right after. Once again, there are exceptions. Some people find that strenuous exercise helps them fall asleep quickly soon afterward. Experiment to learn if this applies to you.

You might think that having a baby precludes your ability to get out and exercise. On the contrary! Your baby gives you the perfect excuse for a daily walk behind the stroller. If winter weather gets in your way, head for an indoor play center or a shopping mall with room to roam. This may not work for you every day, and you may have to leave your wallet at home, but many parents find it an effective way to squeeze in a walk. Plus, most babies love it and benefit from the stimulation (which may in fact help baby sleep, too).

Here are a few other ways to incorporate daily exercise into your life:

If you work at home:

- After you put your little one down for a nap, use a treadmill, stationary bike, or other gym equipment.
- Jog up and down your stairs.
- Bring your baby outside and do some gardening.

If you work outside the home:

- At lunchtime or during a break, climb up and down the stairs, or take a walk around the block.
- Create a routine to take advantage of an employee gym or workout room.
- Take frequent brisk walks to the copy machine, mail room, or bathroom.

Ideas for everyone:

- Exercise with your baby.
- Put on some music and dance with your baby.
- Look for small ways to add exercise into your day such as parking farther away from the store, using the stairs instead of the elevator, walking instead of driving to a close destination, walking your older kids to school, or playing outside with your children.
- Plan family activities that involve movement and action, such as hikes, bike rides, or romps at the beach or park.

Make Your Environment Favorable to Sleep

Take a good look at your bedroom and make sure that it is conducive to relaxation and healthy sleep. Every person is different, but here's a checklist for you to review.

- **Comfort.** Is your mattress comfortable? Do you like your blanket or comforter, or is it a source of aggravation in the night? Is your pillow the right softness and thickness? Do what you can to improve these details.
- **Temperature.** If you are too cold or too hot during sleep, you will wake frequently. Experiment until you find the best temperature. If your partner has different preferences, find a way to please both of you by changing the type of pajamas you wear, using a fan, or adding an extra blanket just for the person who needs it.
- **Noise.** Some people sleep better in perfect silence, while others prefer background music or white noise. Again, if one sleep partner likes noise, but the other wants silence, experiment: Try earplugs or a personal headset for music or sound.
- **Light.** If you sleep better in complete darkness, cover your windows. If you like light, open the blinds, or use a night-light. (Be cautious about using lights during the night if you wake up to use the bathroom or tend the baby. Bright light will fool your biological clock into thinking it's morning. Rely on low-wattage night-lights.) Here again, if your partner likes the blinds open and you like them shut, decide whose needs are greater or find a compromise. You might buy yourself a soft eye mask made just for that purpose, or leave the blinds open on one side of the room, closed on the other—facing the closed window will give you more of a sense of darkness.

Have Your Own Bedtime Routine

You may have implemented a bedtime routine to help your baby sleep better. This same idea can work for you, too. Often, we parents have a very pleasant routine for putting our children to bed. After that relaxing hour, when we have just about fallen to sleep reading the bedtime story, we jam into high gear and rush about the house tending to all those duties that await our attention until we look up and—oh no! It's midnight!

Your own prebedtime routine can greatly improve your ability to fall asleep and stay asleep. It can include anything that relaxes you, such as reading, listening to music, sipping a cup of tea, meditating, or talking about your day. Avoid stimulating your mind or body in the hour before bed. Activities like answering your email or posting online, doing heavy housecleaning, or even watching television, can keep you awake long after you've finished them.

If possible, try to keep the lights dim in the hour before bed, as bright light strongly signals your body to leap into daytime action. Lower lights and quieter sounds will help prepare you for a good night's sleep.

Eat Right and Eat Light Before Sleep

You'll likely sleep best with your stomach neither too full nor too empty. A large meal can make you feel tired but will keep your body working to digest it, thus disturbing sleep. An empty stomach can keep you up with hunger pangs. A happy medium is usually best. Have a light snack about an hour or two before bedtime. Avoid gassy, fatty, sugary, or spicy foods. Some foods that have been found to help people sleep better are milk, eggs, cottage cheese, turkey, and cashews. Experiment to find which choices are best for you.

Encourage Relaxation and the Onset of Sleep

Often, when we lie in bed waiting for sleep, our mind and body are primed for action. The wheels are turning and our thoughts keep us awake. A helpful method for bringing on sleep is to focus your mind on peaceful, relaxing thoughts. Here are a few ways to accomplish this:

- Repeat a familiar meditation or prayer to release the mind from daily action and prime it for sleep. Yoga stretches can help relax your muscles.
- Focus on your breathing while repeating the word *relax* in a slow pattern tied to your exhales. Or imagine your breathing is moving in and out along with a wave at the beach.
- Use progressive relaxation to coax all the parts of your body to relax. Begin at your feet. Feel the weight of your feet, have them go limp and relaxed, and then imagine that they have a gentle warmth moving over them. Then, move up to your right leg, repeat the process. Move on to your left leg, and continue on up to your head. (Most people are asleep or nearly asleep by the time they get that far!) You may want to adapt some of the relaxation exercises you learned in childbirth classes.
- If you find you can't quiet your thoughts, try listening to an audiobook as you nod off. Choose a relaxing story or one that you've read several times for the best results.

When Engorgement Is the Problem

There is often an adjustment period when a breastfed baby begins to sleep through the night. It's hard to believe, but your breasts *will* develop their own clock system. Decreased production during the night is quite normal, and within a week of your baby's new sleep habits, your milk production pattern will parallel your baby's new feeding pattern. Your breasts will still produce milk constantly, so if your baby wakes once in a while to nurse, they'll find enough there for comfort. Interestingly enough, if your baby suddenly begins to wake again because of teething, illness, or growth spurts, your milk production will shift right along with their needs (as long as you feed on demand). What a great miracle breastfeeding is!

Mother-Speak

"Last night we had our best sleep night ever—my little guy slept seven whole hours. The problem is that I woke up in the middle of the night with rocks on my chest! My breasts were leaking, and they hurt. After working so hard to get him to sleep, I didn't dare wake him up. I've so longed for the time my baby would sleep through the night—I never dreamed I would wish he would wake up to nurse!"

Elisa, mother of nine-month-old Jahwill

Adjustment Period Solutions

Here are a few tips for getting through the adjustment period.

- Give your baby a complete, both-sides feeding before bed and in the morning.
- Sleep in your roomiest bra with nursing pads or washcloths tucked inside.
- If you wake engorged, apply warm compresses and pump a small amount (either by hand or with a breast pump). Don't pump a full feeding because you'll trick your body into thinking your baby is still needing that nighttime feeding. Just release enough to get comfortable.

- Try taking a warm shower and massaging your breasts under the spray of water. You might want to lean forward so that gravity helps you express some milk. This may help you release enough milk to get comfortable until your baby wakes up to nurse.
- Apply a cold compress to your breasts, or use ibuprofen to minimize any pain or discomfort.
- If you are in pain and cannot pump, go ahead—pick up your sleeping baby and breastfeed. Most babies can nurse in their sleep, and yours may suck just enough to help you get back to sleep. Even if your baby wakes during this feeding, they will fall right back to sleep easily during the nursing session.
- Be prepared for additional daytime feedings for a bit. Some babies who suddenly begin sleeping longer at night will make up for the lost feedings by nursing more during the day.
- If you have experienced plugged ducts or breast infections in the past, avoid any repeats by pumping or nursing your baby enough to soften your breasts. Just try to minimize this so that you can work the nighttime feeding out of your schedule. Remember that your body will adjust production to match your baby's new sleep schedule.
- Don't stop breastfeeding! Your breasts still need to be emptied, and frequent daytime feeding will help you move past this uncomfortable condition.

Pay Attention to Your Own Health

If you have chronic insomnia or other unusual sleep problems, or other health problems, be smart. See a doctor.

How to Handle Unwanted Advice

When you have a baby in the house you may find that family and friends are eager to impart their advice, especially when it comes to the topic of sleep. It may be stressful and difficult for you to deal with this, especially when you are struggling with sleep issues. So, let's talk about how to handle unwanted advice and reduce this frustrating stressor.

Point to Remember
Your baby is the center of the universe for you—and for other people who love them, also.

The important place to start is to understand that just as your baby is an important part of your life, your little one is also important to others. People who care about you and your baby are bonded to you in a special way, and if they see you struggling with sleep issues, they can't help but provide their opinion. Most of this advice is given because they really feel they can help you, and they believe that what they are telling you is correct. Knowing this may give you a reason to handle the interference gently, in a way that leaves everyone's feelings intact.

Regardless of the advice, however, *this is your baby*, and in the end, you will raise your child the way that you think best. So, it's rarely worth creating a war over a well-meaning person's comments (or even over comments that aren't well-meaning but bossy or controlling!). The good news is that you can respond to unwanted advice in a variety of ways that end the interference without ending the relationship:

Listen First

It's natural to be defensive if you feel that someone is judging you; but chances are you are not being criticized; rather, the other person is sharing what they feel to be valuable insight. Try to listen—you might learn something valuable. But if not, you can still listen quietly . . . and then promptly ignore what you've heard.

Disregard the Suggestion

If you know that there is no convincing the other person to change their mind, simply smile, nod, and make a noncommittal response, such as, "Interesting!" Then go about your own business . . . your way.

Agree with Something

You might find one part of the advice that you agree with. If you can, provide wholehearted agreement on that topic and steer the person away from the point of conflict.

Pick Your Battles

If your mother-in-law insists that your baby wear socks at naptime, go ahead and pop some on those little feet. However, don't capitulate on issues that are important to you or the health or well-being of your child.

Steer Clear of the Topic

If your brother is pressuring you to let your baby cry to sleep, but you would never do that, then don't complain to him about your baby getting you up five times the night before. If he brings up the topic, then distraction and a change of topic are definitely in order.

Educate the Other Person

If your "teacher" is imparting information that you know to be outdated or wrong, share what you've learned on the topic. You may be able to open the other person's mind. Refer to a study, book, or article that you have read.

Quote a Doctor

Many people accept a point of view if a professional has validated it. If your own pediatrician agrees with your position, say, "My doctor said it's normal for an eight-month-old baby to wake up during the night for feeding." If your own doctor doesn't back your view on the issue, then refer to another doctor—perhaps the author of a baby care book or a study.

Be Vague

You can avoid confrontation with an elusive response. For example, if your friend asks if you've started to have your baby sleep in her own room (but you are many months away from even starting the process), you can answer with, "We're moving in that direction." Then, change the subject.

Ask for Advice!

Your friendly counselor is possibly an expert on a few issues that you can agree on, even if unrelated to your current clash. Search out these points and invite their guidance. They'll be happy that they can help you, and you'll be happy you have a way to avoid a showdown about topics that you don't agree on.

Memorize a Standard Response

Here's a comment that can be said in response to almost any piece of advice: "This may not be the right way for you, but it's the right way for me. Let's talk about something else now."

Be Honest

Try being honest about your feelings. Pick a time free of distractions, be calm and choose your words carefully, such as, "I know how much you love Harry, and I'm glad you spend so much time with him. I know you think you're helping me when you give me advice about his sleep, but I'm comfortable with my own approach, and I'd really appreciate if you'd understand that."

Find a Mediator

If the situation is putting a strain on your relationship with the advice-giver, you may want to ask another person you trust to step in for you.

Search for Like-Minded Friends

Join a support group with people who share your parenting philosophies. Talking, texting, or posting with others who are raising their babies in a way that is similar to your own can give you the strength to face people who don't understand or support your viewpoints.

12

Final Thoughts

When my own sleep journey first began, my baby was twelve-months-old and waking every hour to nurse. The desperate longing for sleep filled my nights; a frantic and relentless search for something—anything—that would help him sleep consumed my days. Through it all, though, one criterion guided me. Whatever ideas I tried, I would not allow my baby to cry himself to sleep. After all, we were in the same boat: We both needed sleep and couldn't figure out how to make it happen.

That's not to say that my tears didn't threaten occasionally. I remember nights when he woke me for the sixth time and I prayed, "Please, God, just let him sleep." Like you, my readers and friends, I learned that when one is deprived of sleep, sleep becomes the absolute priority in life.

Now that I'm standing on the other side of the bridge (or shall I say, bed?), sleep is no longer a major issue in my life. Sleep has once again become a simple matter of maintenance in our home.

My test parents followed the same path. They began the trip with bags under their eyes and anguished pleas for help:

Mother-Speak

"I hate to say it, but I have become obsessed with sleep."

Caryn, mother of six-month-old Blaine

"By morning, I'm a walking zombie. I'd do anything for a full night's sleep; it's become my ultimate obsession."

Yelena, mother of seven-month-old Samantha

"I am ALWAYS exhausted. I walk around all day in a fog. I really, really can't let my baby cry, but I really, really want sleep."

Neela, mother of eighteen-month-old Abhishek

These parents ended their journey revitalized and ready to move forward to the next milestone in their baby's lives:

Mother-Speak

"I'm amazed at how far we've come. I can't believe this is the same baby. I feel like a new mother. A happy, energetic mother who sleeps all night and wakes up refreshed and joyful."

Robin, mother of thirteen-month-old Alicia

"Josh now goes gracefully to bed almost every single night. And I have the whole evening to work, take a shower, eat dinner, fix his lunch for day care. It's like having two days in one."

Shannon, mother of nineteen-month-old Joshua

"Kailee is in bed every night by 8:00 P.M., and the earliest I ever hear from her is 6:30 A.M. It has totally changed our lives. It's a new freedom that we enjoy wholeheartedly."

Marsha, mother of eight-month-old Kailee

We Are Alike

As I have worked with my group of test parents, I have discovered how alike we all are. Different names, different places, but the same heart. We love our babies absolutely; we can't bear to hear them cry, nor can we easily tolerate the cries of other babies. Our lives have been irrevocably and completely changed the minute a child entered our lives. And as our babies grow, the special place in our hearts reserved just for them grows bigger, too.

We also have strong opinions about parenting and are not easily swayed by the media, our friends, or even our pediatricians or other "experts." We know in our hearts what our babies need; we feel what they want. Blessed by, and mindful of, advances in medicine, and wary of philosophies developed in the interest of convenience, we are determined to heed our strong instincts. We are even willing to suffer ourselves, if it means the best for our babies. We are mother bears and father tigers. We parent by heart.

If You've Just Begun

If you have just embarked on this journey toward better sleep, I know that you are frustrated and anxious. Because you are determined not to let your baby cry, I know that the feedback you get from family and friends isn't always helpful or supportive.

Talking with others who share your parenting philosophies really does help. If you are lucky enough to find someone nearby who believes as you do, make sure that you both take advantage of this by talking to each other frequently. If you don't have a local friend, you can find support online.

You may find that having someone to talk to—either in person, by phone, or online—can mean the difference between depression and commitment. I encourage you to find the support you need to help yourself through this challenging time.

Living for the Moment?

As your sleep issues cast lengthening shadows over your life, you may begin to live purely for the moment. Your sleep-deprived, foggy brain may focus so intently on sleep that you can't think beyond the next few hours of rest. What you lack is perspective. To gain it back, ask yourself these questions:

1. Where will I be five years from now?
2. How will I look back on this time?
3. Will I be proud of how I handled my baby's sleep routines, or will I regret my actions?
4. How will the things I do with my baby today affect the person they will become in the future?

I know I've said this already, but having older children has afforded me the perspective I lacked the first time around. My children have taught me how very quickly babyhood passes. I struggle now to remember the difficulties of those first years of parenthood, as they were so fleeting. And I am proud that I didn't cave in to the pressures of others around us; instead following my heart as I gently nurtured all of my babies.

I look upon my three grown children, and I like what I see. They are kind, sensitive, and caring young people. When their baby brother was born, they were eight-, ten-, and twelve-years-old. When he cried, all three of them ran to his aid. My kids knew what to do in part because it hadn't been very long since

they were babies themselves. They could still relate to the desperation of a baby's cry. It was simple for them because children
are free of adult baggage and clutter. They instinctually know that
a baby's cry is communication and that it deserves attention.

It's not all instinct, however. And, of course, it isn't always
easy. Attaining anything of true value rarely is.

Point to Remember

When a baby cries, the right response is, well, response. It's that
simple.

Baseball Babies

My three older children all played baseball, so when Coleton
was a baby, he and I spent much of our springtime at the ball-
park. During his first baseball season, he was five months old.
Because I was a coach on my daughter's team, Coleton spent his
time in the dugout and on the field nestled in his sling, watching
the action and listening to the cheers, chants, and noise of the
play. Between swings at bat the girls would often pass him
around from one to the other, entertaining him and trying to
make him giggle. That same season I met another mother with
a baby boy the same age as Coleton. She always arrived with her
little son belted into his car seat–stroller travel system. There he
would remain, parked at the edge of the bleachers. His reclining
position in the seat gave him a view of the sky and trees. When
he fussed, his mother would prop a bottle in his seat, and he
would drink until he fell asleep. As I chatted with this other
mother, as baseball moms do, I discovered the difference
extended beyond the field. While Coleton's nights were spent

sleeping with his mommy by his side, nursing whenever he felt the need for comfort, the other mother was practicing sleep training—putting her baby in his crib at bedtime and ignoring his cries until the appropriate morning hour, "teaching" him to "self soothe" himself to sleep.

Both Coleton and this other baby were quiet babies. Rarely would you hear either one of them cry. But, as I contemplated the lives of these children, I wondered how their early experiences would color their futures. Coleton's early life was filled with people—their warm arms, happy faces, cuddles, and touches. He was always in the middle of life, not only enjoying his own experiences but also observing the experiences of others. His nights were no different than his days: someone was always there to heed his call. This other baby's early months were spent strapped in his stroller, hearing people, but from an uninvolved distance except for the occasional visitor who leaned over his seat. His nights were vast hours of loneliness, his cries ignored.

Coleton's early life was filled with the golden communication of humanity, where he now gravitates as a young adult who is a natural leader and a gregarious, joyful participant in life. The other baby was shown independence and aloneness during the first part of his life, and I still wonder what he is like as a young man. Yes, they both may have been content babies, but content with entirely different worlds—one that was people-centered and one revolving around separateness from people. How will these early experiences color the men these babies will become as they find their partners in life and perhaps become fathers themselves? As you move through these early months with *your* baby, take the time to consider how today's actions will affect your child in the long run. This process will help you toss off unhelpful advice as you work through your own sleep solutions.

Parent-Speak

"I've been rocking and cuddling my baby to sleep since the day he was born, and people tell me it's a bad habit. I mentioned this to a nurse at my clinic recently. She said that she did the same thing with her son, and everyone warned her that she would still have a teenager sleeping in her bed. And then she told me a story.

She said that a few weeks ago, her teenage son came home from school very upset. He didn't want to talk, and just went to his room and listened to his music. The mother gave her son space. Nighttime came, and she went to bed.

Just as she was about to turn off her light, the door opened, and her fifteen-year-old son padded into the room. Saying nothing, he climbed into the bed next to her, laid his head on her shoulder and cried. After a while, he told her all about the girl that broke his heart, all about the friends who laughed, all about the stresses of his life.

She told him about her first broken heart, about friends who'd been cruel, and told him she understood. They talked in the dark for hours, until he fell asleep on her bed, still sad but relieved after their talk. She fell asleep, still sad for him, but relieved after their talk.

'So, you see,' she said to me, when she finished the story, 'I was so scared that I would wind up with a teenager who would 'need me at night,' that I never stopped to consider how beautiful that would really be.'"

Original author unknown

Patience, Patience, and Just a Little More Patience

Take a deep breath and repeat after me, "This too shall pass." You're in the middle of it all right now, and it's hard. But in no time at all, your baby will be sleeping, and so will you. And your concerns will turn to the next phase in this magnificent, challenging, and ultimately rewarding experience we call parenthood. I wish you and your family a lifetime of happiness and love.

Part V

Safety Information and Checklists

Safety First

Yes, you're tired, too tired perhaps to read through the vast body of information and guidelines out there on the subject of safety. Maybe you'll get to it soon, but your good intentions are not enough to keep your baby safe, and you need this information right now.

To help get you started, I have gathered safety information from a wide variety of reputable sources and authorities. And from all this, I have created sleeping-safety checklists for your review. Please read over this section and give it serious consideration.

Keep in mind that this chapter covers safety issues relating to sleep at home. You should, of course, be aware of many other safety issues—at home and away. Also, because safety precautions are updated constantly—and because all babies (and their families) are different—no checklist is fully complete and appropriate for every child. Do your homework and please, put safety first.

Sudden Infant Death Syndrome (SIDS) — What It Is and Ways to Reduce the Risk

I know that this is a difficult and uncomfortable topic to talk about, but it's one we need to discuss so that you can take all the known steps to protect your baby. For most parents, SIDS is the most terrifying fear of babyhood. The term *SIDS* is applied to the unexplained death, usually during sleep, of a seemingly healthy baby less than a year old. According to the American SIDS Institute, the rate of SIDS worldwide has decreased dramatically in the last 30 years, particularly since the 1990s when the emphasis on "back to sleep" was initiated; however, even the loss of one baby to SIDS is too many. In this section we'll cover what we know about SIDS and describe the things that can reduce your baby's risk.

SIDS Is Different from Accidental Death

Some professionals prefer the use of the terms "sudden unexpected death in infancy" (SUDI) or "sudden unexpected infant deaths" (SUID) for clarity. This would include any unexplained death including SIDS. SIDS itself is a medical condition whereas accidental death is related to a specific risk factor. The death of a baby by suffocation or smothering is not SIDS but is a separate tragedy by a different cause. However, too much of what is written about these two issues lump them together in any discussion about baby sleep safety.

The CDC, in a paper about SIDS, says, ". . . although the causes of death in many of these children can't be explained, *most occur while the infant is sleeping in an unsafe sleeping environment.*" The fact here is that where and how the baby is sleeping can be a major risk factor. For example, when bed-sharing is not done according to safety protocol it may increase the risk of overheating, airway obstruction, tummy-sleeping, head-covering and exposure to tobacco smoke—which are all *risk factors for SIDS*. In addition, unsafe bed arrangements introduce the risk of entrapment, falls, smothering, and strangulation. Deaths due to these factors are often incorrectly labeled as SIDS, which is why these conditions are frequently discussed together. (See pages 369–373 for the safe bed-sharing tips.)

The Triple-Risk Model and How it Relates to SIDS

There have been, and continue to be, many studies about what causes SIDS, still we do not yet have definitive answers. However, research continues to uncover more information. The U.S. Department of Health and Human Services tells us this:

> More and more research evidence suggest that infants who die from SIDS are born with brain abnormalities or defects. At the present time, there is no way to identify babies who have these abnormalities, but researchers are working to develop specific screening tests.

Scientists believe that brain defects alone may not be enough to cause a SIDS death. Evidence suggests that other events might also have to occur for an infant to die from SIDS. Researchers use the Triple-Risk Model to explain this concept:

The Triple-Risk Model
The triple-risk model is used to describe the series of events that takes place when a baby dies of SIDS.

The Vulnerable Infant
An underlying defect or brain abnormality makes the baby vulnerable. Certain factors—such as defects in the parts of the brain that control respiration or heart rate or genetic mutations—confer vulnerability.

Critical Developmental Period

During the infant's first six months of life, rapid growth and changes in homeostatic controls occur. These changes may be evident (e.g., sleeping and waking patterns), or they may be subtle (e.g., variations in breathing, heart rate, blood pressure, and body temperature). Some of these changes may destabilize the infant's internal systems temporarily or periodically.

Outside Stressor(s)

Most babies encounter and can survive environmental stressors, such as a stomach-sleep position, overheating, secondhand tobacco smoke, or an upper respiratory tract infection. However, an already vulnerable infant may not be able to overcome them. Although these stressors are not believed to single-handedly cause infant death, they may tip the balance against a vulnerable infant's chances of survival.

According to the Triple-Risk Model, all three elements must be present for a sudden infant death to occur:

1. The baby's vulnerability is undetected.
2. The infant is in a critical developmental period that can temporarily destabilize his or her systems.
3. The infant is exposed to one or more outside stressors that he or she cannot overcome because of the first two factors.

Even though the exact cause of SIDS is unknown, there are ways to reduce the risk of SIDS and other sleep-related causes of infant death. If caregivers can remove one or more outside stressors, such as placing an infant to sleep on his or her back instead of on the stomach to sleep, they can reduce the risk of SIDS."

**The U.S. Department of Health and
Human Services, "Safe to Sleep®**

Things That Reduce the Risk of SIDS

Researchers have uncovered a variety of specific things that they believe can reduce the risk of SIDS. Because so little is known about what causes SIDS, it cannot absolutely be prevented; however, it is wise to follow the known prevention factors that almost all major medical and scientific groups now agree upon:

1. **Put your baby to sleep on their back—for naps and night sleep.** There's no question that back-to-sleep is important. The incidence of SIDS has been reduced significantly in places where this recommendation is followed. It's critical that all caregivers know this fact since babies accustomed to sleeping on their backs who are suddenly put to sleep on their stomachs are at much higher risk. Even when you bed-share you can gently shift your baby to the back-lying position after feedings.

2. **Have your baby sleep on a firm, unyielding surface with snug, secure sheets.** Soft surfaces pose a breathing risk to small babies who are not able to control their head, neck and body muscles. Don't let your baby sleep on sofas,

"The American Academy of Pediatrics believes that breastfeeding is the optimal source of nutrition through the first year of life. We recommend exclusively breastfeeding for about the first six months of a baby's life, and then gradually adding solid foods while continuing breastfeeding until at least the baby's first birthday. Thereafter, breastfeeding can be continued for as long as both mother and baby desire it."

American Academy of Pediatrics (AAP),
Policy statement regarding breastfeeding

recliners, cushions, pillows, nursing cushions, waterbeds, or soft pillow-top mattresses.

3. **Breastfeed your baby, if possible.** The American Academy of Pediatrics Task Force on Sudden Infant Death Syndrome concluded that many factors associated with breastfeeding combine to result in a significantly lower incidence of SIDS over formula feeding.

"Breastsleeping"

Dr. James J. McKenna, one of the world's leading experts on mother-baby sleep, and director of the Mother-Baby Behavioral Sleep Laboratory at the University of Notre Dame, along with Dr. Lee T. Gettler, of the Hormones, Health and Human Behavior Laboratory at the University of Notre Dame, have coined a new term to define the bed-sharing/breastfeeding dyad which defines the close relationship between breastfeeding and sleeping: "Breastsleeping." In an interview with *Kindred* magazine, Dr. McKenna explains:

> . . . based on empirical data there really is no way to measure normal human infant sleep nor any way to measure what constitutes normative patterns of breastfeeding, that is numbers of times per night and sleep architecture that goes along with it, unless you have the two conjoined together, because in fact it is a biological and behavioral system that co-evolved and is indeed simply one system. We are now a breastfeeding-normal culture, and the point of the word *breastsleeping* is to indicate that where you find one you find the other, and it is because of the biological interdependence of the two. They are functionally interdependent systems.

McKenna explains that it is safer for a breastfed baby to bed-share with the mother over a parent and bottle-fed baby pair, "The baby and the mother on a physiological and behavioral level are differentially situated compared with what happens when bottle feeding and bed sharing."

I love this concept and found it to be extremely helpful as a busy, working mother of four children. "Breastsleeping" allowed me to get my sleep without having to roam the halls all night tending to my youngest child, or trying to stay awake during many night feedings. I became highly in tune with my baby and woke at the slightest noise or movement. It almost seemed that I would wake up just before my baby awoke and easily shift position for feeding, and apparently according to Dr. McKenna's research, this is common. This easily arousable state of sleep is safer for babies and bed-sharing mothers, which is why things like alcohol, medications, or even having the other parent or a sibling sleeping directly next to the baby can be dangerous because these things can impact that extreme level of awareness between breastfeeding mother and baby.

In light of this research, if your baby is bottle-fed it is wise to hold off on bed-sharing until your child is a bit older.

4. **Remove blankets, pillows and toys from your baby's sleep area.** Any item that could present a risk of suffocation, strangulation, or entrapment has no place in your baby's bed. This includes things such as pillows, blankets, comforters, bumper pads, and stuffed animals. You can add child-sized versions of blankets and pillows, and child-safe stuffed animals once your baby is past infancy.

5. **Take your baby for regular well-baby check-ups.** Keep your baby healthy by sticking to your health care provider's suggested newborn visit schedule, and discuss and research

Vaccinations and Your Baby: Do Your Research

Vaccination is another of those confusing baby care topics rife with passionate emotions and filled with false information, so let's stop a minute and discuss. When you are making decisions about your baby's vaccinations, and health care in general, *do your homework*, and keep in mind these points:

- Social media is not the best source for accurate, up-to-date information.
- Opinions from your friends and family may not reflect the most recent scientific knowledge on any topic, and it will be heavily weighted by their personal experience and opinions.
- Scientific research is ongoing and changes with new information. Check the date of material you read. If it is more than a year old it may be outdated and new research might provide different outcomes.
- Check multiple, reputable sources, and consider personal agendas that may be behind the information. You must gather all the facts in order to make the best decision for your own baby's health and welfare.

recommended vaccinations. Proper health care has been shown to have a definite effect in protecting your baby.

6. **Don't permit anyone to smoke near your baby or in places where your baby sleeps or plays.** Secondhand smoke affects a baby's developing heart and brain, including the brain center area that controls breathing, which greatly increases the risk of SIDS. Your baby's sleeping areas, play areas, and the cars they travel in should be free of smoke and smoke residue. (Due to the effect of smoke

on a baby's developing system, babies whose mothers smoked during pregnancy have a higher risk of SIDS, which warrants a separate sleeping surface [crib or cradle] for these newborns.)

7. **Make sure your baby doesn't get overheated.** Studies show that overheating inhibits a baby's ability to arouse from a risky sleep condition. Most babies should be dressed in no more than one extra layer over what you are comfortable wearing. Don't cover your baby's head for sleep unless your doctor advises you to. (Premature babies or cold environments might warrant head-covering, but check with a doctor.) At the other extreme, your baby should not be chilled. Your baby's chest, neck, back, and stomach should feel warm and dry, and hands and feet should be pink and warm. Sweating is a sign that your baby is too warm. It's a natural desire to bundle up babies to make them cozy and to get them to sleep longer stretches, but particularly in infancy it is a biologically protective device for them to stir and wake up regularly.

8. **Consider offering your baby a pacifier for sleep.** Once breastfeeding is established, or if your baby is bottle-fed, it is fine to offer your baby a pacifier to help them fall asleep. There is no evidence that using a pacifier creates any health or developmental problems for young babies, unless they are overused and used in place of feeding. Some studies show that pacifier use might reduce the risk of SIDS, although it is unclear why the connection exists. At this time, medical organizations no longer discourage the use of pacifiers for naps and nighttime sleep for babies up to one year of age. They do not make a recommendation of pacifier use for all babies, but if your baby benefits from having a pacifier for sleep you can rest assured that it is fine to use one.

Some scientists and breastfeeding groups feel that more research needs to be done before a blanket recommendation on pacifier use can be made, since pacifier use might interfere with the quantity or length of breastfeeding, so watch the news and talk this over with your lactation consultant or health care professional.

9. **Do not use any commercially available products marketed as SIDS protection.** As of this writing, there are no products known to protect a baby from SIDS. There are no sleep positioners, nests, special mattresses, wedges, or monitors that are deemed safe for use with babies, and some can pose dangerous risks. Just because something is sold does not ensure that it is safe. Watch the news and do your homework, as new products could become available over time.

10. **Create a safe sleeping environment for your baby.** There is one recommendation for safe sleep that is often mentioned by professional groups: Have your baby sleep in your bedroom, but in a separate, safe sleep area, such as a crib, cradle, or bassinet.

While all the experts agree your newborn should sleep in *your bedroom*, there is much conflicting information about bed-sharing versus separate-surface sleep. However, professionals and groups who do approve of bed-sharing agree that there are safe-sleep parameters to be followed. These safety factors are outlined in detail for you in the next section, "Where Should my Baby Sleep?," and in the safety checklist, page 365. If you bed-share with your baby, please scrutinize this information and pay close attention to creating a safe situation—every night, and for every nap.

Where Should My Baby Sleep?

When it comes to the question of where to have your baby sleep the opinions are passionate and the voices are loud. So, if you think you are too confused when it comes to deciding where to have your baby sleep, you aren't. You are exactly the right amount of confused—because this is a topic that doesn't have a precisely perfect answer.

So, should you bring your baby into bed with you, or have your baby sleep in a crib (down the hall or in your room), or in a bed-side cradle attached to your bed? This is a question that is difficult to answer and becomes more challenging the more you research it. And then, it becomes far more perplexing once you add your baby's opinion. No matter what your plan is, babies have a tendency to shake up your life and everything in it. What you thought was the plan may not match your baby's plan—and believe it or not, that little munchkin often has a bigger vote than you do!

Where New Babies Commonly Sleep

Around the world, the most common locations for babies to have their night's sleep fall into these four main categories:

- **Bed-sharing** (often referred to as *co-sleeping* or *the family bed*)—Your baby sleeps in your bed with you.
- **Room-sharing** (also called *rooming-in* or *co-sleeping*)—Your baby sleeps in your room, but in a separate bed, such as a cradle or bassinet. Often the baby's bed is placed directly beside the parent's bed, sometimes in a bedside crib attached to the side of the adult's bed with one side open to the parent for ease of access and to provide the benefits of proximity. ("Co-sleeping" traditionally meant having your baby in your bed with you, but the definition is changing to mean room-sharing, but sleeping on separate sur-

faces. However, the terms co-sleeping and bed-sharing are often used interchangeably.)

- **Separate bedroom**—Your baby sleeps in a crib in a separate room from you.
- **Combination of these**—Baby spends part of the night in one location and part in another. This is a popular scenario during the first year when babies wake up often throughout the night.

Crib, Cradle, and Bassinet Sleep

Many parents choose to have their baby sleep mainly in a crib, cradle, or bassinet. There are four important safety factors regarding this type of sleeping arrangement:

- Always put your baby on their back for sleep (not on their tummy or side, unless your doctor tells you to).
- Make sure the crib and room are safe (see the safety list on pages 368–369).
- Keep your baby's bed in your bedroom during the newborn months, or even better, for the first year.
- Don't fall asleep while feeding your baby on a sofa, recliner, or rocking chair.

If you plan to use a crib or cradle exclusively, or if you start off with your newborn sleeping in their own bed, you may be tempted to skip the rest of this chapter. If you do, you might need to revisit this section later. Many babies resist independent sleep, so while it may not be your plan to bed-share, it's possible you'll "accidentally" wind up with your baby in your bed from time to time, or even all the time. In addition, it can be very dangerous to fall asleep while feeding your baby in a recliner, chair, or sofa—and this happens frequently during those drowsy middle-of-the-night feedings. Therefore, it's not a bad idea to skim this section so that you'll know the ways to create a safe family bed, if you find you need or want one.

Bed-Sharing: Should You Bring Your Baby into Your Bed?

If a full-time crib or cradle isn't your first choice, you may be wondering if it's safe to have your baby sleep in your bed with you. Many parents consider the idea of bed-sharing, or find themselves sharing sleep with their baby by accident, and they want to know if it is safe to do so. If you are looking for an exact yes or no answer to this question, you won't find it here, and I'll explain why. After spending more than thirty years watching the news, scanning research reports, reading books on this topic, and having four babies of my own, I've learned that this is a complex question for which there is no simple answer.

My Personal Experience

I want you to know that I brought all four of my babies into bed with me. Over the years we've had a full-time family bed, part-time bed-sharing, a bedside cradle, bedroom hopping, a "sibling bed in the sleeping room," and possibly every other combination you can think of! We loved the closeness and convenience that a family bed provided. (Between you and me, I really miss those lovely times.)

My four children are now all young adults. They are all independent, successful people, and all of them are tightly bonded to us. Our home is rarely without at least one of them brightening my day. We sincerely believe that this bond began with our close connections to them from the day they were born, which was enhanced by shared family sleep. Clearly my experience colors my opinions on this topic. My primary focus here is to provide you with the known information about bed-sharing so that you can make the best and safest choice for your own unique family.

The Impact on Night Waking

Studies tell us that babies who sleep beside their breastfeeding mothers wake up more often throughout the night. But here's the kicker—the mothers actually get *more overall sleep* than those whose babies are in cribs. This is partly because of the ease of waking beside your baby, flipping them to the other side, and dozing right back off—sometimes so quickly you barely recall the wake up. (Does it sound like I know what I'm talking about here?) You don't have to turn on a light, get out of bed, perhaps travel to the kitchen to prepare a bottle, remove baby from the bed, and then wait for baby to finish feeding, then return them to the crib, before you return to your bed. The difference results in more net sleep for baby and mother when neither one must leave their comfortable bed.

The Debate Over the Safety of Bed-Sharing

The safety of bringing a baby into an adult bed is a subject of ongoing debate. Many professional groups advise against it; however, there are other reputable groups that tout the many benefits of bed-sharing, some even believing that the baby–breastfeeding-mother dyad might protect against SIDS.

I would be remiss if I just conveyed my personal experience and gave you a big thumbs-up for bed-sharing without providing a summary of the information and recommendations that exist. There is much research yet to be done on this topic, and it's important that you do your own homework, watch for new science, and make the best decision for your own family. To help get you started, I'll provide some information here, plus provide links to places for more information.

The Difference Between SIDS and Accidental Death

Far too many books and articles link SIDS and bed-sharing. Therefore, even if you are sure that bed-sharing is right for your family, and even if you've done your homework and created a 100 percent safe sleeping environment for your baby, there may still be a tiny voice in the back of your head that keeps reminding you that SIDS is out there and wondering if bed-sharing is creating that risk. Let me first remind you that SIDS used to be called "crib death" because it happened to babies *asleep in their cribs*. SIDS is a *medical condition*. It can happen to babies *no matter where they sleep*. There is a difference between SIDS and accidental death that occurs during bed-sharing—and the majority of the risks of accidental death while bed-sharing can be controlled by following all the safety rules.

What the Professionals Say

The American Academy of Pediatrics (AAP) recommends "the arrangement of room-sharing without bed-sharing, or having the infant sleep in the parents' room but on a separate sleep surface (crib or similar surface) close to the parents' bed."

The Canadian Paediatric Society also recommends that your baby sleep in your room for at least the first six months, but in a separate bed.

These groups, and others like them, have not done any research to ascertain that bed-sharing is safe, so I personally suspect that they err on the side of extreme caution in their recommendations on this topic. In their book *The Science of Mother-Infant Sleep, Current Findings on Bedsharing, Breastfeeding, Sleep Training, and Normal Infant Sleep*, Wendy Middlemiss, Ph.D., and Kathleen Kendall-Tackett, Ph.D., IBCLC, FAPA say, "Breastfeeding cannot protect an infant from risks introduced by hazardous parental behavior, and so guidance that infants are safest sleeping in a crib next to their parents' bed is defensible as a general public health message; but this message must also acknowledge that not all parent-infant bedsharing is inherently dangerous, and that breastfeeding, bedsharing mothers and infants are a particularly low-risk group."

Bed-sharing is a common practice worldwide. According to some sleep polls, over 50 percent of families follow some sort of bed-sharing arrangement in their home, and among breastfeeding mothers this number appears to be as high as 60 to 70 percent.

There are a number of groups who present arguments for the benefits of bed-sharing, such as these:

- The Academy of Breastfeeding Medicine, a worldwide organization of physicians dedicated to the promotion, protection and support of breastfeeding, supports *safe bedsharing* as one method to facilitate the success of breastfeeding.

  In their ABM Clinical Protocol they state: "There is currently not enough evidence to support routine recommendations against co-sleeping. Parents should be educated about risks and benefits of co-sleeping and unsafe co-sleeping practices and should be allowed to make their own informed decision."

  For more information, visit their website at http://www.bfmed.org.

- La Leche League International (LLL), a nonprofit organization that distributes information on and provides support for breastfeeding mothers is in support of safe bed-sharing. La Leche League International says, "Exclusive breastfeeding for the first six months is recommended by virtually every health authority in the world. Breastfeeding mothers *will* bedshare. Failure to provide safe bedsharing information may result in more harm than good."

Studies show that if we give a blanket warning against bed-sharing, it will *not* stop the practice, but it can make parents hide the fact that they are bringing their baby into their bed. It makes much more sense to provide information about how to make bed-sharing safe for those parents who choose this practice.

- Helen Ball, Ph.D., head of Anthropology at Durham University, United Kingdom, and a director of the Parent-Infant Sleep Lab sums up the confusion about bed-sharing research and recommendations when she says:

  "The issues surrounding bed-sharing are not simple, and so many of the questions posed do not have simple answers. The research evidence is contradictory, and so is the guidance issued by different organizations. Most of the questions are also not easy to research, because bed-sharing is difficult to disentangle from many other aspects of parenting that contribute to various outcomes, and very little research into bed-sharing risks considers breastfed and non-breastfed infants separately. What we know, therefore, is incomplete, and guidance comes with a certain 'spin' that reflects the remit or priorities of the organization providing the guidance."

- The Lullaby Trust, Public Health England, and Unicef UK Baby Friendly Initiative:

  "Babies should sleep in a clear sleep space, which is easy to create in a cot or Moses basket. We know however, that families also bed share, and so recommend making your bed a safer place for baby whether you doze off accidentally or choose to bed share. Our advice on co-sleeping with your baby will tell you how." For more information, visit their website at www.lullabytrust.org.uk.

Professional Views on Bed-Sharing

Most mainstream groups, such as the American Academy of Pediatrics, the Centers for Disease Control and Prevention (CDC), and the Canadian Paediatric Society, have made separate surface sleep a factor in their recommendations. You can read their viewpoints on this and other infant health issues on their websites:

- **American Academy of Pediatrics**—http://www.aap.org
- **Centers for Disease Control and Prevention (CDC)**— http://www.cdc.gov/
- **Canadian Paediatric Society**—http://www.cps.ca/en/

While the above-named groups recommend having your baby sleep on a separate surface, other groups question the policy of a directive advising all parents against bed-sharing, and a few even suggest that when done according to very specific safety guidelines bed-sharing might reduce the risk of unexpected death. In addition, creating a purposeful and safe bed-sharing situation is considerably safer than accidentally falling asleep with your baby in an unsafe environment, such as on a recliner, rocking chair, or sofa.

Point to Remember
The Danger of Falling Asleep with
Your Baby on a Sofa or Chair
Sleep-deprived new parents can easily fall asleep while feeding their baby on a sofa, rocking chair, or recliner, particularly in the middle of the night. This situation is far more dangerous for your baby than purposefully setting up a safe bed-sharing environment. (See the safety list on pages 369–373.)

Parent-Speak

"With our first baby I often fell asleep nursing on the recliner. Once I was jolted awake because she wasn't on my lap—she had slipped down sideways—but she was still sound asleep. It was a terrifying close call. I had the illogical fear put into me about her sleeping in my bed, but I was so exhausted I couldn't always stay awake when I was nursing her. For our second baby, we carefully constructed the safest family bed possible and now I can doze off confidently."

**Sarah, mother of two-year-old Charlotte
and three-month-old Hayley**

Sources for Bed-Sharing Information

If you are bed-sharing already, or if you are considering bed-sharing with your baby, you will want to do it as safely as possible. You may want to check out some of the following sources of information for safe bed-sharing:

- James J. McKenna, Ph.D., Mother-Baby Behavioral Sleep Laboratory, University of Notre Dame— http://cosleeping.nd.edu/

  Professor McKenna is recognized as the world's leading authority on mother-infant sleep in relationship to breast-feeding. His website contains articles and information regarding bed-sharing.
- The Academy of Breastfeeding Medicine— http://www.bfmed.org

  In their *Guideline on Co-Sleeping and Breastfeeding* the Academy states: "Parents should be educated about risks and benefits of co-sleeping and unsafe co-sleeping practices and should be allowed to make their own informed decision."

- **La Leche League International (LLL)—**
  http://www.llli.org/

  In regards to bed-sharing, LLL says: "The latest research shows that breastfeeding mothers and babies who meet very clear criteria, which we call The Safe Sleep Seven, are low-risk and can bed-share with confidence. (1–No smoke. 2–Sober parents. 3–Breastfeeding mother. 4–Healthy baby. 5–Baby on back. 6–No sweat. 7–Safe surface.) They add, "A tired mother may not plan to fall asleep with her baby. A prepared bed makes it safer if she does."

- **Attachment Parenting International—**
  http://www.attachmentparenting.org/infantsleepsafety/

  Attachment Parenting International (API) is a non-profit organization that promotes parenting practices that create strong, healthy emotional bonds between children and their parents. They provide infant sleep safety guidance which includes information about co-sleeping and bed-sharing.

- **Australian Breastfeeding Association—**
  https://www.breastfeeding.asn.au/

  The ABA's Position Statement on Safe Infant Sleeping states: "The Association aims to provide factual and up-to-date information on safe sleeping practices so that parents who choose to co-sleep with their baby can do so fully informed about the potential risks and benefits for their particular circumstances. Co-sleeping can benefit babies by supporting breastfeeding and therefore a baby's health. It is unlikely that co-sleeping per se is a risk factor for SUDI (Sudden Unexplained Death in Infancy) but rather the particular circumstances in which co-sleeping occurs. If a parent decides to co-sleep with their baby, they should be made aware of [safe-sleeping rules.]"

- **The Lullaby Trust, with Public Health England and Unicef UK Baby Friendly Initiative—** http://www.lullabytrust.org.uk

   "Babies should sleep in a clear sleep space, which is easy to create in a cot or Moses basket. We know however, that families also bed share, and so recommend making your bed a safer place for baby whether you doze off accidentally or choose to bed share. Our advice on co-sleeping with your baby will tell you how."

   The Lullaby Trust has worked with Public Health England, Unicef UK Baby Friendly and Basis on publications to support families with safer sleep advice and advice on co-sleeping more safely. They have also collaborated on a guide for health professionals to have more open and productive discussions with families about safer sleep and co-sleeping. These can be downloaded at their website.

The Very Safest Bed-Sharing Situation

Based on research and statistics from a wide variety of sources, when bed-sharing is a family's chosen location for their baby's sleep, the very safest situation is this:

A nonsmoking, breastfeeding mother, who is sober and free from all drug use (prescription, over-the-counter, and recreational), sleeping beside her healthy, full-term baby, in a bed that has been purposefully set up for bed-sharing per the safety list on pages 369–373.

I appreciate that fathers, grandparents, caregivers, and formula-feeding mothers may wish to bed-share with their babies; however, in the name of safety I suggest you wait on this experience until your baby is older, which is the recommendation of pro-bed-sharing organizations. The best alternative for you during the early months is to use a bed-side cradle, crib, or bassinet so that your baby is safe and snug at arm's-length from where you sleep. This way you can stay close and attend to your baby's needs easily throughout the night.

The Benefits of Safe Bed-Sharing

Mothers who safely bed-share with their babies often list the following reasons for their choice:

- Having their baby close at their side all night makes nighttime breastfeeding easier, so it increases the chance of breastfeeding success.
- Sleeping with the baby by their side is easier than having to get up and down all night to tend to their baby's nighttime needs and is less disruptive to everyone's sleep.
- Cuddling quietly throughout the night is a peaceful balance to busy days and allows a special brand of bonding.

Those in favor of bed-sharing believe that it can be done safely, and many millions of parents do safely share sleep with their babies. I've researched a wide array of available information

Professional-Speak

"Overwhelmingly, bed-sharing deaths are associated with at least one independent risk factor. These include an infant being placed prone (on their stomach), placed in an adult bed without supervision, the absence of breastfeeding, or other children in the bed, or infants being placed in an adult bed on top of a pillow, or those who bed-shared even though the mothers smoked during the pregnancy (therein potentially compromising the infant's ability to arouse), or drug or alcohol use."

Dr. James J. McKenna

on this topic to compile the safety list on pages 369–373. To create a safe sleeping environment for your child, I recommend that if your baby sleeps with you, or any adult, either for naps or at nighttime, you should adhere to the listed safety guidelines. In addition, watch the news for ongoing research on this subject.

Making Your Own Best Decision

You likely came into this chapter confused and indecisive, and I'm sorry that I didn't help that situation! This is just the first in a lifetime of parenting decisions that you have ahead of you. This is a very complex topic and requires diligence and thoughtfulness. My advice is to do your research, discuss the situation with your parenting partner or others who are involved in raising your baby, and then make the best decision for your unique baby and your family.

The Sleeping Safety Checklists

General Sleeping Safety Precautions for All Families

- During the newborn months, put your infant to sleep on their back for naps and night sleep, unless your doctor specifically says it's safe for your baby to sleep in other positions.
- Have your infant sleep all night in *your bedroom* for the first six to twelve months. (Check with your medical care provider for the appropriate length of time for baby.) The American Academy of Pediatrics (AAP) says "*sharing a room with an infant can reduce the risk of SIDS by up to 50 percent.*"
- Keep the bedroom at a comfortable sleeping temperature, usually between 65°F and 72°F (18°C to 22°C). Be careful not to let your baby get overheated or chilled. If your baby

comes home from delivery wearing a newborn hat, ask if this should be removed for sleep, as a hat can contribute to overheating.

- Do not allow anyone to smoke around your child, or in rooms where your child spends time. This holds true whether your baby is asleep or awake. Children exposed to secondhand smoke face an increased risk of SIDS and health complications, such as allergies, asthma, sleep apnea, and other sleep disruptions. If you are a smoker, avoid smoking before breastfeeding, as nicotine levels peak in breastmilk 30 to 60 minutes after smoking and are gone after three hours. So the more time you can place between smoking and your baby's feedings, the better.

- Do not use pillows, adult blankets, or comforters under or over your child as these can entangle them or become a suffocation hazard. Instead, dress your child in warm pajamas layered with an undershirt when the temperature warrants, and use small baby-sized blankets. Hold off on using a child-sized pillow until your child is about eighteen months old.

- Dress your child in snug-fitting sleepwear, not oversize, loose-fitting cotton clothing. Billowy or cotton fabrics pose a burn hazard in case of fire.

- Do not allow your baby to sleep on a very soft sleeping surface such as a pillow, waterbed, beanbag, foam pad, nursing pillow, featherbed, or any other flexible surface. Babies should sleep only on a firm, flat mattress, with a smooth, wrinkle-free sheet that stays securely fastened around the mattress.

- Keep nightlights, lamps, white noise machines, and all other electrical items away from where your child sleeps.

- Make sure you have a working smoke detector in your baby's sleeping room and check it as often as the manufac-

turer suggests. Have a carbon-monoxide alarm in the home
if necessary. Replace batteries as recommended.

- Do not put a child to sleep near an accessible window, window blinds, cords, or draperies.
- Keep your child's regular appointments for checkups. If your child is sick or feverish, call your medical care provider or hospital promptly.
- Never shake or hit your baby. (Child abuse often occurs when a parent is sleep-deprived and at the end of their rope. If you feel like you may lose your temper with your child, put your baby in a safe place or with another caregiver and go take a breather. Ask someone for help.)
- Never tie a pacifier to your child or their bed with a string, ribbon, or cord, as any of these can become wound around your child's finger, hand, foot, or neck.
- Follow all safety precautions when your child is sleeping away from home, whether in a car seat, stroller, a friend or family member's home, daycare, a hotel, or any other place.
- Never leave a child unattended while in a stroller, baby seat, swing, or car seat.
- Never leave a pet with access to a sleeping baby. Even the most gentle, protective pet could unintentionally harm your baby.
- Learn how to perform infant CPR. Be sure that all other caregivers for your child are also trained in CPR. (Check with your local hospital or fire department for classes, or at a minimum watch a few YouTube videos produced by reputable medical sources.)
- Keep your child's environment clean. Wash bedding often. Wash your hands after diapering your child and before preparing food. Wash child's hands and face frequently.
- Pay attention to your own health and well-being. If you have feelings of anxiety, panic, sadness, or hopelessness,

you may be suffering from postpartum depression. Please talk to a professional (such as your doctor, lactation consultant, doula, or midwife). This condition is common and treatable. Call someone now and ask for help so that you can be the best parent for your baby.

Safety Precautions for Cradles and Cribs

- Make certain your child's crib meets all federal safety regulations, industry standards, and guidelines of the U.S. Consumer Product Safety Commission's most recent recommendations (www.cpsc.gov). Look for a safety certification seal. Avoid using an old or used crib.
- Make sure the mattress fits tightly to the cradle or crib, without gaps on any side. (If you can fit more than two fingers between the mattress and side of the crib, the mattress does not fit properly.)
- Make certain that your crib sheets fit securely and cannot be pulled loose by your child thus creating a dangerous tangle of fabric. Do not use plastic mattress covers or any plastic bags near the crib.
- Remove any decorative ribbons, bows, or strings. Don't use bumper pads.
- Be certain that all screws, bolts, springs, and other hardware and attachments are tightly secured, and check them from time to time. Replace any broken or missing pieces immediately. (Contact the manufacturer for replacement parts.) Make sure your crib has a sturdy bottom and wide, stable base so that it does not wobble or tilt when your baby moves around. Check to see that all slats are in place, firm, and stable—and that they are spaced no more than $2\frac{3}{8}$ inches (60 mm) apart.

- Make sure that corner posts do not extend more than $\frac{1}{16}$ inch ($1\frac{1}{2}$ mm) above the top of the end panel. Don't use a crib that has removable decorative knobs on the corner posts, or headboard and footboard designs that present a hazard, such as sharp edges, points, or pieces that can be loosened or removed. When you raise the side rail, lock it into position.
- Don't hang objects over a sleeping or unattended baby—that includes mobiles and other crib toys. There is a risk of the toy falling on your child.
- If you are using a portable crib, make sure the locking devices are properly and securely locked.
- Make sure your child is within hearing distance of your bed or that you have a reliable baby monitor turned on. It is highly recommended that your baby sleep overnight in the same room as you during the newborn period, and possibly longer.
- Check the manufacturer's instructions on suggested size and weight limits for any cradle, bassinet, or crib. If a there is no tag, call or write the manufacturer for this information or check their website.
- Make sure that any place your child sleeps when away from home meets all the above safety requirements.

Safety Precautions for Bed-Sharing
- It is much wiser to create a safe condition in an adult bed than to fall asleep on a sofa, recliner or chair with your baby in your arms, or lying on you, which all carry a high level of risk.
- Bed-share only with a healthy, full-term infant, or an older baby unless your doctor approves otherwise.

- If you choose to bed-share with your newborn, it's important that you breastfeed your baby, as the breastfeeding mother–infant pair is considered safest for infant co-sleeping. Dr. James McKenna, a leading authority on infant–mother sleep, states, "Bottle-feeding babies should always sleep alongside the mother or father *on a separate surface* rather than in the same bed." A bedside cradle adjacent to your bed keeps the baby close enough to touch, but on a separate surface.
- Avoid bed-sharing if either parent is a smoker, because secondhand smoke and smoke residue can affect a baby's developing lungs and increase the risk of SIDS.
- Your bed must be absolutely safe for your baby. The best choice is to place the mattress on the floor, making sure there are no crevices that your baby can become wedged in. Make certain your mattress is flat, firm, and smooth. Do not allow your baby to sleep on a soft surface such as a waterbed, beanbag, soft pillow-top, or any other flexible surface.
- Make certain that your fitted sheets stay secure and cannot be pulled loose.
- If your bed is raised off the floor, use mesh guardrails to prevent your baby from rolling off the bed, and be especially careful that there is no space between the mattress and headboard or footboard. (Many guardrails are designed for older children and are not safe for infants, because they have gaps that small babies can get stuck in.)
- If your bed is placed against a wall or against other furniture, check every night to be sure nothing has shifted to create a space between the mattress and wall or furniture where your child could become stuck. Make this part of your bedtime routine.
- The majority of professionals agree that infants should be placed between Mother and the wall or guardrail. Yes, of

course Father, siblings, caregivers, and grandparents love your newborn every bit as much as Mother does! Once your baby is a bit older it will be safe, but science shows that others don't have the same instinctual awareness of an infant's location as mothers do. Mothers, pay attention to your own sensitivity to your baby. Your little one should be able to awaken you with a minimum of movement or noise—often even a sniff or grunt is enough to wake a mother sleeping next to her baby. If you find that you are such a deep sleeper that you only wake up when your baby makes a loud cry, you should consider moving your baby into a bed-side cradle or crib.

- Use a large, firm mattress to provide ample room for everyone's space and movement.

- With a premature newborn, or a newborn with special needs, you might consider a sidecar arrangement in which your child's crib, bed, or mattress sits beside or close to your bed. Many three-sided co-sleepers are now available to give your baby a designated space of their own attached to your bed.

- Well before your child reaches their first birthday, make certain that the room your child sleeps in, and any room they might have access to, is child-safe. (Imagine your child crawling out of bed as you sleep. Even though they're too young now, time passes quickly, and they eventually will!)

- Do not ever sleep with your baby if you have been drinking alcohol, if you have used any drugs or medications that could make you drowsy or affect your senses, if you are ill and unable to respond to your baby's needs, if you are an especially sound sleeper, or if you are suffering from sleep deprivation and find it difficult to awaken.

- Never swaddle your baby when bed-sharing. Your baby's arms and legs should be free to move about. In addition, swaddling during bed-sharing can increase the risk of overheating.

- Do not sleep with your baby if you are a large person, as a parent's excess weight has been determined to pose a risk to child in a bed-sharing situation. Examine how you and your child settle in next to each other. If your child rolls toward you, or there is a large dip in the mattress, or if you suspect any other dangerous situation, play it safe and move your child to a bedside crib or their own bed.
- Remove pillows and blankets during the newborn period. (You might be able to use a small, firm pillow under your own head.)
- Do not wear any nightclothes with strings or long ribbons.
- Don't wear jewelry to bed, and if your hair is long, put it up.
- Don't use any strong-smelling perfumes or lotions that may affect your baby's delicate senses.
- Do not allow other children or pets to sleep in bed with your newborn. Save this treat for when your child is older.
- Until your baby is past the newborn stage, when not actively breastfeeding they should be sleeping on their back, the safest position during newborn sleep.
- Never leave your baby alone in an adult bed unless that bed is perfectly safe for your child, such as a mattress on the floor in a childproof room, and when you are nearby or listening in on your child with a reliable monitor.
- As of this writing there are no proven safety devices for use in protecting a baby in an adult bed. However, as a result of the great number of parents who wish to bed-share safely with their babies a number of new inventions are appearing in baby catalogs and stores. You may want to look into some of these nests, wedges, and cradles—but check the safety factors, watch the news, and do your homework. Just because something is sold does not ensure that it is safe, and as of this writing there are no devices deemed safe for use in the family bed.

Index

About the Author

Parenting educator Elizabeth Pantley is president of Better Beginnings, Inc., a family resource and education company. Elizabeth is frequently quoted as a parenting expert in magazines worldwide and on thousands of parent-focused Web sites. She publishes articles that are distributed in schools, daycares, medical offices, childbirth educator programs, lactation centers, doula and midwife offices, and parent programs everywhere.

Elizabeth is the author of twelve popular parenting books, available in twenty-nine languages, and read by over two million people. Her books include the best-selling *No-Cry Solution* series:

- *The No-Cry Sleep Solution, Second Edition*
  Gentle Ways to Help Your Baby Sleep Through the Night
- *The No-Cry Sleep Solution for Toddlers and Preschoolers*
  Gentle Ways to Stop Bedtime Battles and Improve Your Child's Sleep
- *The No-Cry Nap Solution*
  Guaranteed Gentle Ways to Solve All Your Naptime Problems
- *The No-Cry Sleep Solution for Newborns*
  Amazing Sleep from Day One—for Baby and You
- *The No-Cry Picky Eater Solution*
  Gentle Ways to Encourage Your Child to Eat—and Eat Healthy
- *The No-Cry Separation Anxiety Solution*
  Gentle Ways to Make Good-Bye Easy from Six Months to Six Years

Hunter, five-months-old, and Nana Elizabeth Pantley

- *The No-Cry Discipline Solution*
  Gentle Ways to Encourage Good Behavior Without
  Whining, Tantrums and Tears
- *The No-Cry Potty Training Solution*
  Gentle Ways to Help Your Child Say Good-Bye to Diapers

Elizabeth and her husband, Robert, are the parents of four children, Angela, Vanessa, David, and Coleton, and are grandparents to Hunter.

For more information, excerpts and parenting articles visit the author at:

Website
http://www.nocrysolution.com

Blog
http://elizabethpantley.com/

Follow Her on Social Media:

Facebook
https://www.facebook.com/ElizabethPantleyNoCryAuthor

Pinterest
http://www.pinterest.com/nocrysolution/

Blogger
http://www.kidsinthehouse.com/blogs/Elizabeth-Pantley

Instagram
https://instagram.com/elizabethpantley/